"Distinguished authors from the United States, China, and Europe address the implications of China's growing power not only for great power politics in East Asia but also for European security and economic affairs. The volume is especially important for its analyses of China's growing economic presence in Europe, for the effects of America's response to China's challenge to America's Asian interests on the U.S. contribution to NATO and to European security, and for European interests regarding Russia's actions in the Middle East."

– *Robert J. Art, Brandeis University, USA*

"Tapping deep wisdom of veteran specialists from the United States, China and Europe and brilliance of newly minted experts from Europe and the United States, this volume explains well how acute US–China rivalry and weakened European unity foreshadow waning globalization and decline of the liberal international order and institutions that will be difficult to rebuild."

– *Robert Sutter, George Washington University, USA*

US–CHINA FOREIGN RELATIONS

This book examines the power transition between the US and China, and the implications for Europe and Asia in a new era of uncertainty.

The volume addresses the impact that the rise of China has on the United States, Europe, transatlantic relations, and East Asia. China is seeking to use its enhanced power position to promote new ambitions; the United States is adjusting to a new superpower rivalry; and the power shift from the West to the East is resulting in a more peripheral role for Europe in world affairs. Featuring essays by prominent Chinese and international experts, the book examines the US–China rivalry, the changing international system, grand strategies and geopolitics, foreign policy, geo-economics and institutions, and military and technological developments. The chapters examine how strategic, security, and military considerations in this triangular relationship are gradually undermining trade and economics, reversing the era of globalization, and contributing to the breakdown of the US-led liberal order and institutions that will be difficult to rebuild. The volume also examines whether the adversarial antagonism in US–China relations, the tension in transatlantic ties, and the increasing rivalry in Europe–China relations are primarily resulting from leaders' ambitions or structural power shifts.

This book will be of much interest to students of Asian security, US foreign policy, European politics, and International Relations in general.

Robert S. Ross is Professor of Political Science at Boston College, and Associate and Executive Committee member at John King Fairbank Center for Chinese Studies, Harvard University, Cambridge USA.

Øystein Tunsjø is Professor and Head of Asia Program at the Norwegian Institute for Defence Studies at the Norwegian Defence University College, Oslo.

Wang Dong is Associate Professor in the School of International Studies; Executive Director of the Institute for Global Cooperation and Understanding; and Deputy Director of Office for Humanities and Social Sciences, Peking University, China.

ASIAN SECURITY STUDIES

Series Editors: Sumit Ganguly, *Indiana University, USA*, Andrew Scobell, *Research and Development (RAND) Corporation, USA*, and Alice Ba, *University of Delaware, USA*.

Few regions of the world are fraught with as many security questions as Asia. Within this region it is possible to study great power rivalries, irredentist conflicts, nuclear and ballistic missile proliferation, secessionist movements, ethnoreligious conflicts and inter-state wars. This book series publishes the best possible scholarship on the security issues affecting the region, and includes detailed empirical studies, theoretically oriented case studies and policy-relevant analyses as well as more general works.

Hizbut Tahrir Indonesia and Political Islam
Identity, Ideology and Religio-Political Mobilization
Mohamed Nawab Mohamed Osman

China and International Nuclear Weapons Proliferation
Strategic Assistance
Henrik Stålhane Hiim

Reshaping the Chinese Military
The PLA's Roles and Missions in the Xi Jinping Era
Edited by Richard A. Bitzinger and James Char

India's Nuclear Proliferation Policy
The Impact of Secrecy on Decision Making, 1980–2010
Gaurav Kampani

China's Quest for Foreign Technology
Beyond Espionage
Edited by William C. Hannas and Didi Kirsten Tatlow

US–China Foreign Relations
Power Transition and its Implications for Europe and Asia
Edited by Robert S. Ross, Øystein Tunsjø and Wang Dong

For more information about this series, please visit: www.routledge.com/Asian-Security-Studies/book-series/ASS

US–CHINA FOREIGN RELATIONS

Power Transition and its Implications for Europe and Asia

Edited by Robert S. Ross, Øystein Tunsjø, and Wang Dong

Routledge
Taylor & Francis Group

LONDON AND NEW YORK

First published 2021
by Routledge
2 Park Square, Milton Park, Abingdon, Oxon OX14 4RN

and by Routledge
52 Vanderbilt Avenue, New York, NY 10017

Routledge is an imprint of the Taylor & Francis Group, an informa business

Library of Congress Cataloging-in-Publication Data
Names: Ross, Robert S., 1954-editor. | Wang, Dong, 1977-editor. | Tunsjø, Øystein, editor.
Title: US-China foreign relations: power transition and its implications for Europe and Asia/edited by Robert S Ross, Dong Wang, Øystein Tunsjø.
Other titles: United States-China foreign relations
Description: Abingdon, Oxon; New York: Routledge, 2021. | Series: Asian security studies | Includes bibliographical references and index.
Identifiers: LCCN 2020020528 (print) | LCCN 2020020529 (ebook) | ISBN 9780367521400 (hardback) | ISBN 9780367521349 (paperback) | ISBN 9781003056683 (ebook)
Subjects: LCSH: United States–Foreign relations–China. | China–Foreign relations–United States. | United States–Foreign relations–21st century. | China–Foreign relations–21st century. | Asia–Foreign relations–1945- | Europe–Foreign relations–1989-
Classification: LCC E183.8.C5 U175 2021 (print) | LCC E183.8.C5 (ebook) | DDC 320.73051–dc23
LC record available at https://lccn.loc.gov/2020020528
LC ebook record available at https://lccn.loc.gov/2020020529

ISBN: 978-0-367-52140-0 (hbk)
ISBN: 978-0-367-52134-9 (pbk)
ISBN: 978-1-003-05668-3 (ebk)

Typeset in Bembo
by Deanta Global Publishing Services, Chennai, India

CONTENTS

ILLUSTRATIONS

Figures

Tables

CONTRIBUTORS

Jo Inge Bekkevold is Senior Advisor at the Norwegian Institute for Defence Studies, Norwegian Defence University College. He has written extensively on Chinese foreign policy and Asian security, and ongoing projects include Chinese geopolitics and China–India relations. Bekkevold is the editor of *Sino-Russian Relations in the 21st Century* with Bobo Lo (Palgrave Macmillan, 2019), *China in the Era of Xi Jinping: Domestic and Foreign Policy Challenges* with Robert S. Ross (Georgetown University Press, 2016), and *International Order at Sea: How it Is Challenged. How it Is Maintained* with Geoffrey Till (Palgrave Macmillan, 2016). In 2012–2015, he took part in the international research project AsiArctic, examining drivers and consequences of China and Asian countries' entry into Arctic affairs, which resulted in the volume *Arctic: Commerce, Governance and Policy*, co-edited with Uttam Sinha (Routledge, 2015). Bekkevold is a member of the expert pool of the European Centre of Excellence for Countering Hybrid Threats (Hybrid CoE). Bekkevold is a former career diplomat in the Norwegian Foreign Service, with several postings to Asia, and he has previously also worked as a market analyst in Beijing.

Ian Bowers is an Associate Professor at the Institute for Military Operations, Royal Danish Defence College in Copenhagen. His research focuses on sea power, the strategic impact of new military technology, Asian security, and deterrence. Bowers has published in leading international journals including the *Naval War College Review*, the *Journal of Strategic Studies*, and *Pacific Review*. His monograph *The Modernisation of the Republic of Korea Navy: Seapower, Strategy and Politics* was published in 2018. His latest work *Grey and White Hulls: An International Analysis of the Navy-Coastguard Nexus* (co-edited with Collin Koh) was published by Palgrave in 2019. Bowers holds a PhD in War Studies from King's College London.

Rosemary Foot is a Senior Research Fellow in the Department of Politics and International Relations, University of Oxford, an Emeritus Fellow of St Antony's

College, Oxford, and a Research Associate of Oxford's China Centre. In 1996, she was elected a Fellow of the British Academy. She is the author of several books, including *The Wrong War: American Policy and the Dimensions of the Korean Conflict, 1950-53* (Cornell University Press, 1985); *The Practice of Power: US Relations with China since 1949* (Oxford University Press [OUP], 1995); *Rights Beyond Borders: The Global Community and the Struggle Over Human Rights in China* (OUP, 2000); and with Andrew Walter as co-author, *China, the United States, and Global Order*, (Cambridge University Press, 2011). Two recent edited books include *China Across the Divide: The Domestic and Global in Politics and Society* (OUP, 2013), and, with Saadia M. Pekkanen and John Ravenhill, *The Oxford Handbook of the International Relations of Asia* (OUP, 2014). In May 2020, Oxford University Press published her current book entitled *China, the UN, and Human Protection: Beliefs, Power, Image*. Her research interests cover security relations in the Asia-Pacific, human rights, Asian regional institutions, China and world order, and China–US relations.

Avery Goldstein is the David M. Knott Professor of Global Politics and International Relations in the Political Science Department, Inaugural Director of the Center for the Study of Contemporary China, and Associate Director of the Christopher H. Browne Center for International Politics at the University of Pennsylvania. His research focuses on international relations, security studies, and Chinese politics. He is the author of *Rising to the Challenge: China's Grand Strategy and International Security* (Stanford University Press, 2005), *Deterrence and Security in the 21st Century: China, Britain, France and the Enduring Legacy of the Nuclear Revolution* (Stanford University Press, 2000), and *From Bandwagon to Balance of Power Politics: Structural Constraints and Politics in China, 1949-1978* (Stanford University Press, 1991). Among his other publications are articles in the journals *International Security, International Organization, Journal of Strategic Studies, Security Studies, China Quarterly, Asian Survey, Comparative Politics, Orbis, and Polity* as well as chapters in a variety of edited volumes. Goldstein is also a Senior Fellow at the Foreign Policy Research Institute in Philadelphia.

Gerlinde Groitl (Dr. phil, University of Regensburg) serves as Assistant Professor of International Politics and Transatlantic Relations at the University of Regensburg, Germany. She is particularly interested in US, German, and European foreign and security policy, the changing dynamics of European–American relations as well as questions of world order, great power relations, and the sources of strategic success or failure. Her latest monograph dealt with US-civil–military conflict over post–Cold War intervention policy (2015). She is currently working on her next book on the strategic competition of Russia, China, and the West over the future of the international order. In recent years, visiting fellowships have led her to LSE IDEAS at the London School of Economics and Political Science, the Johns Hopkins University's Center for Transatlantic Relations, and to the "American–German Situation Room," a joint initiative of the American Institute for Contemporary German Studies (AICGS) and the German Marshall Fund in Washington, DC.

Committed to policy-relevant scholarship and cross-professional exchange, she is, among others, an alumna of the multi-year Young Leaders in Security Policy program of the German Federal Academy for Security Policy in Berlin.

Isaac B. Kardon is an Assistant Professor at the US Naval War College (NWC) in the Department of Strategic and Operational Research. He is a core member of the China Maritime Studies Institute (CMSI), where he researches and writes on maritime disputes, the law of the sea, Indo-Pacific maritime security and commerce, and China–Pakistan relations. Isaac also serves as managing editor of the CMSI Red Book series of monographs on Chinese maritime power, and teaches classes on Chinese politics and foreign policy to American and foreign students at NWC. Kardon's book *China's Law of the Sea* covers PRC approaches to its maritime disputes and is forthcoming from Yale University Press. His work has been published by Stanford University Press, Routledge, the University of Pennsylvania's *Asian Law Review*, *Global Asia*, and elsewhere. Kardon earned a PhD in Government from Cornell University, an MPhil in Modern Chinese Studies from Oxford University, and a BA in History from Dartmouth College. He was formerly a Research Analyst at the National Defense University's Center for the Study of Chinese Military Affairs, and a Visiting Scholar at NYU Law, the PRC National Institute for South China Sea Studies in Hainan, and Academia Sinica in Taipei. He studied Chinese (Mandarin) at Peking University, Tsinghua University, Hainan University, and National Taiwan Normal University.

Philippe Le Corre is a Research Associate at the Harvard Kennedy School (Ash Center for Democratic Governance & Innovation and Mossavar-Rahmani Center for Business & Government), and a Non-resident Senior Fellow with the Carnegie Endowment for International Peace. He is also an Associate in Research with the John K. Fairbank for Chinese Studies at Harvard. Le Corre was previously a Fellow at The Brookings Institution. He served as a Special Assistant for international affairs to the French Defense Minister from 2004 to 2007, and as a Senior Policy Adviser on Asia in the Defense Ministry's policy planning staff. Mr. Le Corre has been specializing in EU–China relations, outbound Chinese direct investments, and great powers competition. Mr. Le Corre has spoken on the subject at Harvard, Princeton, Johns Hopkins, and Boston University, and contributed to numerous publications, including *The Wall Street Journal*, *The Financial Times*, *The National Interest*, *Nikkei Asian Review*, and *Foreign Affairs*. His latest book is *China's Offensive in Europe* (Brookings Institution Press, 2016). He is also the author of several recent reports on the subject, including *China's Rise as a Geoeconomic Influencer: Four European Case Studies* (Carnegie Working Paper, October 2018) and *Kazakhs Wary of Chinese Embrace as BRI Gathers Steam* (National University of Singapore, February 2019).

Robert S. Ross is Professor of Political Science at Boston College, Associate and Executive Committee member, John King Fairbank Center for Chinese Studies, Harvard University. From 2007 to 2016, he was Adjunct Professor, Institute for Defence Studies, Norwegian Defence University College. He has taught at Columbia University and at the University of Washington. Professor Ross's research focuses on Chinese security policy, East Asian security, and US–China relations. His recent publications include *Strategic Adjustment and the Rise of China: Power and Politics in East Asia*; *China in the Era of Xi Jinping: Domestic and Foreign Policy Challenges*; and *Chinese Security Policy: Structure, Power, and Politics*. His other major works include *China's Ascent: Power, Security, and the Future of International Politics*; *Normalization of U.S.-China Relations: An International History*; *Great Wall and Empty Fortress: China's Search for Security*; *Negotiating Cooperation: U.S.-China Relations, 1969-1989*; and *The Indochina Tangle: China's Vietnam Policy, 1975-1979*. Professor Ross is also the author of numerous scholarly and policy articles in *World Politics*, *The China Quarterly*, *International Security*, *Security Studies*, *European Journal of International Relations*, *Naval War College Review*, *Orbis*, *Foreign Affairs*, *Foreign Policy*, *The National Interest*, and *Asian Survey*. His books and articles have been translated in China, Taiwan, South Korea, Japan, and various European countries.

Shi Yinhong is Distinguished Professor of International Relations, Chairman of Academic Committee of the School for International Studies, and Director of the Center on American Studies at Renmin University of China in Beijing. He is also a non-resident specially-invited Professor at the School of Governmental Administration, Nanjing University. He has served as a Counsellor of the State Council of PRC since February 2011. He mainly engages in history and ideas of international politics, strategic studies, East Asia security, and foreign policies of both China and the United States. His previous positions include Professor of International History at Nanjing University, and Professor of International Relations and Director of the Center for International Strategic Studies at International Relations Academy in Nanjing. Professor Shi received a PhD in international history from Nanjing University in 1988. He was a visiting fellow at Harvard–Yeching Institute at Harvard University from 1983 to 1984, a Fulbright research visiting scholar at the University of North Carolina at Chapel Hill from 1995 to 1996, and taught graduate courses at University of Michigan at Ann Arbor and Aichi University in Nagoya. He has published 19 books and over 630 professional articles and essays, as well as 17 translated books mainly on strategic history and international politics.

Joshua Shifrinson is an Assistant Professor of International Relations at Boston University's Pardee School of Global Studies, where his research focuses on US foreign policy, international security, and great power politics. A graduate of MIT and Brandeis University, his work has appeared in *International Security*, *The Journal of Strategic Studies*, *Foreign Affairs*, *The Washington Quarterly*, and other publications. Shifrinson's first book, *Rising Titans, Falling Giants: How Great Powers Exploit Power Shifts*, was published by Cornell University Press; his next volume explores when, why, and how great powers suppress or abet the rise of new peer competitors, drawing heavily from the United States' post–Cold War engagement with Western Europe and China.

May-Britt U. Stumbaum (PhD), is Team Leader of #APRAN, the EU's Asia-Pacific Research and Advice Network, an internal think tank serving the EEAS and EC Services, run by a consortium of Konrad Adenauer Foundation, Clingendeal, and Chatham House. Previous positions included Director, NFG Research Group "Asian Perceptions of the EU," Fellow at Einstein Programme on East Asian Security, both at Freie Universität Berlin; Senior Research Fellow and Executive Director, China and Global Security Programme at the Stockholm International Peace Research Institute (SIPRI); Fritz Thyssen Fellow at WCFIA, Harvard University; Director, International Forum on Strategic Thinking/Senior Researcher, German Council on Foreign Relations (DGAP); Director, Asia Department, Berlin Partner and Seminar Leader for the Bosch Foundation. May-Britt U. Stumbaum has lectured and worked as a Visiting Fellow at several renowned European, Asian, and Chinese think tanks, research institutions, and governmental entities. She served as president for Women in International Security Deutschland (WIIS.de), and as board member and first female president for the German international leaders' association "Tönissteiner Kreis." Current involvements encompass e.g. Board Member, Clausewitz Society, member of the CSCAP EU Committee, and annual stints as LTC (R) German Airforce at the Ministry of Defence/security policy section. May-Britt U. Stumbaum graduated with an MSc in European Politics and Governance from the London School of Economics and Political Science (LSE) and received her PhD from the Freie Universität Berlin on EU-China relations (trade/security).

Øystein Tunsjø is Professor and Head of Asia Program at the Norwegian Institute for Defence Studies at the Norwegian Defence University College. Tunsjø is author of *The Return of Bipolarity in World Politics: China, the United States and Geostructural Realism*, (Columbia University Press, 2018); *Security and Profits in China's Energy Policy: Hedging Against Risk* (Columbia University Press, 2013); and *US Taiwan Policy: Constructing the Triangle* (London: Routledge, 2008). Tunsjø is co-editor with Robert S. Ross of *Strategic Adjustment and the Rise of China: Power and Politics in East Asia* (Ithaca: Cornell University Press, 2017); co-editor with Robert S. Ross and Peter Dutton of *Twenty-First Century Seapower: Cooperation and Conflict at Sea* (London: Routledge, 2012, translated into Chinese, *21 Shiji Haiyang Daguo: Haishang Hezuo yu Zhongtu Guanli,* by Shehui Kexue Wenxian Zhubanshe, Beijing, 2014) and co-editor with Robert Ross and Zhang Tuosheng of *US-China-EU Relations: Managing a New World Order* (London: Routledge, 2010, translated into Chinese, *Zhong Mei Ou Guanxi: Goujian Xin de Shijie Zhixu* by the World Affairs Press, Beijing, 2012). Tunsjø has published articles in journals such as *The National Interests, Survival, International Relations, Cooperation and Conflict*, and *World Economy and Politics* (in Chinese) and contributed with book chapters to several edited volumes. Tunsjø holds a PhD in International Relations from the University of Wales, Aberystwyth, 2006, an MSc from the London School of Economics, 2002, and an MA from Griffith University, Australia, 2000. Tunsjø was a visiting Fulbright scholar at the Fairbank Center for Chinese Studies, Harvard University, during the spring term of 2010.

Wang Dong is Associate Professor in the School of International Studies; Executive Director of the Institute for Global Cooperation and Understanding (iGCU); and Deputy Director of Office for Humanities and Social Sciences, Peking University. He also serves as Member of the Steering Committee of the "East Asia Security Forum," Chinese Overseas Educated Scholars Association, International Advisory Committee Member of the Shanghai Academy of Area Studies, and Global Governance, Advisory Committee Member for the Carter Center-Global Times "US-China Young Scholars Forum," and Secretary General of the Academic Committee of the Pangoal Institution, a leading China-based public policy think tank. Wang Dong received his bachelor degree from Peking University and PhD from UCLA. He had previously taught at York College of Pennsylvania, with a tenure-track appointment. Dr. Wang has written extensively on international relations and China's foreign policy. His articles appear in *Diplomatic History, Journal of Conflict Resolution, The Pacific Review, The Diplomat, The New York Times* as well as other top academic and news outlets. He sits on the editorial committees of several top academic journals. He has provided consultation to the Chinese government on matters important to Chinese foreign policy, and has served as Chinese speaker/delegate for preeminent international fora such as the World Economic Forum, Munich Security Conference, and Shangri-La Dialogue. Dr. Wang has received many awards and was named a "Munich Young Leader" in 2016. He was selected by the inaugural program of "Preeminent Young Scientists" of Beijing in 2018 (ranked number one in humanities and social sciences).

Zhang Tuosheng is Chairman of Academic Committee and Director of Foreign Policy Center, China Foundation for International and Strategic Studies (CFISS). He is also a council member of the Chinese Arms Control and Disarmament Association, the Academy of International and Strategic Studies of Peking University and a member of the Academic Committee of CISS, Tsinghua University. Previously, he was the Deputy Defense Attaché at the Chinese Embassy in the United Kingdom, a Research Fellow in the Institute of Strategic Studies of PLA National Defense University, and a drillmaster at the PLA Military College. His main research interests are Sino–US relations, Sino–Japan relations, Asia-Pacific security, security crisis management, and China's foreign policy. He has authored or co-authored lots of research publications including papers, reports and books. He received an LLM in modern Chinese history in 1986 from the Central Party School of the Chinese Communist Party.

ACKNOWLEDGMENTS

The editors are grateful to the Norwegian Embassy in Beijing, and to the Norwegian Ministry of Foreign Affairs and Ministry of Defence, for the financial support that made this project possible. They also appreciate the assistance and staff support from the School of International Studies, Peking University, which contributed to the success of the workshop in Beijing in 2019. The Norwegian Institute for Defence Studies hosted the second workshop in 2019, and we are especially grateful to Vibeke Hoffman for her organizational support. The editors thank Christopher Weidacher Hsiung for his assistance in compiling the chapters for the final manuscript for Routledge.

1

THE NEW US–CHINA SUPERPOWER RIVALRY

Challenges for Asia and Europe

Øystein Tunsjø and Wang Dong

This volume addresses the impact of the rise of China on the United States, Europe, transatlantic relations, and Asia. In a previous study, we examined the US–China–EU "diplomatic triangle."[1] Several developments suggest that focusing on triangular relations is no longer the best approach to study the relationship between China, the United States, and Europe. The most important development over the last decade is the unprecedented rise of China. The international system is entering a new bipolar era and China has emerged as a peer-competitor of the United States.[2] The power shift is fuelling a more conflictual US–China relationship. Thus, the contributors to this volume examine this new superpower rivalry and focus on how it affects Asia and Europe in unprecedented ways.

A period of engagement, shaped by absolute gains and mutual cooperation within a diplomatic triangle is now gradually replaced by a more competitive and strategic US–China relationship, resulting in a gloomy outlook for stability and prosperity. The relationship between China, the United States, and Europe has entered a more uncertain era in which the security–economic nexus of the US–China superpower rivalry dominates. The main consequences of this development are beginning to emerge. First, arguably, the process of globalization is gradually being reversed, and trade, investments, and value chains are undermined, fragmented, or reshaped. Second, global norms, rules, and institutions are reconfigured. Third, confidence-building measures and crisis management are compromised. Fourth, Asian and European states are seeking to avoid having to choose between the US and China. Fifth, transatlantic ties are challenged. Sixth, Europe is awakening to a new reality of power politics and geopolitical tension. Seventh, the risk of conflict in East Asia and Europe has heightened.

These implications of growing Sino-US rivalry and competition show that since the publication of our previous volume, US–China relations have gradually deteriorated. This began under the period of the Obama administration, accelerated with the emergence of the new Chinese leadership, and has currently culminated with the Trump administration. Over the last decade and looking towards the future, we observe that the main actors in China–Europe relations and transatlantic relations are individual European states and not so much the EU. The EU is lacking a coherent foreign, economic, and security policy toward China and the United States. While we examine the potential for the EU to rise to the challenges posed in this new age of uncertainty and develop a more coherent foreign, economic, and security policy, the volume focuses more on individual European states.

When examining the explanations for worsened US–China relations and discussing potential implications, uncertainty became a buzzword in the discussions among our contributors. There is a new era of uncertainty related to power shifts and the future world order. The structure of the international system is changing. The unipolar era is ending. A US–China bipolar system is emerging with a "mosaic" of orders primarily shaped by China, the United States, European states, and the EU.

The uncertainty we are witnessing also relates to structure and agency. Trump has undermined US credibility and transatlantic ties, but the diverging threat perceptions of China have also contributed to weakening the relationship between the US and Europe. Europe and the US are likely to remain divided in their views of China's conventional military threat. However, China's rise provides structural incentives that could unite the transatlantic alliance on governance, ideology, international law, and human rights issues, and in new and unconventional security domains, including cybersecurity, the economic–security nexus, regulations and standards on investment and technology. Arguably, US–China relations have worsened not only because of, at the personal level, political leaders' strong personalities and ambitions but also because of, at the structural level, the relative power rise of China and the relative decline of the United States. Leaders alone are unlikely to reverse the deteriorating trend and the conflicting trajectory in US–China relations.

For the first time in more than 100 years, the United States is facing a peer competitor that is rising, while it is in relative decline. The United States is not only uncertain about Chinese capabilities but also uncertain about itself and the role it should play in world affairs. The US needs a new grand strategy for the twenty-first century. President Xi and many others in China have a "China dream" and a vision for the rejuvenation of China's role as a preeminent regional power and a leading global power in the new era. New strategies and policies are a result of a strong leader and a more powerful China. However, the People's Republic of China (PRC) is not accustomed to having power. It is uncertain about how it should use its power.

There is also uncertainty over what this new era means for the EU and states in Europe and East Asia. In contrast to Europe, there is no collective security in East Asia. The EU and European states can seek more independence from the superpower rivalry and aspire to take a more active role in East Asian affairs. While both European and East Asian states hedge, aiming to avoid taking sides and cooperating with both China and the United States, increased US–China rivalry compels states to choose sides. The US is facing a potential regional peer competitor in East Asia, not in Europe. From a regional perspective, East Asia is bipolar and Europe is multipolar. Thus, the US is more likely to prioritize its resources toward the Asia-Pacific and sustain its security commitments to East Asia rather than Europe. Such developments could increase the risk of conflict in both East Asia and Europe. The United States' balancing and containment of China increases the risk of a limited war in the maritime domain of East Asia, and potential US retrenchment from Europe increases the risk of conflict on the European continent.

Superpower rivalry and great power politics are back on the agenda in international politics. China is consolidating and enhancing its strategic partnership with Russia, but there are few signs of a traditional alliance emerging. There is a potential for closer US–Russian ties in order to balance China, but such a strategic shift is unlikely in the years to come. In short, US–China relations will shape security, the international economy and the new international order, and the security and economic nexus is becoming vital. Crisis management and confidence building are becoming more challenging.

This volume examines the new US–China rivalry, the changing international system and order(s), grand strategies and geopolitics, foreign policy and security flashpoints, geo-economics and institutions, Europe–China relations, transatlantic relations, and military and technological developments. Although the contributors do not necessarily endorse each other's view, together, they show how strategic, security, economic, and military considerations in this triangular relationship are gradually undermining trade and economics (more relative gains, decoupling and zero-sum thinking), slowing down if not reversing the era of globalization and contributing to the breakdown of the US-led liberal international order and institutions that will be difficult to rebuild.

Organization of the volume

The volume is divided into four parts. The first part examines power shifts, China's new ambitions, and increased US–China rivalry. The second part deals with the implications of growing US–China rivalry for Europe and transatlantic ties. The third part explores new strategies developed in the US, China, and Europe in response to global power shifts and a new era of uncertainty. The fourth part considers the implications of US–China rivalry for crisis management and mitigating conflict.

The chapters in Part I address different aspects of the sharp relative increase in China's combined capabilities, including the narrowing power gap between the United States and China and the widening power gap between the two top-ranking powers (US and China) and any third-ranking power.

Avery Goldstein's Chapter 2 notes that China has emerged as the only plausible candidate to end the post–Cold War unipolar era of American supremacy. He argues that once that reality dawned, each country recognized that the other was its most capable strategic competitor and that there would not be third parties weighty enough to alter the balance of power between them. The ongoing shift in the distribution of power helps explain both the sharp increase over the past decade in American concerns about China's growing international economic role and its expanding (if still limited) military presence from Africa to the Arctic, as well as China's sensitivity to US measures that address those concerns. Goldstein shows how bipolarity encourages zero-sum thinking that fosters acute attentiveness to the capabilities and behavior of one's most important potential adversary. The slogan of "America first" and China's strive for "national rejuvenation" contributes to zero-sum thinking, which is gaining more influence on economic policies.

Wang Dong provides in Chapter 3 a critical review of the liberal international order. The chapter surveys the contending views and challenges confronting the liberal international order. Wang argues that the liberal international order is not an accurate description of the post–World War II international order. Rather than being a "singular" liberal order as assumed by the narrative of the liberal international order, the post–World War II order is in fact mosaic-like, composed of different layers of sub-orders including a multilateral political order centered on the United Nations and a multilateral, international financial order centered on the World Bank and the International Monetary Fund. The author concludes by noting that in the future, there will be a multipolar world, one without dominant powers, but diverse ideals and government structures.

In Chapter 4, Øystein Tunsjø compares what he defines as the origins of a new bipolar international system and the superpower rivalry between the United States and China with the previous bipolar system and the superpower rivalry between the United States and the Soviet Union. Tunsjø argues that there are significant differences when it comes to economic interdependence, ideology, technology, and institutions, but that the most important difference shaping balancing and stability when comparing the two bipolar systems is geopolitics. Different geopolitical factors explain why there is less arms-racing and balancing in the new bipolar system; why the risk of a limited war is relatively higher; and why the United States and China are likely to focus their military rivalry on East Asia and be less involved in proxy wars in the periphery. While Tunsjø emphasizes the differences between the two bipolar systems of the twentieth and twenty-first centuries, he notes that current economic, ideological, technological, and military rivalry resembles some of the developments during the previous superpower rivalry in the twentieth century.

Chapter 5, by Robert S. Ross, examines how China's naval build-up is challenging the regional balance of power. As China has modernized and expanded its capabilities, the US Navy has experienced relative decline. The Chinese Navy now possesses a larger fleet than the United States Navy, and advanced technologies, challenging US maritime supremacy in East Asia. Ross shows that the United States retains advantages, but these advantages are eroding and the trend of China's rise persists. US declining capabilities has prompted the region's secondary powers to reconsider their alignments within the US–China great power competition; they are moving toward equidistance between the great powers. In conclusion, Ross contends that China's economic growth rate will slow, but there is little likelihood that the United States can halt the trend in the maritime balance. Rather, as the regional balance of power continues to evolve, the regional order will continue to evolve.

Part II considers how increased US–China rivalry and adversarial antagonism is affecting Europe. Where once Europe perceived itself to be in a tutelage role with respect to China, and the United States sought engagement with a China that it could recognize as a "responsible stakeholder", there is far greater equivalence in today's relationships and less agreement between Europe and the United States on how best to deal with a resurgent China.

Rosemary Foot's Chapter 6 examines how deterioration in Sino-American relations, a more ambitious China, together with a disruptive force in Washington has led European governments to face several policy dilemmas. A primary dilemma involves addressing the divisive challenges posed to Europe by China's growing material power and political influence, and the continent's continuing interest in the actual economic benefits that come from a close trading and investment relationship with Beijing. A second requires dealing with the turbulence that the Trump presidency has introduced into Europe–US relations. This includes determining how closely to align with the antagonistic approach that the Trump administration has adopted with respect to China. Foot argues there is a fluidity in policies not seen in earlier periods of discord that presages increased fragmentation across the Western world.

Following on from Foot's chapter, Gerlinde Groitl's Chapter 7 examines how the European model and the transatlantic partnership is in an existential crisis. This comes exactly at a time when rival powers such as Russia and China assert themselves on the world stage. Groitl argues the Western-shaped structures and Europe's regional order erode from within as much as they are challenged from non-Western competitors like Russia or China from without. The two established templates for European security, the alliance with the United States as well as European integration and political transformation, have become mired in crisis. In considering changed power realities and gridlock in international institutions, Groitl points out that it is not surprising to see the US act more unilaterally, disrupting the status quo. However, she maintains that the Trump challenge goes beyond previous crises in transatlantic ties as he sets out to destroy the liberal international order his predecessors had cultivated. As such, Groitl warns that Trump threatens to upend the political, economic, and normative grand strategic consensus that has tied Europe and the United States together for more than 70 years.

In Chapter 8, Philippe Le Corre focuses on how European states and the EU have adjusted to Chinese foreign direct investments (FDI) and the Belt and

Road Initiative (BRI) linking China and the European continent. From the early 2000s, China's "going global" policy encouraged Chinese companies, both state-owned and private, to pursue opportunities abroad in order to acquire technologies and expand their footprint, using Chinese state aid to develop. While the Chinese government has been promoting the BRI towards European countries, the reality is that most Chinese FDI, including by state-owned enterprises, has been targeting countries that did not officially join the BRI. Overall, Le Corre argues, Chinese FDI, especially state-backed, has tended to target the strong industries in advanced economies. This includes advanced manufacturing industries, with automotive, chemical, agribusiness, energy, and machinery taking a significant share of non-infrastructure (non-greenfield) investment. As Le Corre shows, it is mainly in those countries where infrastructure is weaker and who have a connection to the BRI that China has focused on building up railways and ports to connect its commerce routes. This is particularly the case with Greece and Balkan countries, which have attracted most "BRI-labelled investments."

Part III examines how the United States, China, the EU, and European states are adopting to new uncertainty. Anarchy and the rise and fall of great powers have been an enduring theme in international politics. The new superpower rivalry and uncertainty inherent in an anarchic international system reinforces security concerns about interdependence that have recently come to the fore with greater clarity in US–China relations. The US is now for the first time facing a potential power transition whereby it is the declining power.

In Chapter 9, Joshua Shifrinson shows that this has spurred the most intense grand strategy debate in the United States since after the Cold War. He discusses four grand strategies: Second Generation Primacy; Deep Engagement; Offshore Balancing; and Restraint. Regardless of what emerges, American grand strategy – its foundational "theory" over how to create security for itself using the political, economic, and military tools at its disposal – will be substantially different from those that preceded it. All things being equal, Second Generation Primacy and Deep Engagement are poised to gain traction the longer proponents can plausibly argue American unipolarity (or something close to it) endures. Conversely, the strategy is poised to lose salience in bipolar or multipolar conditions. Offshore Balancing and Restraint, on the other hand, gain traction the more the world shifts from unipolarity – albeit under different conditions. Just as the US grand strategy debate is itself in flux, so too are the international conditions that will drive the appeal of the different strategies. Shifrinson maintains that despite the uncertainty surrounding the international conditions that will drive the appeal of the different strategies, China and Asia are increasingly the focus of US strategy debates.

Just as the US grand strategy debate is in flux, so too is China's, argues Shi Yinhong in Chapter 10. He maintains that the US and China are increasingly slipping into the "Thucydides trap," the seemingly destined power struggle between the rising power and the established power. To avoid the Thucydides trap requires both China and the United States to exercise strategic self-restraint. This is not only challenging for the United States, accustomed to primacy for three decades, but a more powerful China is searching for a new grand strategy that reflects its new power status. To maintain its peaceful rise, China needs to adapt to a changing domestic and external environment. As the economy slows down, Shi contends that China needs to prioritize and balance between domestic, regional, and global ambitions. Shi advocates a period of strategic retrenchment, whereby China conducts, in Deng Xiaoping's words, a new type of "taking a low profile while doing something" strategy throughout the next five or six years. He argues that China should make strategic retrenchment in a sufficiently great degree, while conduct, in a Great Leap Forward manner, the improvements of its practices of trade and business, based on broadening, deepening, and speeding up domestic economic reform. A major strategic purpose of doing so, argues Shi, is to "strive for demobilization of its antagonists, before making new advances."

In Chapter 11, May-Britt Stumbaum argues that the EU and European states are seeking to translate strategies into initiatives and to let deeds follow words. The new Commission President Ursula von der Leyen, the former German Defence Minister, claims that she will be heading a "geopolitical Commission" that needs to develop a new relationship about power, and about exercising power. Asia is the most important trade and production region for the EU and Asian countries such as Japan, Korea, India, and China, as well as ASEAN and its member states, have concurrently increased their interest in working with the European Union – ranging from trade issues to climate change and cooperative security. Stumbaum contends that in an ever more Asia-centric era and amidst growing rivalry between two of the EU's prime strategic partners, the EU strives to maintain a rule-based order and avoid bipolar confrontations that force European states to choose sides between the United States and China. The EU Global Strategy's (EUGS) five key priorities – coping with mass migration resulting from the disaster- and conflict-induced displacement of people, maritime security, cybersecurity, and counterterrorism – resonate with the challenges of Asian partners, including the EU's strategic partners South Korea, Japan, India, and China.

In Chapter 12, Jo Inge Bekkevold argues that the forming of a China–Russia military alliance is a concern for the United States, and it would have implications for European security. The US preoccupation with China would be a lesser concern for Europe if Russia had a strained relationship with China, forcing Moscow to build a credible deterrence on its Asian flank. However, Sino-Russian ties are now better than ever, contends Bekkevold. The existing "strategic partnership" between China and Russia serves both parties well. It allows them to keep their strategic rear safe, and to channel resources into more pressing theaters, without any significant commitments to each other. This security arrangement is a major achievement for both China and Russia. The costs associated with entering into a formal alliance with mutual defense responsibilities might be larger than the benefits. Bekkevold maintains that even though the current Sino-Russian security arrangement serves their geopolitical interests well, it still has a way to go before it resembles an alliance.

Part IV examines the prospect for crisis management and confidence building in a new era of Sino-US confrontation. Chapter 13, by Zhang Tuosheng, examines China's security flashpoints, including the Korean Peninsula, the Taiwan Strait, the East China Sea, the South China Sea, and the China–India border area. Zhang argues that China's higher crisis-management awareness and the strengthening of crisis management are important factors explaining why none of these security flashpoints have erupted into a military conflict and war. He also shows how these mechanisms are improved, including (1) strengthening Chinese security decision-making through the Central Foreign Affairs Commission; (2) improving means of communications through the establishment of hotlines and security talks with the US, Japan, Russia, India, and other neighbors; (3) enhancing confidence-building measures through memorandums of understanding (MOUs) on air and maritime encounters and on prior notification of military activities between China and the US and with ASEAN countries; and (4) China's increased participation and hosting of regional security dialogues, such as ARF, ADMM plus, Shangri-La Dialogue, CICA, SCO meetings, and the Beijing Xiangshan Forum.

In Chapter 14, Isaac Kardon, argues that despite enhanced crisis management and confidence-building mechanisms, competition, not cooperation, is the watchword of the new era in US–China relations and that the absolute number of potential crises has increased. The new era does not bode particularly well for US–China maritime flashpoints, even as the costs of such an event mount. Given the growing capability fielded in the region and its increasing points of contact on water, in the air, and in the public arena, the perceived stakes are larger. While mechanisms for communication exist, and in some cases have been improved, Kardon maintains that the scope for cooperation appears to be narrowing as both sides adopt more adversarial postures. China's insecurity along its maritime frontier and US persistence in seeking access to those vulnerable points breed a spiraling dynamic. In this new era of great power competition, some of the brakes on conflict are being tested. The maritime flashpoints of East Asia are increasingly important sites to watch and manage some acute risks of Sino-US miscalculation and potential conflict. Overall, the several long-standing flashpoints of potential US–China crisis and conflict in the maritime domain are now riskier because of increasing capabilities, higher stakes, and growing geopolitical competition.

In Chapter 15, Ian Bowers develops a broader view of conflict management and arms-racing. He argues that a conventional arms dynamic coupled with potential technological and doctrinal advances is a new source of increasing uncertainty, therefore undermining US–China relations and East Asia stability. The interaction between Chinese conventional missile capabilities and US responsive strategies is already producing an arms competition. Advances in US counter-systems in part influence China's pursuit of numerical and technological superiority in its conventional missile force. Given the strategic and operational importance of Chinese conventional missile forces and the US focus on countering them, combined with the technological and economic resources of both sides, it is likely that both sides will continue to design around each other's advances. Such efforts suggest that even in its relatively nascent stage, this form of arms competition may lead to arms-race instability.

Further, these sources of instability, while being developed for the Asian theater of operations have substantial implications for European stability. The challenge posed by China is likely the primary driving force behind the acceleration of US weapon and doctrinal development; the capabilities that will result from this development will have strategic utility in Europe. Core concepts such as Prompt Global Strike, JAM-GC, and IAMD have global applicability and therefore influence the Russia–NATO dynamic. As the arms competition in Asia continues it will not remain confined to that region. Because the doctrines and weapons being developed have global implications, it is likely that Russia as a third party is now being forced to respond to ensure its own strategic interests are met. It is evident that both China and the US are engaged in an arms dynamic that may have unforeseen consequences in the conventional and nuclear realms as technology matures and both sides view the military balance with uncertainty. While there are few clear current off-ramps, arms control may not be impossible but will involve difficult choices for all involved.

In Chapter 16, Robert S. Ross concludes by summarizing the core themes of the volume. He starts out by examining how the US–China power transition affects the international politics of East Asia and Europe. He argues that the power transition is reshaping regional alignments, with heightened uncertainty and increased instability. The source of this instability and uncertainty is the changing US–China balance of power, reinforced by domestic political change and leadership characteristics. Together, these developments contribute to diminished confidence in East Asia and Europe in great power security commitments.

Notes

1 Robert S. Ross, Øystein Tunsjø, and Zhang Tuosheng, "Introduction," in Robert S. Ross, Øystein Tunsjø, and Zhang Tuosheng, eds., *US-China-EU Relations: Managing the New World Order* (New York: Routledge, 2010), 1–4.
2 Øystein Tunsjø, *The Return of Bipolarity in World Politics: China, the United States and Geostructural Realism* (New York: Columbia University Press, 2018).

PART I

Structure, order, and US–China relations

2

THE PRESENT AS PROLOGUE

The gloomy outlook for US–China relations

Avery Goldstein

Relations between China and the United States reached a turning point in 2019. Bilateral ties that had been characterized by a pattern of ups and downs over the past quarter century took a clear and possibly irreversible turn for the worse, reflected most vividly in the collapse of negotiations focused on an array of economic disagreements. The speed with which this deterioration occurred surprised many. Although there had been changes in the relationship that set the stage for what transpired, few had seen the present state of affairs as inevitable, let alone imminent. Many, however, now see the newly fraught relationship as irretrievably altered. Is it?

This chapter analyzes the trajectory of US–China relations in recent decades. In doing so, I draw on a taxonomy offered by Chas Freeman.[1] Freeman distinguishes among relations he labels "competitive transactionalism" (where two states pragmatically identify areas of mutual benefit), "rivalry" (where each seeks strategic advantages but neither seeks to undermine the other's interests or capabilities), "adversarial antagonism" (where each seeks strategic advantages but also seeks to undermine the other side's interests and capabilities), and "enmity" (where each targets the other to eliminate the threat it represents). Using these labels, I first briefly trace the shift from a US–China relationship that had been marked by various combinations of cooperation and conflict typical of competitive transactionalism after the Cold War, to one of rivalry in about 2010, and now to one best described as adversarial antagonism – though not yet enmity – during the Trump administration. Next, I identify the causes that produced this shift. I conclude by considering their implications for the future of US–China relations.

Shifting US–China relations

From competitor to rival

Once the Cold War ended, China and the US were no longer partners in an entente that had been forged to oppose the Soviet Union. Beginning in the

1990s and extending through the first decade of the twenty-first century, the United States and China reworked their relationship with an eye to enhancing cooperation (especially economic exchange) and isolating areas of conflict (especially disagreements about human rights and unresolved sovereignty disputes in East Asia). In the 1990s, President Clinton reciprocated President Jiang Zemin's interest in building a "constructive strategic partnership." In the 2000s, President Bush continued with a substantively similar approach, though his administration referred to it as a "candid, cooperative, and constructive relationship."[2] In retrospect, however, this continuity in bilateral ties over two decades looks like an artifact of the September 11, 2001 terrorist attacks on the US.

When the Bush administration first took office, observers had expected that the new administration would move away from Clinton's effort to build a strategic partnership and would instead deal with China as a strategic competitor or rival. President Bush's future national security adviser Condoleezza Rice had previewed this policy shift during the 2000 presidential campaign and, after the election, Secretary of Defense Donald Rumsfeld began drafting a Quadrennial Defense Review that aimed to transform the US military in preparation for challenges from a rising China.[3] Events unexpectedly intervened, however, derailing the planned changes in US–China policy. With the September 11 terrorist attacks against the United States, the Bush administration's strategic focus immediately turned to the "global war on terrorism" that entailed major military efforts in Afghanistan and Iraq. The protracted nature of those wars, the counterinsurgency operations they required, and ultimately the broadening of American struggles to deal with other dangerous nonstate actors across the Middle East and North Africa, precluded devoting much attention or resources to the strategic implications of a rising China. Moreover, China was cooperating with the American counterterrorism efforts, and then when the great recession occurred in 2007–2008 China became a useful partner in mitigating the worst effects and greatest risks of a global economic downturn. But as the recession eased, and as the US started to disengage from its protracted wars at the end of the decade, US–China relations changed.

After 2008, China's increasing wealth and power and its more active regional role altered American perceptions. Its remarkably rapid growth and, especially after accession to the WTO in 2001, its expanding international economic role, had put it on track to become the world's second largest economy and largest trading nation. In addition, its economic strength was accelerating a program of military modernization that had already benefitted from decades of generous budget increases and, increasingly, from the improving technological sophistication that a more advanced economy made possible. Along with these growing capabilities, China was adopting a more active foreign policy in East Asia that some labeled "assertive," and that fed concerns in Washington that drove new tensions in US–China relations.[4]

Concerns about the challenge a rising China might pose to US interests in the Western Pacific resulted in the Obama administration's rollout of its "strategic rebalance" or pivot. The rebalance included (1) American support for the con-clusion of the Trans-Pacific Partnership to counter China's growing regional economic influence, (2) reaffirmations of American alliance commitments to those facing challenges from China's stronger military, and (3) announcement of a reallocation of US military assets to the Asia Pacific.[5] This US declaration of its new strategic priorities elicited a strong reaction from Beijing which saw it as an attempt to contain China and forestall its rise.[6] After a decade's delay, the more competitive relationship that had been anticipated at the outset of the Bush administration was emerging.

The US and China were settling into a pattern of rivalry as both countries maneuvered for advantage while still seeking to avoid direct confrontations. In the South China Sea, China began fortifying its territorial holdings and maritime claims; the US publicized its military maneuvers asserting navigational rights in international waters, reiterated the American commitment to the Philippines under the mutual security treaty, and signaled its support for Manila's appeal to an international arbitral panel to rule on maritime disputes with China. In South Korea, Seoul agreed to deploy the American THAAD antimissile defense sys-tem for protection against a growing ballistic missile threat from North Korea; Beijing objected that THAAD's radar would adversely affect China's security by eroding the viability of its own nuclear deterrent and responded by adopt-ing economic policies to punish America's Korean ally.[7] Rivalry also character-ized regional economic developments as the US accelerated efforts to finalize the Trans-Pacific Partnership while China rolled out its plans for a new Asian Infrastructure Development Bank that would give Beijing a leading role in its own multilateral organization.[8]

From rival to adversary

By the end of the Obama administration, it was clear that the next US president would be managing a more contentious relationship with China. After Donald Trump became president, US–China rivalry deepened and ultimately moved in the direction of adversarial antagonism. This change did not occur imme-diately, despite the harsh rhetoric about China used by President Trump in the 2016 campaign. During his first year in office, the President and his more moder-ate advisers on China policy initially embraced personal diplomacy and summitry in an effort to achieve the ambitious transformation of the bilateral economic relationship that candidate Trump had promised. But when the attempt to "win without fighting" failed, the moderates lost influence or left the administration and President Trump quickly shifted to a new, tougher approach encouraged by advisers who backed a broadly confrontational stance toward China.

At the end of 2017, the Trump administration's view of China was formally articulated in its National Security Strategy and National Defense Strategy. For the first time in such a document, China was explicitly identified as a revisionist power whose rise threatened to undermine American interests. And from the fall of 2017, China's leader, Xi Jinping, began delivering major speeches in which he boldly proclaimed China's determination to realize the country's rejuvenation that would make it one of the world's leading military and economic powers by the middle of the twenty-first century, implicitly declaring a timeline for ending the era of American primacy that had followed the Cold War.[9]

The views being outlined in the two capitals reinforced each side's deepening concerns about the other. Rivalry was evident on four fronts. First, Washington ramped up the publicity for and tempo of US Navy challenges to Beijing's position in the South China Sea; China criticized these operations as provocations that challenged its interests and complicated its efforts to work with ASEAN states to reduce tensions by negotiating a Code of Conduct.[10] Second, recurrent hints that the US would strengthen its support for Taiwan exacerbated China's concern that Taiwan's newly elected leader, Tsai Ing-wen, would be emboldened to abandon the fragile consensus on "one-China" that Beijing thought had been agreed at Singapore in 1992.[11] Third, Xi Jinping's ambitious and ever-expanding international economic development program, the Belt and Road Initiative (BRI), elicited a newly strident response from the Trump administration which criticized the BRI as a scheme to advance China's global influence through "debt-trap diplomacy." And fourth, as the world edged closer to adopting potentially revolutionary 5G technologies in telecommunications, the anticipation of China's major stake in its deployment around the world was met with a fierce US response warning others, most importantly American allies and partners, that permitting China's companies to participate would put their national security and relations with the United States at risk. Typifying the shift from rivalry to adversarial antagonism, the US objection to China's principal player in 5G, Huawei, was not based mainly on the economic concern about unfair competition but on the fear that this Chinese company could be required to comply with directives from the CCP that threatened the security of the US and its allies. Washington argued that this threat justified completely excluding Huawei from the telecom infrastructure. The Trump administration put Huawei on the "entities list" that effectively prohibited US companies from selling it components and software crucial to its operations. Huawei defiantly argued that the American security concerns were groundless, while the Chinese government retaliated by creating its own entities list to target US companies with big stakes in China.[12]

The transition from limited competition to rivalry to adversarial antagonism in less than a decade seems, at first blush, surprisingly swift. But, as noted above, that is mainly because for the first decade of the twenty-first century, the United States had turned its strategic attention elsewhere. Although counterfactual reasoning is unavoidably inconclusive, the transition would likely have occurred sooner, if more gradually, had the Bush administration not been diverted from its initial strategic vision when it came to office in 2001 since the causes that produced swift changes later were already in play by the late 1990s. The next section identifies these causes.

Causes of the shift from competitor to rival to adversary

The constraints of the international system, as well as national attributes distinctive to the US and China, have both shaped the transformation of bilateral relations described in the previous section. Chief among the international constraints are the structural condition of anarchy in which all states find themselves and the distribution of power that defines the system's polarity. The national attributes most relevant to understanding the evolution of US–China relations are the countries' geographic locations, their technological capabilities, and their domestic politics. A brief review of these causes operating at the international and national levels suggests that the shift from limited competition to rivalry was very likely, perhaps overdetermined, even if its timing was unpredictable.[13]

International constraints

Anarchy

The condition of anarchy, the absence of an authority that can reliably resolve disputes among states, constrains all to think about the possibility that they will need to provide for their own security. When the intensity of such security concerns deepens, states are more likely to worry about their vulnerabilities, including those resulting from economic interdependence. While US–China relations were characterized by limited competition, each was comfortable with a focus on the mutual benefits they derived from economic exchanges. As the Chinese side frequently put it, these were "win–win outcomes." As rivalry took root, however, attention shifted from "win–win" to "who wins more?", especially on the American side where growing calls for reciprocity in all areas of US–China exchanges after 2010 reflected the perception that China was benefiting disproportionately from the relationship.[14] The view that engagement with China was helping to make it richer and stronger led to American objections and concerns that China's gains could ultimately jeopardize US security.[15] As the relationship moved toward rivalry, there was growing concern about relative gains and the security implications of the vulnerabilities that interdependence entails.

In response to such worries, Washington strengthened its regulation of prospective Chinese investments in the US. Typifying the new concern, President Trump decided to block China's Huawei from expanding its minor role in the US telecom sector.[16] Trepidation about the vulnerabilities that interdependence creates spread beyond economic relations and led Washington to tighten visa regulations governing the access of China's scholars to educational experiences at universities and research labs in the US. Exchanges previously deemed mutually beneficial were treated as problematic once the US worried that they might result in China acquiring expertise that could enhance its economic or military power.[17]

These American measures reinforced China's concerns about the implications of its own vulnerability. Particularly worrisome was the dependence on American sources for crucial inputs to technologically advanced sectors at the heart of Beijing's vision for the next stage of China's economic modernization. Washington's actions against Huawei demonstrated that the US would not hesitate to exercise the kind of leverage dependence created (and that had been previewed when the US banned sales to China's ZTE in April 2018, nearly putting that major telecom company out of business).[18] Although some modification of the draconian US policy toward Huawei could be included as part of a future US–China agreement to contain their economic disputes, the experience has already prompted Beijing to attach greater urgency to ending China's heavy dependence on American suppliers for critical components. China's gnawing doubts about future behavior in an anarchic international system where even formal treaties are ultimately self-enforcing contracts (a universal concern compounded by recent US decisions to withdraw from major international agreements) will limit its confidence in any reassurances that a deal might provide. The uncertainty inherent in an anarchic international order reinforces security concerns about interdependence that have recently come to the fore with greater clarity in US–China relations.

A shifting distribution of power: From unipolarity to bipolarity

The evolution of US–China relations during the past two decades has unfolded not only in the shadow of anarchy, but at a time when the distribution of power in the international system was shifting. This shift together with the concerns rooted in anarchy, undermined the feasibility of managing competition and fostered the emergence of rivalry and then a more adversarial relationship.

After the mid-1990s, China's rapid rise and the failure of any other state to follow a comparable trajectory initiated a transition in the structure of the international political system – away from the post–Cold War condition of unipolarity marked by America's position as peerless superpower. Barring a catastrophic collapse in China, that transition pointed toward a bipolar world sometime in the first half of the twenty-first century in which China and the United States would comprise a distinctive pair whose capabilities set them apart from all others on the global stage. Indeed, Oystein Tunsjø convincingly argues that by 2015 China had already drawn close enough to the US along relevant dimensions (mainly economic and military) that it was at least as much a second superpower as the Soviet Union was in the 1950s, and that there was little likelihood other countries could close the yawning gap between their capabilities and China's that would be necessary to raise the prospect of a multipolar, rather than a bipolar, world.[19]

Tunsjø's claim about the timing of this transition to bipolarity notwithstanding, by the turn of the twenty-first century China had emerged as the only plausible candidate to end the post–Cold War unipolar era of American supremacy. Once that reality dawned, both China and the US already had reason enough to focus their attention on one another with consequences that are similar to those that prevail under bipolarity.[20] Each country recognized that the other was, or (in the case of China) would soon be, its most capable strategic competitor and that there would not be third parties weighty enough to alter the balance of power between them. Their own efforts at amassing power would dwarf the contribution they could expect from allies.[21] In the new century, whether China succeeded in forging close ties with Russia to address shared concerns about American power, and whether the US succeeded in maintaining its close ties with Pacific partners to address shared concerns about a rising China, would not matter as much and could not substitute for the efforts undertaken by the two giants themselves. That reality was easy to foresee even before 2015, by which time China had significantly distanced itself from those in the next tier of powerful states (Japan, Germany, India, Russia, France, Britain) heralding the transition to a bipolar world.[22]

The sharp increase in China's capabilities reshaped relations with the US. Prior to the mid-1990s, speculation about China one day being a peer competitor for the US had been just that – speculation about a still lagging middle power.[23] Addressing China's growing, if still limited, international role at the time required only the modest competitive efforts undertaken by President Clinton to ensure the health of Cold War vintage alliances in Asia in 1996–1997.[24] However, China's economic development and global engagement accelerated shortly thereafter and its military began to reap some of the dividends of slow and steady modernization helped by selective purchases of advanced equipment from Russia. At the end of the 1990s, the dawning realization in the US that it had to anticipate the emergence of a new rival superpower motivated the Bush administration's initial plans to deal with China as a strategic competitor. And by the time the US redirected its strategic focus to the Asia Pacific under President Obama, the significance of China's economic and military rise had become unmistakable. If unipolarity had not yet ended, the handwriting was on the wall. In a league of their own, set apart from others by their massive capabilities, Beijing and Washington viewed one another not only as rivals but as rivals whose potential threats could not be countered by looking to others. As is expected in a bipolar world, they began to monitor one another more closely and compete more widely lest the other's gain be their loss. Each began to craft its economic and military policies with an eye to the challenge the other could pose. This ongoing shift in the distribution of power helps explain both the sharp increase over the past half-decade in American concerns about China's growing international economic role and its expanding (if still limited) military presence from Africa to the Arctic, as well as China's sensitivity to US measures that address those concerns. Bipolarity encourages zero-sum thinking that fosters acute attentiveness to the capabilities and behavior of one's most important potential adversary.

National attributes

The constraints of international structure are an important part of the explanation for changes in US–China relations. But the changes also reflect the fact that the two states responding to these constraints are the United States and China.

Geography

As anarchy and intimations of bipolarity encouraged China and the US to focus their attention on one another, that focus increasingly turned to the geographic space where the two countries' interests intersect, the waters of the western Pacific Ocean. Both see vital interests in the region. China's interests include securing the periphery of the homeland and defending contested sovereignty claims to land forms and associated maritime spaces in East Asia. US interests include upholding the credibility of America's international commitments, in this case manifest in security treaties with allies along China's periphery in the Western Pacific, several of whom have disputes with China, and upholding principles of international relations for which the US proclaims support – the peaceful settlement of international disputes and the rules governing freedom of navigation that are embodied in UNCLOS.

Before China's rise caught the attention of observers in Washington, conflicts over these interests in the Western Pacific were muted.[25] To be sure, in the 1990s both sides recognized that they had important interests in the region—especially tied to Taiwan and its adjacent waters, but also in the East and South China Seas where China was beginning to clarify and defend its claims. And both sides recognized the ability and willingness of the other to run risks in defense of their interests—as demonstrated during the 1995–1996 tensions in the Taiwan Strait. But, given China's relative weakness at the time, such concerns were not sufficient to overwhelm the desire of the US and China to limit their competition and preserve a bilateral relationship that benefitted both countries.

As China grew stronger and the US became more attentive, however, both began making contingency plans and deploying new forces that would be needed if their emerging rivalry resulted in armed confrontation. Importantly, the maritime arena on which the US and China were focused introduced some distinctive problems. Unlike the fixed positions of rivals based on land (e.g., the central front in Europe during the Cold War), even when forces at sea are not directly challenging one another they patrol, maneuver, and exercise in areas where units from both sides are present. Surveillance, tracking, trailing, warnings, and other naval actions institutionalize a posture that nurtures an adversarial psychology and increases the risk of incidents that can trigger military conflict.[26]

Technology

Technologies useful for coercion or military action have also shaped threat perceptions and the security concerns altering US–China relations. I discuss two key technologies – nuclear weapons and advancements in electronics, communications, and computers at first lumped together as marking a "revolution in military affairs" but now more often subsumed in discussions about the prospect of cyberwarfare.

Nuclear weapons

Unlike conventional military balances of power in which relative numbers are important because they can determine the outcome of battles and wars, when potential adversaries possess nuclear weapons, absolute numbers and blunt threats to punish are what matter most. Once a nuclear weapons state is confident that adversaries must worry that its arsenal provides an ability to inflict unacceptable retaliatory punishment, it has satisfied the requirements of a deterrent strategy that dissuades others from challenging its vital interests. Possession of nuclear forces, then, should mute the incentives for rivals or potential adversaries to compete in building ever-larger arsenals. But, as ever, reality is not so simple; strategic logic is only one influence on national decisions. In a bipolar world, or one that is emerging, the leading powers' close focus on the capabilities and intentions of their most important prospective military adversary induces exaggerated fears that any relative advantage *might* matter. The experience of the US and the Soviet Union during the Cold War suggests at least three ways bipolarity confounded the expectation of a muted nuclear competition that should follow from possession of what Bernard Brodie aptly termed "absolute weapons."[27]

First, the massive resources superpowers can muster allows them the luxury of hedging against unlikely but conceivable scenarios. During the Cold War, speculation about remote possibilities and Byzantine scenarios in which nuclear weapons could be used for purposes other than simple strategies threatening punishment accounted for much of the massive buildup in US and Soviet cold war arsenals beyond the requirements deterrence.[28] Second, when a single rival becomes the key benchmark for one's international position, invidious comparisons are readily drawn. These create political pressures that drive arms build-ups for reasons that have only a tenuous connection to military considerations. During the Cold War, a focus on the relative size and sophistication of the two superpowers' nuclear arsenals fueled concerns in both countries about their international status and triggered speculation about ways in which a perceived advantage in the balance of nuclear power might somehow affect their competition for influence around the globe.[29] Third, with a sole rival as the key measuring stick, invidious comparisons of nuclear warheads and delivery vehicles are readily invoked in domestic political debates. Armed services, weapons manufacturers, and politicians whose careers are tied to the national nuclear arsenal, benefit from funding its modernization and expansion. They have an incentive to play up security concerns about the grave risks the adversary's nuclear advantage might pose since this helps them make the case that the government needs to spend more on the weapon systems in which they have a stake.[30]

For two reasons, these sorts of strategically dubious concerns about the nuclear balance of power that can arise under bipolarity have not yet played an important role in US–China rivalry. One reason may be that American thinking about the nuclear balance has continued to focus on the superpower-sized nuclear inheritance that a declining Russia has maintained. Nevertheless, Washington has recently begun paying greater attention to the nuclear modernization of the rising Chinese superpower it will face in coming decades.[31] The US decision in 2019 to withdraw from the Intermediate Nuclear Forces Treaty mainly reflected concerns about Russian violations of the agreement. But Washington also objected to the treaty's restrictions because they prevented the US from deploying forces to counter the expanding arsenal of intermediate-range missiles that China, not party to the treaty, was deploying in Asia. And looking ahead, as the deadline to renew the US–Russia New Start Treaty approaches, Washington has also expressed its interest in including China in any new strategic arms control treaty that would constrain American deployments (a suggestion that China has rejected as at least premature given the still small size of its long-range nuclear arsenal compared to the US and Russia).

A second important reason for muted nuclear competition thus far has been Beijing's doctrinal embrace of a relatively simple deterrent strategy and the modest arsenal that it requires.[32] Adherence to this nuclear posture, however, has long reflected China's resource constraints and, when these eased, the higher priority Beijing attached to funding the modernization of its conventional forces. It remains to be seen if China's nuclear restraint will hold as its economic growth and technological progress provide an ever more adequate resource base for military investment, as rivalry with the United States deepens, and as institutional interests in China favoring a larger arsenal make their case. If Beijing does abandon its traditional restraint, the intensity of a US–China nuclear rivalry likely to further aggravate bilateral relations would, in part, also be shaped by the exaggerated beliefs about the importance of relative numbers in a bipolar world. The Cold War experience suggests that such strategically dubious beliefs will encourage a wasteful diversion of national wealth to deploy superfluous nuclear weapons systems.[33]

Cyberweapons

The technologies that enable cyberwarfare are also sharpening the rivalry between China and the US in at least four ways.[34] First, because military effectiveness is now dependent on networks that are typically more vulnerable than weapons themselves, both the US and China have reason to ramp up their readiness for taking the initiative should conflict occur, before the other side can disrupt their ability to coordinate action and assess threats.[35] Second, both the US and China have incentives to invest more resources in coping with the risks of cyberwarfare by building redundant capabilities to hedge against the risk of catastrophic failures in the networks necessary for the effective use of military capabilities. Third, both countries also have incentives to build ever larger traditional military arsenals for the blunt use of kinetic-force air, sea, missile, or space weapons – so that they have the option of launching preemptive strikes to neutralize the sources of cyberattacks before they begin.[36] And fourth, because the lines between cyberthreats posed to civilian and defense networks and between operations undertaken by a foreign government and those undertaken by private actors can be hazy, uncertainty fosters a broadening of fears about vulnerabilities to cyberattack beyond government and the military to commercial and educational sectors. This compounds US and Chinese concerns about interdependence and vulnerability discussed earlier.

Domestic politics

Domestic politics have also contributed to the worsening of bilateral ties between the US and China and sharpened their focus on one another as potential adversaries.

Because it is a liberal democracy, competitive electoral pressures in the US periodically transform policy analysis into partisan debate. As US policy toward a rising China has become a more salient issue, incumbents are often pressed to defend their approach to the challenges it may pose to American prosperity or security. Presidential aspirants, in particular, have an incentive to critique the incumbent's China policy, question its results, and assert that they could more effectively ensure US interests. Until recently, the political incentives to accuse one's rivals of being too soft on China produced a familiar electoral cycle in which winning presidential candidates came to office having pledged to get tough with China, only to decide once in office that the costs of confrontation outweighed the benefits of sustaining engagement.[37] But under President Obama doubts about the wisdom of continued engagement grew, and under President Trump doubts turned to deep skepticism.[38] Having entered what appears to be the post-engagement era for American China policy, one in which there is bipartisan consensus on viewing China as a dire challenge that must be countered, there is little reason to expect the previous pattern of moderation after elections to reemerge. The pressures of US politics now seem set to push candidates to argue even more forcefully for confronting China, and to constrain those who win elections from significantly moderating their position after victory.

In China, the domestic political pressures affecting relations with the US are not the result of electoral competition but of the authoritarian regime's concerns about performance legitimacy. Successfully delivering on its promises to improve the quality of life for the Chinese people and to stand up for China's interests on the world stage are the keys for the CCP to maintain domestic political support. Consequently, when US economic policies impose costs on China that jeopardize continued growth (such as the insistence that China must fully accede to the Trump administration's sweeping demands outlined early in bilateral economic negotiations), or when US security policies contest China's self-defined core interests (such as moves by the US Congress and the Trump administration to upgrade the 40-year old quasi-official American relationship with Taiwan that China has grudgingly tolerated but never accepted, or to increase well publicized challenges to China's maritime claims by US military ships and planes in the South China Sea) Beijing's CCP leaders have powerful incentives to stand firm rather than compromise, even if this fosters more adversarial US–China relations.[39]

Values

The values informing American and Chinese foreign policies reflect the different history and cultural traditions of each country. Such differences have not precluded cooperation when both countries have had common interests. But when common interests are weak or absent and relations have grown contentious, these differences in values have exacerbated tensions.

The American embrace of liberal values that developed during the Western Enlightenment, and the belief that political rights based on these values are a universal entitlement for all human beings, has long informed an idealistic streak in US foreign policy. When growing American power resulted in a more active international role beginning in the twentieth century, spreading these values around the world became a distinctive national purpose, one whose salience rose in the unipolar era of American preponderance after the Cold War ended.[40] Recently, this mission has increasingly colored American policy statements about China, perhaps most notably in US Vice President Michael Pence's highly publicized rollout of a harsher American view in October 2018. Pence not only cited Washington's concerns about the economic and military threat China posed, but also the challenge that China posed to values that the US insists are universal. His speech, and remarks by others in the Trump administration that focused on China's violations of values the US holds dear, contrast sharply with the more muted disagreements over such issues as late as the Obama administration.[41]

The values that imbue the thinking of leaders in the PRC arise out of a different tradition. They reflect pride in China's long history as the revered center of Sinitic civilization. This fuels a mission to restore the country to its former greatness destroyed through more than a century of domestic turmoil and foreign depredation ("the century of humiliation") that ended with the CCP's consolidation of power in 1949 and which a rising China is now better able to pursue. On a variety of issues, China's growing self-assurance and pride in regaining its international standing have affected relations with the US. In their ongoing economic dispute, Beijing has bridled at American demands and reminded the US that the days of a moribund Chinese regime agreeing to unequal treaties are over. The CCP depicted the terms on which the US was insisting in the economic negotiations during 2018–2019 as tantamount to an American ultimatum that would undermine China's interests and infringe on its sovereignty.[42] Similarly, the CCP has condemned the mounting American criticism of the regime's record on human rights, in particular its treatment of rights lawyers, democracy activists on the mainland and in Hong Kong, feminists, its massive detention and forced assimilation of Uyghurs in Xinjiang, and its restrictions on internet content. These are lambasted as brazen attempts to interfere in the country's internal affairs by a US that seeks to weaken a now strong, renascent China.

Conclusion

A shift towards rivalry in US–China relations, delayed by nearly a decade during which the US diverted its strategic attention elsewhere, accelerated after 2010. Recently, it has moved towards adversarial antagonism. The array of factors discussed above that have contributed to the deterioration in ties suggests that it will be increasingly difficult to return to the pragmatic sort of managed and limited competition that characterized the era of engagement during which both countries mainly focused on mutual benefits. China and the US are now mostly focused on relative rather than absolute gains, and on how those gains might affect the risks and threats they pose to one another. This is, as has been widely recognized, a significant change in bilateral relations. But it is important to add that this downturn in US–China relations does not necessarily presage a further deterioration in which antagonism feeds the sort of enmity that makes military conflict likely.[43] On the contrary, the experience of the Cold War suggests that nuclear-armed rivals are more likely to recognize the dire consequences of daring to move from even deep hostility to warfare.[44] Fear of the potential for prompt, obviously catastrophic outcomes provides powerful incentives for contemporary superpowers to recognize that their interests are best served by learning to live as adversaries despite their antagonism.[45]

One might hope, however, that even the lesser dangers and costs of their current confrontational posture would be incentive enough for China and the US to move away from the adversarial stance they are now adopting towards one another. After all, both should be able to recognize the limited advantages each gets from competing in the deployment of military forces when their use will be constrained by the fear of nuclear escalation. And both should be able to recognize the significant benefits available from sustaining some version of a rules-based, relatively open international economic order that can provide a framework for trade and investment as well as a setting within which they can address the inevitable disputes these generate.

Unfortunately, the current concerns about relative position and security – resulting from strong international constraints and domestic political pressures—that feed mutual mistrust are now so deeply entrenched that a return to a more moderate sort of US–China rivalry looks implausible. Though unlikely, it is certainly possible that the accumulating consequences of deepening antagonism will provide incentives that induce Beijing and Washington to make an effort to reverse the current trend. Acting on this impulse, however, would also require strong leadership in Washington and Beijing from those who want to fashion more productive bilateral ties. Such leaders would have to be strong enough to buck the domestic political pressures and international constraints that would make this sort of bold initiative so difficult.

Under current circumstances, it is hard to be optimistic about the chances for such a reversal of recent trends. Instead, the future of US–China relations seems set to resemble the fraught present rather than the hopeful past. If so, the dawning era of adversarial antagonism in US–China relations is likely to be protracted, peaceful, and pitiable – protracted, because there is little prospect that the conditions that have produced the current, more hostile relationship will change; peaceful because the consequences of war make it unlikely leaders would actually run the risk of uncontrolled escalation during a military confrontation; and pitiable because the US, China, and others will be worse off than they would be if they could manage their rivalry short of adversarial antagonism.[46] As others have emphasized, the new era seems unlikely to reprise the Cold War in which global ideological contestation paralleled the military and economic competition of power politics.[47] But given the international and national causes shaping and shoving the US and China, on their present course they seem headed for a twenty-first-century relationship that will share many unfortunate similarities with the decades-long era of US–Soviet antagonism.

Notes

1 Chas W. Freeman Jr., "A New Era in US-China Relations," *Remarks to the Watson Institute, Brown University, and the Fairbank Center, Harvard University,* November 13 and 14, 2018, https://chasfreeman.net/a-new-era-in-us-china-relations

2 Bonnie S. Glaser, "U.S.-China Relations: Fleshing Out the Candid, Cooperative, and Constructive Relationship," *Comparative Connections,* July, 2002, http://cc.pacfo rum.org/wp-content/uploads/2017/06/0202qus_china.pdf

3 Condoleezza Rice, "Campaign 2000 - Promoting the National Interest," *Foreign Affairs,* vol. 79, no. 1 (January-February 2000): 45–62. See "Quadrennial Defense Review Report," *United States Department of Defense,* September 30, 2001, http://www .defenselink.mil/pubs/qdr2001.pdf; Michael E. O'Hanlon, *Defense Policy Choices for the Bush Administration.* Second ed. (Washington, DC: Brookings Institution, 2002): chapter 1; Martin Kettle, "US Told to Make China Its No 1 Enemy: US Told to Target China Special Report: George Bush's America," *The Guardian,* March 24, 2001, https://www.theguardian.com/world/2001/mar/24/china.usa

4 See Michael D. Swaine and M. Taylor Fravel, "China's Assertive Behavior, Part Two: The Maritime Periphery," *China Leadership Monitor,* no. 35 (Summer 2011): 1–34; Andrew Scobell and Scott W. Harold, "An "Assertive" China? Insights from Interviews," *Asian Security,* vol. 9, no. 2 (May 1, 2013): 111–131; "Stirring up the South China Sea (I)," *Asia Report No. 223* (Brussels: International Crisis Group, April 23, 2012), http://www.crisisgroup.org/~/media/Files/asia/north-east-asia /223-stirring-up-the-south-china-sea-i.pdf; and "Stirring up the South China Sea (II): Regional Responses," *Asia Report No. 229* (Brussels: International Crisis Group, July 24, 2012), http://www.crisisgroup.org/~/media/Files/asia/north-east-asia/229 -stirring-up-the-south-china-sea-ii-regional-responses. For a view that questions the empirical warrant for the claims, see Alastair Iain Johnston, "How New and Assertive Is China's New Assertiveness?" *International Security,* vol. 37, no. 4 (Spring 2013): 7–48. See also Avery Goldstein, "U.S.-China Interactions in Asia," in David L. Shambaugh, ed., *Tangled Titans: The United States and China* (Lanham, MD.: Rowman & Littlefield, 2013): 263–291.

5 Though some saw this new American approach compensating for the Bush administration's alleged inattention to East Asia, the US had remained engaged in the region's

affairs even as its top priority was prosecuting the wars in Iraq and Afghanistan. See Thomas J. Christensen, *The China Challenge: Shaping the Choices of a Rising Power* (New York: W. W. Norton, 2015).

6 See "Foreign Ministry Spokesperson Liu Weimin's Regular Press Conference on November 17, 2011, *Ministry of Foreign Affairs, the People's Republic of China*. http://www.fmprc.gov.cn/eng/xwfw/s2510/2511/t879769.htm; Chris Buckley, "China Looks Across Asia and Sees New Threats," *Reuters*, November 10, 201. http://www.reuters.com/article/2011/11/10/us-china-asia-idU.S.TRE7A91CY20111110; Keith B. Richburg, "U.S. pivot to Asia makes China nervous," *The Washington Post*, November 16, 2011, http://www.washingtonpost.com/world/asia_pacific/us-pivot-to-asia-makes-china-nervous/2011/11/15/gIQAsQpVRN_story.html?; Barbara Demick, "China's Fury Building over Obama's New Asia Policy," *Los Angeles Times*, November 21, 2011. http://latimesblogs.latimes.com/world_now/2011/11/china-obama-asia-policy.html; "Chinese Spokesman Rebukes U.S.-Australian Military Alliance," *Xinhua*, November 30, 2011, http://news.xinhuanet.com/english2010/china/2011-11/30/c_131280105.htm

7 On China's concerns, see Li Bin, "The Security Dilemma and THAAD Deployment in the ROK," *Carnegie Endowment for International Peace*, August 3, 2016, http://carnegieendowment.org/2016/08/03/security-dilemma-and-thaad-deployment-in-rok-pub-64279; Ankit Panda, "THAAD and China's Nuclear Second-Strike Capability," *The Diplomat*, March 8, 2017, https://thediplomat.com/2017/03/thaad-and-chinas-nuclear-second-strike-capability/ On the vulnerability of China's nuclear arsenal to US counterforce strikes, see Charles L. Glaser and Steve Fetter, "Should the United States Reject Mad? Damage Limitation and U.S. Nuclear Strategy toward China," *International Security*, vol. 41, no. 1 (Summer 2016): 49–98. See Bonnie S. Glaser, Daniel G. Sofio, and David A. Parker, "Snapshot–the Good, the THAAD, and the Ugly: China's Campaign against Deployment, and What to Do About It," *Foreign Affairs*, February 15, 2017, https://www.foreignaffairs.com/articles/united-states/2017-02-15/good-thaad-and-ugly; Bonnie S. Glaser and Lisa Collins, "Snapshot: China's Rapprochement with South Korea: Who Won the THAAD Dispute?," *Foreign Affairs*, November 7, 2017, https://www.foreignaffairs.com/articles/china/2017-11-07/chinas-rapprochement-south-korea

8 See "The United States in the Trans-Pacific Partnership," Office of the United States Trade Representative, http://www.ustr.gov/about-us/press-office/fact-sheets/2011/november/united-states-trans-pacific-partnership; Xue Litai, "The Role that U.S. Plays in Asia," *China Daily*, November 24, 2011, http://www.chinadaily.com.cn/opinion/2011-11/24/content_14151883.htm; John Ross, "Realities behind the TransPacific Partnership," *China.org.cn*, November 18, 2011, http://www.china.org.cn/opinion/2011-11/18/content_23953374_2.htm; Zhou Luxi, "A Meeting of Minds, or U.S.-China Faceoff?" *China.org.cn*, November 11, 2011, http://www.china.org.cn/opinion/2011-11/11/content_23889056.htm; Natalie G. Lichtenstein, *A Comparative Guide to the Asian Infrastructure Investment Bank*. First Edition. ed. Oxford, United Kingdom: Oxford University Press, 2018.

9 Most notably, his speeches at the 19th CCP Congress in October 2017 and at the 13th National People's Congress in March 2018.

10 See Wei Fenghe, "Speech at the 18th Shangri-La Dialogue by Gen. Wei Fenghe, State Councilor and Minister of National Defense, PRC," *PLA Daily*, June 2, 2019, http://english.pladaily.com.cn/view/2019-06/02/content_9520790.htm

11 As China ramped up pressure on Tsai's Taiwan, the US Congress and the Trump administration called into question the American willingness to abide by its own long-standing "one-China policy" that sought to preserve a peaceful status quo in the Strait. Richard C. Bush, "A One-China Policy Primer," *Brookings Institution*, March, 2017, https://www.brookings.edu/wp-content/uploads/2017/03/one-china-policy-primer-web-final.pdf

12 See "Addition of Entities to the Entity List: A Rule by the Industry and Security Bureau," *Federal Register*, May 21, 2019, https://www.federalregister.gov/document s/2019/05/21/2019-10616/addition-of-entities-to-the-entity-list; Celia Chen, "Huawei among More Than 140 Chinese Entities on Us Trade Blacklist," *South China Morning Post*, May 30, 2019, https://www.scmp.com/tech/big-tech/article /3012321/huawei-among-more-140-chinese-entities-us-trade-blacklist; Teng Jing Xuan, "China to Set up Own 'Unreliable Entity' List for Foreign Firms," *Caixin Global*, May 3, 2019, https://www.caixinglobal.com/2019-05-31/china-to-set-up -own-unreliable-entity-list-for-foreign-firms-101422286.html

13 By contrast, the shift from rivalry to adversarial antagonism serves as a reminder that national- and international- level constraints and the theories that draw on them can only explain the broad contours of international affairs. Unexpected events (like the 9/11 attacks on the US that delayed the shift to rivalry), and the choices made by individual leaders (like Presidents Trump and Xi whose decisions have accelerated the deterioration of bilateral relations) affect the nature and timing of outcomes. See Kenneth N. Waltz, *Theory of International Politics* (Menlo Park, Ca: Addison-Wesley Publishing Co, 1979): 72. See also Avery Goldstein, "Structural Realism and China's Foreign Policy: Much (but Never All) of the Story," in Andrew Hanami, ed., *Perspectives on Structural Realism* (New York: Palgrave Macmillan, 2003): 119–154.

14 See Elizabeth C. Economy, "China's New Revolution," *Foreign Affairs*, vol. 97, no. 3 (May/June 2018): 60–74. See also Jennifer M. Harris, "Writing New Rules for the U.S.-China Investment Relationship," *Council on Foreign Relations*, December 12, 2017, https://www.cfr.org/report/writing-new-rules-us-china-investmen t-relationship; Brock Erdahl, "Restoring Reciprocity to U.S.-China Relations," *International Policy Digest*, April 15, 2018, https://intpolicydigest.org/2018/04/15/r estoring-reciprocity-to-u-s-china-relations/

15 That possibility had led the US Congress to create the US–China Security Economic Review Commission in 2000. Its mandate was precisely to consider whether the depth and breadth of US engagement with China might be jeopardizing American security interests. But while the top US strategic priority was prosecuting the global war on terrorism the Commission's effects on US China policy were limited. See https://www.uscc.gov/about

16 The Foreign Investment Risk Review Modernization Act of 2018 updating the rules for CFIUS reviews so that they could better deal with the new challenges China posed. "S.2098 – Foreign Investment Risk Review Modernization Act of 2018: 115th Congress (2017-2018)," *Congress.gov*, May 22, 2018, https://www.congress .gov/bill/115th-congress/senate-bill/2098; Demetri Sevastopulo, Kiran Stacey, and Nian Liu, "Donald Trump Issues Executive Order Laying Ground for Huawei Ban," *Financial Times*, May 16, 2019, https://www.ft.com/content/c8d6ca6a-76ab-11e9 -be7d-6d846537acab

17 Elizabeth Redden, "Stealing Innovation: FBI Director Addresses Efforts by China to Steal Academic Research and Technology," *Inside Higher Ed*, April 29, 2019, https://www.insidehighered.com/news/2019/04/29/fbi-director-discusses-chinese -espionage-threat-us-academic-research; see also "Director Addresses Council on Foreign Relations: Wray Says China Is 'Stealing Its Way Up the Economic Ladder'," *FBI News*, April 26, 2019, https://www.fbi.gov/news/stories/director-addresses-cou ncil-on-foreign-relations-042619. See also Lucy Hornby and Archie Zhang, "China Warns of Growing Difficulties Facing Students in US," *Financial Times*, June 4, 2019, https://www.ft.com/content/da0d5022-85df-11e9-a028-86cea8523dc2

18 Claire Ballentine, "U.S. Lifts Ban that Kept ZTE from Doing Business with American Suppliers," *New York Times*, July 13, 2018, https://www.nytimes.com/2018/07/13/ business/zte-ban-trump.html

19 Building on the seminal work of Kenneth Waltz, Tunsjø emphasizes that bipolarity is defined not by the equivalence of the two leading states in the international system but by the large gap between their capabilities and the next group of powerful states.

Øystein Tunsjø, *The Return of Bipolarity in World Politics: China, the United States, and Geostructural Realism* (New York: Columbia University Press, 2018); see also Yan Xuetong, "Why a Bipolar World Is More Likely than a Unipolar or Multipolar One," *New Perspectives Quarterly*, vol. 32, no. 3 (July 2015): 52–56. Yan Xuetong, *Leadership and the Rise of Great Powers*, The Princeton-China Series (Princeton, NJ: Princeton University Press, 2019).

20 Power transition theory similarly highlights the attention a rising challenger and a dominant power pay to one another, though it mainly addresses the motivations for war launched by the dominant power (to forestall the arrival of a competitor) or the challenger (to overcome the dominant power's resistance to its rise). See A.F.K. Organski and Jacek Kugler, *The War Ledger* (Chicago, IL: University of Chicago Press, 1980); Dale C. Copeland, *The Origins of Major War* (Ithaca, NY: Cornell University Press, 2000); Ronald L. Tammen, *Power Transitions: Strategies for the 21st Century*; Graham T. Allison, *Destined for War: Can America and China Escape Thucydides's Trap?* (Boston, MA: Houghton Mifflin Harcourt, 2017); cf. Lawrence Freedman, "Destined for War: Can America and China Escape Thucydides's Trap?," *Prism*, vol. 7, no. 1 (2017): 175–178, http://cco.ndu.edu/Portals/96/Documents/prism/prism_7-1/15-BR_Freedman.pdf?ver=2017-09-14-133601-573
   Whatever its merits as an explanation for great power war, the mutual suspicion it highlights as relative power shifts echoes the closer attention that results once the prospect for a shift from unipolarity to bipolarity is recognized.

21 As during the Cold War, allies are useful and often desirable, but for dealing with the top priority of the other superpower they are neither necessary nor sufficient. China's support of the Soviet Union early in the Cold War augmented Moscow's international role; but Soviet security depended on the massive military might the regime was able to deploy. China's shift to supporting the US in confronting the Soviets after 1970 which required Moscow to face the prospect of a two-front war and the military contribution of America's NATO allies both augmented the US ability to discourage Soviet adventurism in Europe; but the US ability to secure its vital interests in Europe and elsewhere ultimately depended on the outsized American military contribution.

22 See Tunsjø, *The Return of Bipolarity in World Politics*, esp. chapter 4.

23 See Avery Goldstein, "Great Expectations: Interpreting China's Arrival," *International Security*, vol. 22, no. 3 (Winter 1997/98): 36–73. See also, Thomas J. Christensen, "Posing Problems Without Catching Up: China's Rise and Challenges for U.S. Security Policy," *International Security*, vol. 25, no. 4 (2001): 5–40.

24 See Avery Goldstein, *Rising to the Challenge: China's Grand Strategy and International Security* (Stanford, CA: Stanford University Press, 2005), chapter 5.

25 See Robert S. Ross, "The Geography of the Peace," *International Security*, vol. 23, no. 81 (Spring 1999): 81–118.

26 These risks may be increasing as China deploys maritime militia and its coast guard in disputed areas, as the US deploys its coast guard as well, and both begin focusing on so-called gray-zone actions that risk escalating to military conflict that could draw in regular naval forces. See Andrew S. Erickson and Ryan D. Martinson, eds., *China's Maritime Gray Zone Operations*, Studies in Chinese Maritime Development (Annapolis, MD: Naval Institute Press, 2019); Chen Xiangmiao, "How the Gray Area Contest Between China and the U.S. in the South China Sea Can Become the Norm," *China-US Focus*, August 09, 2019, https://www.chinausfocus.com/foreign-policy/how-the-gray-area-contest-between-china-and-the-us-in-the-south-china-sea-can-become-the-norm

27 Bernard Brodie, ed., *The Absolute Weapon* (New Haven, CT: Yale Institute of International Studies, 1946).

28 States with tighter resource constraints settled for modest arsenals that satisfied their asymmetric nuclear deterrent strategies. See Avery Goldstein, *Deterrence and Security in the 21st Century: China, Britain, France and the Enduring Legacy of the Nuclear Revolution* (Stanford, CA: Stanford University Press, 2000).

29 Lawrence Freedman, *The Evolution of Nuclear Strategy*. 3rd ed. (Houndmills, Basingstoke, Hampshire/New York: Palgrave Macmillan, 2003): 350; Robert Jervis, "The Political Effects of Nuclear Weapons: A Comment," *International Security*, vol. 13, no. 2 (Fall 1988): 80–90.

30 The effectiveness of such claims can be further strengthened when the adversary boasts about its new nuclear accomplishments, providing fuel to those who have an institutional interest in emphasizing the urgency of competing more vigorously. Classic examples of this during the Cold War include US self-criticism about an emerging "missile gap" in the late 1950s made to appear all the direr because of Nikita Khrushchev's repeated boasting about the significance of the Soviet nuclear buildup.

31 See Office of the Secretary of Defense, "Annual Report to Congress: Military and Security Developments Involving the People's Republic of China 2019," May 2, 2019, https://media.defense.gov/2019/May/02/2002127082/-1/-1/1/2019_CHINA_MI LITARY_POWER_REPORT.pdf; Lara Seligman, "Will Congress Let Trump Build More Nuclear Weapons?," *Foreign Policy*, April 11, 2019, https://foreignpolicy.com /2019/04/11/will-congress-let-trump-expand-americas-nuclear-arsenal/

32 See Alastair Iain Johnston, "China's New 'Old Thinking': The Concept of Limited Deterrence," *International Security*, vol. 20, no. 3 (Winter 1995/1996): 5–42; Goldstein, *Deterrence and Security in the 21st Century*; Yunzhu Yao, "China's Perspective on Nuclear Deterrence," *Air & Space Power Journal*, vol. 24, no. 1 (Spring 2010): 27–30; M. Taylor Fravel and Evan S. Medeiros, "China's Search for Assured Retaliation: The Evolution of Chinese Nuclear Strategy and Force Structure," *International Security*, vol. 35, no. 2 (Fall 2010): 48–87; Fiona S. Cunningham and M. Taylor Fravel, "Assuring Assured Retaliation: China's Nuclear Posture and U.S.-China Strategic Stability," *International Security*, vol. 40, no. 2 (Fall 2015): 7–50.

33 Inklings of such a shift are already evident. Some military analysts in China have begun discussing the force requirements of nuclear warfighting if deterrence fails and have expressed concerns about the adequacy of the retaliatory forces that would survive an American first strike especially when retaliation would have to penetrate improving US missile defenses.

34 The various ways these new technologies are becoming a key arena of US–China rivalry have been reflected in institutional adjustments on both sides—including the growing importance of US Cybercommand as well as restrictions on American internet companies selling technology and software to China, and China's establishment of both its Strategic Support Force in the PLA to better prepare for electronic, space, and cyberwarfare, and in its party and state bodies to more tightly control the civilian internet.

35 In this respect, the technology reinforces institutional preferences in the military for offensive warfighting doctrines and by fostering beliefs in at least the initial advantages of the offense, aggravates the security dilemma between the US and China— with adverse implications for arms buildups and mutual suspicion. See Barry R. Posen, *The Sources of Military Doctrine: France, Britain, and Germany Between the World Wars* (Ithaca, NY: Cornell University Press, 1984).

36 See Avery Goldstein, "First Things First: The Pressing Danger of Crisis Instability in U.S.-China Relations," *International Security*, vol. 37, no. 4 (Spring 2013): 66–68.

37 President Obama's election in 2008 deviated from this pattern at a time when China issues were on the back burner.

38 See David M. Lampton, "The US and China: Sliding from Engagement to Coercive Diplomacy," *PacNet Number 63*, August 4, 2014, http://csis.org/publication/pacnet-63-us-and-china-sliding-engagement-coercive-diplomacy; John J. Mearsheimer, "Can China Rise Peacefully?" *The National Interest*, October 25, 2014, http://national interest.org/commentary/can-china-rise-peacefully-10204; David M. Lampton, "A Tipping Point in U.S.-China Relations Is Upon Us," *U.S.-China Perception Monitor,*

May 11, 2015, http://www.uscnpm.org/blog/2015/05/11/a-tipping-point-in-u-s
-china-relations-is-upon-us-part-i/; Kevin Rudd, "U.S.-China 21– the Future of
U.S.-China Relations Under Xi Jinping: Toward a New Framework of Constructive
Realism for a Common Purpose," *Belfer Center for Science and International Affairs,
Harvard Kennedy School,* April, 2015, http://asiasociety.org/files/USChina21_English
.pdf; Kurt M. Campbell and Ely Ratner, "The China Reckoning," *Foreign Affairs,* vol.
97, no. 2 (March–April 2018): 60–70; Wang Jisi, J. Stapleton Roy, Aaron Friedberg,
Thomas Christensen, Patricia Kim, Joseph S. Nye Jr., Eric Li, Kurt M. Campbell,
and Ely Ratner, "Did America Get China Wrong? The Engagement Debate," *Foreign
Affairs,* vol. 97, no. 4 (July–August 2018): 183–95; Aaron L. Friedberg, "Competing
with China," *Survival,* vol. 60, no. 3 (June–July 2018): 7–64; Jonathan D. Pollack
and Jeffrey A. Bader, "Looking Before We Leap: Weighing the Risks of US-China
Disengagement," *Policy Brief,* July, 2019, https://www.brookings.edu/wp-content/
uploads/2019/07/FP_20190716_us_china_pollack_bader.pdf

39 The CCP can compromise when it wants to and has sometimes done so in ways that
serve China's interests. See Jessica Chen Weiss, *Powerful Patriots: Nationalist Protest in
China's Foreign Relations* (Oxford: Oxford University Press, 2014).

40 See Anthony Lake, "From Containment to Enlargement," Johns Hopkins University,
Washington, D. C. September 21, 1993, https://www.mtholyoke.edu/acad/intrel/la
kedoc.html; Rasmus Sinding Søndergaard, "Bill Clinton's 'Democratic Enlargement'
and the Securitisation of Democracy Promotion," *Diplomacy & Statecraft,* vol. 26,
no. 3 (September 2015): 534–551. This ideologically defined mission for US foreign
policy informed the expansion of NATO membership in Central and Eastern Europe
to grow the community of free-market democracies, military action in Afghanistan,
Iraq, and Libya to effect democratic regime change, and support for mass movements
across the Middle East, North Africa, and Central Asia who called for an end to
authoritarian rule.

41 On the Obama approach set forth by Secretary of State Clinton, see "Clinton:
Chinese Human Rights Can't Interfere with Other Crises," *CNN Politics,* February
22, 2009, http://edition.cnn.com/2009/POLITICS/02/21/clinton.china.asia/
See "Remarks by Vice President Pence on the Administration's Policy Toward
China," *The White House,* October 4, 2018, https://www.whitehouse.gov/briefing
s-statements/remarks-vice-president-pence-administrations-policy-toward-chi
na/; Michael R. Pompeo, "On the 30th Anniversary of Tiananmen Square," *U.S.
Department of State,* June 3, 2019, https://www.state.gov/on-the-30th-anniversary-
of-tiananmen-square/

42 Beijing's response has included a massive patriotic campaign emphasizing national
pride and preparing the country for the possibility of a full-blown trade war. In part,
the campaign taps the raw nerve of historical humiliation and invokes the proud
memory of a much poorer and weaker China's history of resistance under CCP
leadership. See Zhou Xin and Sarah Zheng, "Xi Jinping Rallies China for Decades-
Long 'Struggle' to Rise in Global Order, Amid Escalating UU Trade War," *South
China Morning Post,* September 5, 2019, https://www.scmp.com/economy/china-
economy/article/3025725/xi-jinping-rallies-china-decades-long-struggle-rise
-global

43 In short, war between the two is not inevitable; it is arguably improbable, though
always possible. On these issues, see the hotly debated book by Allison, *Destined for
War.*

44 Still, the crises that punctuated the first 15 years of the Cold War were frightening
learning experiences that effectively chastened leaders in Moscow and Washington
in ways that led them to accept that they would have to live as adversaries rather than
enemies. See Goldstein, "First Things First," 58: 62–63.

45 Or, as John Lewis Gaddis put it, the absence of great power war means that the "Cold
War" might more aptly be labeled the "Long Peace." See John Lewis Gaddis, "The

Long Peace: Elements of Stability in the Postwar International System," *International Security*, vol. 10, no. 4 (Spring 1986): 99–142.

46 A world in which China and the US strive to minimize the vulnerability they see in economic interdependence and the security risks they see in sharing potentially sensitive knowledge and technology will also affect the many countries that have benefitted from being part of global supply chains and from the competition inherent in a relatively open international economy.

47 Thus far, intensifying US–China antagonism has not resulted in much of a competition to establish ideologically defined blocs. Some in the US, however, have suggested that China aims to spread its authoritarian alternative to liberal democracy (either by power of example or by leveraging China's economic and military might to influence others). See Jessica Chen Weiss, "A World Safe for Autocracy? China's Rise and the Future of Global Politics," *Foreign Affairs*, vol. 98, no. 4 (July/August 2019): 92-102. On the prospect of a new cold war, see Hunter Marston, "The U.S.-China Cold War Is a Myth," *Foreign Policy*, September 6, 2019, https://foreignpolicy.com/2019/09/0 6/the-u-s-china-cold-war-is-a-myth/; Odd Arne Westad, "The Sources of Chinese Conduct," *Foreign Affairs*, vol. 98, no. 5 (September/October 2019): 86–95.

3

THE LIBERAL INTERNATIONAL ORDER

A Chinese perspective

Wang Dong

Defining the liberal international order

In the aftermath of World War II, two postwar arrangements emerged: one is the containment system, and the other the Western liberal democratic order. Unlike the order centering on containment, the liberal democratic order survived the Cold War. Today, the liberal international order has become more extensive and consolidated. While developing a liberal international order featuring economic openness, political reciprocity, and multilateral management, the United States ensures that participants in the America-led system can increasingly benefit from it, and thus endows the liberal order with high legitimacy and great persistence.[1]

The concept "liberal international order" refers to the kind of international order with liberalism as its basis. G. John Ikenberry (1999) developed the theory of "structural liberalism." In the post–Cold War era, in the absence of the Soviet threat, the realist balance of power theory would expect Western security organizations, such as the North Atlantic Treaty Organization (NATO), to weaken. International relations will return to a situation where economic rivalry, security dilemma, and arms races will reemerge.[2] Nevertheless, Ikenberry notes that, in the wake of World War II, the United States and its allies created a liberal political, economic, and strategic order that has five main features. The first is the practice of security co-binding as a liberal solution to the problem of cooperation under anarchy. By binding itself with allies and partners through security arrangements such as NATO, the United States was able to reassure allies and partners and alleviate their fear of preponderant American power, therefore helping facilitate security cooperation between the United States and its allies and partners. The second explores the penetrated character of American hegemony and its reciprocal rather than coercive nature, which is mainly demonstrated in transparency, the diffusion of power into many hands, and the multiple points of access to policy-making. The third points to the role of the semi-sovereign as structural features of the Western political order. For example, for Germany and Japan, the "peace constitutions" initially imposed on them have come to be embraced by the German and Japanese publics as acceptable. The fourth feature indicates that economic openness makes it hard to calculate relative gains and gives rise to fast changes of relative gains. The interdependence of industrial sectors enhances liberal democracy. And the fifth is that the common civic identity, shared norms, and political identities give the Western political order cohesiveness and solidarity.[3] Ikenberry argues that the United States established a durable postwar order, and obtained the loyalty of other countries to this order by choosing to restrain its own power, so as to transform its own strength into a durable, legitimate, reciprocal order that is in line with its own interests.[4]

Challenges facing the liberal international order

The liberal international order is faced with multiple challenges. Many Western analysts and politicians argue that the challenges come from the "revisionist states" China and Russia. In Asia, the rise of China threatens to challenge the United States' economic and military hegemony, as Beijing seeks to draw American allies such as the Philippines and Thailand into its political orbit. In the Middle East, the United States and its European allies have failed to guide the region toward a more liberal and peaceful future in the wake of the Arab Spring and have proved powerless to halt the conflict in Syria. Russia's geopolitical influence has reached heights unseen since the end of the Cold War, as the country attempts to roll back liberal advances on its periphery.[5]

Other scholars, however, contend that the rise of China would not pose an existential threat to the American-led postwar liberal order. China does not just face the United States; it faces a Western-centered system that is open, integrated, and rule-based, with wide and deep political foundations. China will not be able to surpass the United States in terms of national power, nor will it be able to exclude the United States from the Western Pacific. It can be assured that although the relative power of the United States may decline, the liberal international order will survive. This is mainly a result of three characteristics of the liberal international order. First, the liberal international order is built around rules and norms of nondiscrimination and market openness, creating conditions for rising states to advance their expanding economic and political goals within it. Second, the stakeholders of the current liberal international order include a coalition of powers arrayed around the United States. Third, the postwar liberal international order is more open and rule-based than any previous order.[6] There are also scholars who expect that China will play a constructive role in shaping the emerging order. For instance, Wu Xinbo (2018) holds that China will aim to preserve the liberal features of the existing order while curtailing its hegemonic nature. Instead of attempting to overthrow the existing order, China would pursue selective and incremental adjustments that will over time lead to a "liberal partnership international order."[7]

And in terms of soft power, a recent index published by Portland, a London consultancy, ranks the United States in first place and China in twenty-eighth place. Moreover, China is a beneficiary of the existing international order. It is one of the five permanent members of the UN Security Council, and its voting rights in the World Trade Organization and the International Monetary Fund are increasing. Besides, China is now the second-largest funder of UN peacekeeping forces and has participated in UN programs related to Ebola and climate change. In recent years, Beijing had joined hands with Washington in developing new norms for dealing with climate change. On balance, China has not tried to overthrow the liberal international order; rather, it aims to increase its influence within the existing order.[8]

Still others hold that challenges confronting the liberal international order stem from inside Western countries. For instance, the European Union expansion has halted, and the United Kingdom is to pull out of the EU. The liberal international order has survived the Cold War. Yet so long as the economies of its leading members remain fragile and their political institutions dysfunctional, the order that they have championed is unlikely to regain the political momentum that helped Western democracy spread across the globe. Instead, it will evolve into a liberal international economic order that encompasses states with diverse domestic political systems.[9]

Some Western analysts deplore that for over the last few decades countries that suffered "democratic setbacks" outnumbered those that registered gains. Yet now, the United States has withdrawn its moral support for the promotion of democracy around the world. The United States also questions the fabric of international cooperation – security treaties, open markets, multilateral institutions and, attempts to address such global challenges as climate change. For Washington, relations are now to be transactional. Therefore, the challenges facing the international order come from inside the West rather than from China or Russia. This is a lesson to learn as populism suddenly returns to the West, which is most evidently shown in Brexit and Mr. Trump's election as US president.[10]

There are scholars who acknowledge that the US-led liberal hegemonic order is in crisis. But they view it as a crisis of authority within the liberal international order and not a crisis of its underlying principles and organizational logic. That is, it is a crisis of the American governance of the liberal international order and not of the liberal international order itself. These scholars argue that the liberal international order does not belong to the United States or Western countries, but to the whole world; that the leading countries in the global system are still on the same path of modernity; and that democracy and the rule of law remain the symbol of modernity and the global standard of legitimate governance. Donald Trump, as a revisionist, is the greatest challenge to the international order. These scholars also believe that the United States or other Western countries may rise and fall within the existing global system, but the liberal characteristics of the system are still beneficial and attractive to most countries. The current crisis cannot prove that liberalism is wrong, but rather liberal governance has some problems, which can only be resolved through reflecting, reconstructing, and expanding the liberal international order.[11]

There are more critical voices that contend that the disintegration of the liberal international order is inevitable, resulting from its inherent flaws from the very beginning. John Mearsheimer offers such a critique. The foundation of a liberal international order is the spread of liberty and democracy in the world, which has encountered significant resistance in the form of national self-determination. In addition, the hyper-globalization brought about by the liberal order has caused economic distresses in the lower and middle classes of many Western countries, which in turn gives rise to populism and anti-globalization, thus undermining the very foundation of the liberal order. Finally, the liberal order has helped accelerate China's rise, which has helped transform the international system from a unipolar system to a multipolar one. A liberal international order is possible only in a unipolar world. The new multipolar world will feature three realist orders: a thin international order that facilitates cooperation, and two bounded orders – one dominated by China, the other by the United States – poised for waging security competition between them.[12]

Re-understanding of the liberal international order

The post–World War II international order: A mosaic order

The liberal international order is not an accurate description of the post–World War II international order. Rather than being a "singular" liberal order as assumed by the narrative of the liberal international order, the post–World War II order is in fact mosaic-like, composed of different layers of sub-orders including a multilateral political order centered on the United Nations and a multilateral, international financial order centered on the World Bank and the International Monetary Fund. Both sub-orders have elements of liberalism, but they also contain the connotation of respecting national sovereignty. Many Western scholars also regard human rights as part of the liberal international order. However, in the wider world, human rights are a political norm or issue advocated by the United States and European Union, who are trying to use it to shape the behavior of and interaction between countries. Different countries and regions have different understandings and interpretations of the specific connotation of human rights. Obviously, the developed world, including the United States and the EU, emphasizes the political aspect: freedom of speech, freedom of assembly, etc., while developing countries call for basic rights to survival and economic development, which belong to the economic aspect of human rights. In short, the post-World War II order is not totally liberal to begin with.

The Western definition of freedom is based on the Atlantic Charter, including freedom of speech, freedom of religion, freedom from want, and freedom from fear. However, the Atlantic Chapter was signed only by Western powers. The only common basis for postwar order is the United Nations Charter, which was based largely on Westphalian principles rather than the liberal principles to which Western powers are committed. Respect for state sovereignty and non-interference are not just norms enshrined in the United Nations Charter. They are also an integral part of the deep operating logic of the international order. Indeed, current debate between the West and non-Western powers such as China and Russia are not so much about the liberal international order itself but about different versions of it.[13]

To sum up, the postwar international order is mosaic. The postwar order has a strong liberal spirit, but it is questionable to use only "liberal" to describe the postwar order. First, the "liberal consensus" of political democracy, market economy, religious tolerance, and individual freedom is only consensus in the Western world, which has minimal support in developing countries, including the Islamic world. Second, the constitutionality embodied in the liberal international order is essentially that the United States restricts itself to obtaining the acquiescence and obedience of other countries. This acquiescence and obedience are fundamental, and one may argue constitutionalism embodies respect for the sovereignty of other countries.

The liberal international order concept suffers some major deficiencies. Most fundamentally, the concept of liberal international order is inward looking and exclusive; it focuses on interactions between states that are members of the liberal international order. "Non-liberal" states such as China and Russia are excluded from the order and are viewed as the "Other," an alien that needs to be "liberalized." This is a serious limitation, and as a result the liberal international order becomes a partial order since it does not (and did not) include key major powers that are not "liberal states" by definition.[14] During the Cold War, for example, the liberal international order did not include the Soviet Union; today, neither China nor Russia is fully included. Consequently, the concept can shed little light on the most important issues in contemporary international relations – specifically, the prospects for peace and cooperation between the United States and its allies, on the one hand, and its competitors, such as China and Russia, on the other.

China and the international order

China was a socialist country during the Cold War and, judging by the ideology of liberalism, it was outside the liberal international order. However, China did not totally belong to the socialist camp. Kissinger-type realists regarded China as a revisionist country that needed to be transformed to be a realist power, following the logic of the balance of power. In the 1970s, with rapprochement between Beijing and Washington, the strategic triangle of China, the United States, and the Soviet Union was formed. China, however, was not part of the liberal international order led by the United States. The perspective adopted by

Kissingerians regarded China as an outsider of the US-led international order. It holds that China is the party that should change, an "oddity" that needs to be transformed and integrated into the US-led liberal international order.

After the Cold War ended, such a Kissingerian epistemology was inherited by US officials, and Washington continued to view China as an "oddity" that needs to be "liberalized" economically and, eventually, politically. The debate in the early 1990s over whether to contain or engage China was essentially based on such a dichotomy. The Clinton administration finally decided to pursue the "engagement" strategy toward China, with the implied premise or expectation that over time, China would not only accept economic liberalism, but also liberalize its political system. In the past two or three years, US–China relations have undergone a "paradigm shift" and many US analysts and politicians declare the bipartisan, decades-long US engagement strategy toward China a colossal "failure." Many US strategists and officials begin to view China as the biggest threat to the US-led liberal international order. Part of such a shift stems from the perception and frustration that China has failed to move from economic liberalization to political liberalization as expected by the US liberal vision of "engagement."

The aforementioned expectation of the United States represents a rigid state of mind, which coincides with the connotation of a Chinese fable, "Marking the Boat to Locate the Sword" (*ke zhou qiu jian*). The story is about a Chu State gentleman in ancient China who went out to travel by boat. When crossing the river, he accidentally dropped the sword that he was carrying into the water. So, he used a knife to engrave a mark on the gunwale. When the boat went ashore, he swam in the marked direction to search for the sword, but failed to find it. The sword that had fallen into the river did not follow the boat, while the boat and the mark constantly moved forward. By the time the boat reached the shore, the mark and the position of the sword in the water had become irrelevant. The moral of this story is that when a situation changes, it cannot be understood by an old way of thinking. The international order is constantly changing, but the way the West treats China is like making a mark on the boat, that is, that the market economy will inevitably bring about freedom and democracy. The West wanted to find the changed China according to this mark, but to no avail. Therefore, when it comes to understanding China, the West, especially the United States, has fallen into an epistemological trap of seeking a sword by marking the boat.

Conclusion: The future of the international order

The future of the international order faces many challenges. In the West, nationalism is on the rise, and for many, China and the United States are increasingly slipping into (should they have not yet fallen into) the "Thucydides trap," the seemingly destined power struggle between the rising power and the established power. To avoid the Thucydides trap requires both China and the United States to exercise strategic self-restraint. The West needs to change the way it understands

China. Previously, the West had always believed that it owned the "intellectual property rights" to the liberal international order, and that whether or not China could join the order depends on its performance. However, the reality is that the world is pluralistic, and the West must acknowledge that there are diverse pathways toward modernity. Each sovereign state has the right to choose its own path of development. Understanding the future of a liberal international order requires the West to get out of this epistemological trap of "marking the boat." After the Cold War, with the disintegration of the Soviet Union, the conditions for the existence of liberal internationalism disappeared. The unipolar world made unilateralism more attractive. Even if the September 11 terrorist attacks had not happened, the United States would have used various pretexts to shirk its responsibilities and get rid of the restraints of the international system. In the future, there will be a multipolar world, one without dominant powers, but with diverse ideals and government structures. The twenty-first century will not be American, nor Chinese, or Asian; it will not be anyone's; it does not belong to any party. The upcoming international system will have multiple and diverse power centers.[15]

For the foreseeable future, the United States is likely to remain the most powerful country in the world. However, the United States will not be able to achieve many of its international goals, such as international financial stability, climate change, and other issues, by acting alone. In a world where borders are becoming more porous, letting in everything ranging from drugs to infectious diseases to terrorism, nations must use soft power to develop networks and build institutions to address common threats and challenges. Success will require the cooperation of others – and thus empowering others can help the United States accomplish its own goals.[16] In this sense, power becomes a positive-sum game: one needs to think of not just the United States' power over others but also the power to solve problems that the United States can acquire by working with others.

Notes

1 John G. Ikenberry, "Power and Liberal Order: America's Postwar World Order in Transition," *International Relations of the Asia-Pacific*, vol. 5, no. 2 (September 2005): 133–152.
2 Daniel Deudney and John G. Ikenberry, "The Nature and Sources of Liberal International Order," *Review of International Studies*, vol. 25, no. 2 (April 1999): 179–181.
3 Ibid.
4 John G. Ikenberry, "The Rise of China and the Future of the West: Can the Liberal System Survive?," *Foreign Affairs*, vol. 87, no. 1 (January/February 2008): 23–27.
5 Kristi Govella and Vinod K. Aggarwal, *Russian Foreign Policy: Challenging the Western Liberal International Order?* (New York: Springer, 2012); Editorial, "The Liberal International Order is Under Fire. The United States Must Defend It," *The Washington Post*, May 21, 2016, https://www.washingtonpost.com/opinions/the-liberal-internat ional-order-is-under-fire-the-united-states-must-defend-it/2016/05/21/dd5a01c6 -1eae-11e6-9c81-4be1c14fb8c8_story.html; Roger E. Kanet, "Russia and Global

Governance: The Challenge to the Existing Liberal Order," *International Politics*, vol. 55, no. 2 (March 2018): 177–188; Catherine Jones, *China's Challenge to Liberal Norms: The Durability of International Order* (London: Palgrave Macmillan, 2018); Evelyn E. Goh, "Contesting Hegemonic Order: China in East Asia," *Security Studies*, vol. 28, no. 3 (2019): 614–644; Matthew D. Stephen and David Skidmore, "The AIIB in the Liberal International Order," *The Chinese Journal of International Politics*, vol. 12, no. 1 (Spring 2019): 61–91.

6 Ikenberry, "The Rise of China and the Future of the West", 24–32.

7 Wu Xinbo, "China in Search of a Liberal Partnership International Order," *International Affairs*, vol. 94, no. 5 (2018): 995–1018.

8 Joseph S. Nye Jr., "Will the Liberal Order Survive? The History of an Idea," *Foreign Affairs*, vol. 96, no. 1 (January/February 2017): 10–16.

9 Robin Niblett, "Liberalism in Retreat: The Demise of a Dream," *Foreign Affairs*, (January/February 2017), http://www.foreignaffairs.com/node/1118826

10 Martin Wolf, "Davos 2018: The Liberal International Order is Sick," *Financial Times*, January 25, 2018, https://www.ft.com/content/c45acec8-fd35-11e7-9b32-d7d59aace167

11 John G. Ikenberry, "The Liberal International Order and Its Discontents," *Millennium: Journal of International Studies*, vol. 38, no. 3, (2010): 514–515.

12 John J. Mearsheimer, "Bound to Fail: The Rise and Fall of the Liberal International Order," *International Security*, vol. 43, no. 4 (Spring 2019): 7–50.

13 Hans Kundnani, "What is the Liberal International Order?" The German Marshall Fund of the United States, *Policy Essay*, November 2017.

14 Charles L. Glaser, "A Flawed Framework: Why the Liberal International Order Concept is Misguided," *International Security*, vol. 43, no. 4 (Spring 2019): 51–87.

15 Christopher Wood, "Book Review Charles A. Kupchan: *No One's World: The West, the Rising Rest, and the Coming Global Turn*," *South African Journal of International Affairs*, vol. 20, no. 2 (August 2013): 316–318.

16 Nye Jr, "Will the Liberal Order Survive?" *Foreign* 10–16.

4

CHINA AND THE UNITED STATES IN A NEW BIPOLAR SYSTEM

Øystein Tunsjø

The international system is returning to bipolarity and the world is entering a new era of US–China superpower rivalry, different from the US–Soviet rivalry of the second half of the twentieth century.[1] While the new superpower rivalry contains political, military, strategic, economic, and technological competition, the current era of globalization and economic interdependence is vastly different from the independence and East–West divide of the Cold War era. The ideological confrontation today is not similar to the capitalist vs. communist polarities of the Cold War years. The contemporary superpowers' possession of a credible nuclear second-strike capability contrasts with the asymmetric nuclear balance in the early Cold War years. The world is entering a fourth industrial revolution with new technologies, accelerated speeds, and higher connectivity that differ from the technological developments of the mid-twentieth century.

The core difference of the new bipolar system, however, can be summarized in the phrase "it's geopolitics, stupid." The United States and the Soviet Union confronted each other on the European continent and along a land border. The features of the previous bipolar system were strong balancing (arms-racing), stability ("the long peace" and the Cold War), and strong competition and rivalry at the periphery (a number of proxy wars). The new superpower rivalry is largely at sea, rather than on land. Because of geopolitics, the systemic effects on balancing, stability, and the periphery are likely to differ.

First, geopolitics and the importance of water barriers postpone contemporary strong balancing. None of the United States' closest allies in East Asia shares a land border with China. The United States and China are therefore unlikely in the near future to pursue an arms race characteristic of the US–Soviet pattern of behavior during the previous bipolar era.

Second, geopolitical factors make superpower rivalry in a bipolar system concentrated on maritime East Asia more prone to conflict than a bipolar system concentrated on continental Europe, despite contemporary strong economic interdependence, the existence of an international institutional order, limited ideological confrontation, and nuclear second-strike capability. Water barriers may prevent a third world war, but it simultaneously increases the risk of a limited war for the control and access to sea-lanes in maritime East Asia.

Third, since China and the United States are likely to be preoccupied with instability, rivalries, and conflict in maritime East Asia, geopolitics will help subdue global-security confrontations and involvement in proxy wars by the superpowers in other regions. This is different from the relative stability that emerged in Europe and the global rivalry and conflict that developed between the superpowers during the previous bipolar period.

Waltz's structural realist theory, based on anarchy and the distribution of capabilities, only compared multipolar and bipolar systems. His core theoretical propositions were that balancing differs between bipolar and multipolar systems and that a bipolar system is more stable than a multipolar system. While Waltz never compared two bipolar systems, structural realism expects roughly similar systemic effects and patterns of behavior when structure remains the same.[2]

This chapter adds geopolitics to structural realism. It explains how geopolitics can account for different stability and patterns of behavior when comparing two bipolar systems. Such a reconfigured structural realist theory is labeled geostructural realism. The new geostructural realist theory contends that although it is important whether the international system is bipolar or has some other structure, balancing and stability are heavily affected by geopolitics and by how geography affects the two superpowers and their relationship.

At times, geopolitics can trump Waltz's structural factors. When comparing a US–China bipolar system concentrated on East Asia, with a US–Soviet bipolar system concentrated on Europe, geopolitics modify the intensity of balancing and arms-racing in the new bipolar system. Geopolitics also shape the intensity of a potential superpower war. The risk of a major or nuclear war is relatively lower in the new bipolar system, but there is a higher risk of a limited war in East Asia than in Europe. Finally, more geopolitical instability at the new power center in East Asia is likely to prevent the new superpower rivalry from being as intense in the periphery as during the previous bipolar system.

Such geostructural realist views do not disregard that today's superpower rivalry affects economics, technology, institutions, and ideology and that this competition differs from the previous bipolar system and the Cold War era. The argument, however, is that the shift in the distribution of capabilities and geopolitics are the main drivers of the new US–China competition and confrontation. Irrespective of the decision-makers in Washington and Beijing, the new bipolar distribution of capabilities compels the United States and China to become peer competitors. As the world enters a new bipolar system, it is likely to push the United States and China toward less economic interdependence, decoupling of technological connectivity, and more ideological rivalry.

The chapter is divided into two main parts and a conclusion. First, since there are conflicting definitions of a pole in great power politics and because there is a debate over the polarity of the contemporary international system, I explain why the international system has become bipolar. Second, I present my arguments about US–China relations in a new bipolar system focusing on stability or the risk of war, balancing, and rivalry on the periphery. Finally, I emphasize that geopolitics is primary in explaining different balancing, stability, and patterns of behavior when comparing the bipolar systems of the twentieth and the twenty-first century.

Defining a pole and measuring polarity

Some observers think that Russia and the United States are in a "new" Cold War. This view is misguided. The only power posing a major challenge to the United States today is China, not Russia. China's nominal gross domestic product (GDP) is about ten times larger than Russia's[3] and its defense spending roughly four times Russia's.[4] The United States and China are the world's lone superpowers and no other state is strong enough to serve as a competitor to these two.

According to Waltz, a pole and polarity can be measured by how states "score on *all* of the following items: size of the population and territory, resource endowment, economic capability, military strength, political stability and competence."[5] However, we cannot know which states are poles, or the polarity of the international system, until we examine the distribution of capabilities among states. This can be achieved by examining: (1) the narrowing power gap between the United States and China; (2) the widening power gap between China and the number-three-ranking power; and 3) the roughly similar distribution of capabilities between the contemporary international system and the origins of the previous bipolar system in 1950.

The power gap between the United States and China has narrowed considerably over the last two decades. China's nominal GDP currently accounts for about 65 percent of that of the United States.[6] This contrasts sharply with the early 1990s when the US nominal GDP was about fifteen times larger than China's or in 2000 when it was approximately eight times larger.[7] While China is not as powerful as the United States, the United States is *no longer* "unrivaled," as the title of Beckley's book suggests.[8]

According to SIPRI, the US and China's defense expenditures in 2018 were respectively $648 billion and $249 billion. This differs from the turn of the century when the US defense budget was more than ten times that of China, not to mention the early 1990s when US defense expenditure was more than 20 times higher. Economically, militarily, and technologically, China has become a peer competitor of the United States. The relative increase in China's combined capabilities, and the narrowing power gap, place China in the top ranking with the United States, even if only barely. The Soviet Union was never as powerful as the United States during the previous bipolar system – China does not need to obtain power parity. It has narrowed the power gap with the United States sufficiently to have entered top ranking.

However, we cannot know whether the unipolar international system has shifted to bipolarity or multipolarity without also examining the power gap between China and other states contending for top-ranking position. If another state were as powerful as China, then it is more likely the international system would be multipolar rather than bipolar. For many years, scholars and policymakers have been referring to the BRICS countries' (Brazil, Russia, India, China, and South Africa) emerging economies and multipolarity.[9] This view is misleading. China's nominal GDP is more than twice as large as the combined nominal GDP of Brazil, Russia, India, and South Africa. The power gap between China and any other third-ranking power has widened enormously and the power gap between China and the third-ranking power is wider than the gap between China and the United States. A bipolar system is "a system in which no third power is able to challenge the top two."[10] Today, two states – the United States and China – are much more powerful than any other states, and this defines the new bipolar international system.

Finally, based on a historical comparison, the distribution of capabilities in the international system today is roughly similar to the distribution of capabilities at the origins of the previous bipolar system. Even though World War II changed the distribution of power, it was not easy to recognize a polarity shift. At the end of World War II, most policy-makers and scholars expected a continuance of the multipolar system with the big three – the United States, the Soviet Union, and the United Kingdom.[11] Nonetheless, in only five years most observers had reached the conclusion that the international system was bipolar. The Soviet Union was not as powerful as the United States, but the gap between the Soviet Union and the third-ranking power (the United Kingdom) had become so large as to warrant a shift to bipolarity.[12] A similar shift in the distribution of capabilities has taken place today. China is much more powerful than any third-ranking power and the gap has become so large that China can be ranked as a superpower with the United States in a new bipolar system.

Why polarity matters

Establishing the contemporary polarity of the international system is important because the superpower(s), great powers, and other states and institutions behave differently within different structures. In the words of Waltz, structure "shapes and shoves." The distinct role and pattern of behavior of the United States and China prior to World War II (multipolar system), during the Cold War era (bipolar system), and in the post–Cold War period (unipolar system), suggest that a new international system is likely to push the United States and China in new directions.

Structural realist theory maintains that a polarity perspective cannot explain much, but it can explain and predict the most important aspects in international politics, namely, how the systemic distribution of capabilities shapes state-balancing behavior and the risk of war among the top-ranking states. From Waltz's theory, we should expect roughly similar balancing and stability when structure remains the same. However, we are not seeing the same internal balancing and arms-racing today as during the origins of the previous bipolar system. As a percentage of their gross domestic product, the United States and China spend less than four and two percent, respectively, on defense. The United States and the Soviet Union spent far more.[13]

Geopolitics and the intensity of balancing

Geopolitics can explain such different systemic effects in a new bipolar system. At the onset of the previous bipolar system, several US allies bordered the Soviet Union or Warsaw Pact countries and the United States was conventionally inferior to the Soviet Red Army in Europe. This fuelled a conventional and nuclear arms race and internal balancing. In contrast to Europe, no US allies in East Asia border China. Instead, water barriers separate the United States and its allies from China's formidable land power. Equally important, the United States remains militarily superior to China in the maritime domain of East Asia. These two factors moderate the intensity of balancing and account for different patterns of behavior when comparing two bipolar systems.

If we were to imagine Japan moved into the Yellow Sea, whereby it would share a long land border with China, similar to how US troops in Germany faced the Soviet Union along the East–West divide, then that would describe a geopolitical configuration similar to that of Europe. Under such geopolitical conditions, it is likely that the current bipolar system would resemble the strong balancing in Europe at the start of the last bipolar era, irrespective of today's economic interdependence, institutions, nuclear second-strike capability, and other differences. By complementing structural realism with geopolitics, a new geo-structural realist theory can better explain balancing behavior and predict that similar internal balancing will be postponed until China obtains more power parity with the United States than the Soviet Union achieved. Geopolitics does not eliminate balancing but shapes the intensity of balancing, whereas structural realism expects similar structural effects across different geopolitical settings.

Rivalry at sea and the role of geopolitics

The most important feature of the new superpower rivalry, increasing the risk of a limited war, is that it will be concentrated in the maritime domain of East Asia and not on the land-mass of Europe. During the previous superpower rivalry concentrated on Europe, the United States was inferior to the Soviet Union's land power. The United States had to rely on nuclear weapons in order to deter and prevent a Soviet attack on Western Europe. There was a high risk that any crisis or conflict could escalate into a major, plausibly nuclear, war. A galloping arms race, severe tension, and profound hostility followed, but Europe remained stable and peaceful.

In contrast to Europe, none of the United States' most important allies in East Asia (Japan, South Korea, the Philippines, and Australia) borders China. Instead, water and US naval preponderance protect these allies from China's formidable land power. Consequently, the United States need not rely on nuclear weapons as heavily as it did in Europe in order to deter China. One might think that this is good for peace and stability, but the temptation of brinkmanship and the risk of war increases when the contenders rely on conventional rather than nuclear deterrence.[14]

A future conflict might erupt in the South China Sea, the East China Sea, or the Taiwan Strait. In any case, the most likely scenario is a limited war confined to the sea, that would not result in an invasion of China, the United States, or its allies, but would likely result in devastating attacks on the military infrastructure of both sides. If core interests are at stake, decision-makers might be willing to risk a limited war or a constrained battle at sea in maritime East Asia, calculating that escalation to a major war is avoidable.

Many have suggested that economic interdependence will prevent a war between the United States and China. This argument is undermined by the fact that the United States and China have been willing to risk economic costs from dueling tariffs and a trade war even when there has not been a security crisis. China is determined to push the United States out of East Asia, but the United States is not willing to let China dominate the region. When geopolitical friction erupts, concern over the regional balance of power and security interests trumps trade and economic interests.

Few believed that a limited war in Europe would not escalate to a major or nuclear war during the Cold War. Today, since the geopolitical realities make an existential battle for territorial sovereignty implausible, the risk of escalation to the use of nuclear weapons is, therefore, less likely. Consequently, we should be aware that this increases the danger that the United States or China might choose a limited war for the control and access to sea-lanes in maritime East Asia instead of trade war in the years ahead.

Rivalry in the periphery?

Within a bipolar world, wrote Waltz, "there are no peripheries." The bipolar structural conditions suggest that any global event involves the interests of the two superpowers that are compelled to intervene across the world to safeguard their interests. A global zero-sum game follows from the condition of a two-power competition, argued Waltz. However, the sameness effect and the zero-sum thinking that are expected from a bipolar system are not evident in US–China interaction in world affairs today. Similar geopolitical factors that heighten the risk of war in East Asia explain the different patterns of behavior by the United States and China as they compete for influence globally.

Geopolitical instability at the center in East Asia mainly accounts for diverging patterns of behavior. In contrast to the previous bipolar system, which experienced stability at the center in Europe and instability at the periphery, contemporary US–China relations are set to be more unstable at the center in East Asia and more stable at the edges. Preoccupation with confrontation, instability, and conflict in maritime East Asia is likely to prevent US–China rivalry from becoming as intense in other regions of the world as US–Soviet rivalry.

After Europe was stabilized into two blocs and spheres of influences during the early Cold War, the superpowers' rivalry and conflict moved instead to other regions. The Korean Peninsula, Indochina, the Middle East, Africa, Latin America, and Central Asia became theaters for the struggles and proxy wars of the two superpowers. In the new bipolar system, disputes in East Asia, from the Korean peninsula to the East China Sea to Taiwan and the South China Sea remain unsettled and are core concerns preventing superpower rivalry from spreading to other regions. Sino-American conflict in maritime East Asia will likely restrain global security confrontations and proxy wars in other regions that defined superpower relations during the Cold War.

Contemporary China remains concerned with its regional ambitions in East Asia, where it challenges the existing status quo and spheres of influence, protects its sovereignty claims in maritime East Asia, expands its presence on land and at sea, and seeks to establish a security buffer at sea by emphasizing the development of anti-access and area-denial capabilities. Since East Asia does not resemble the East–West divide in Europe, a revisionist China is likely to be preoccupied with dominating the region and pushing the United States out of East Asian waters. In contrast, the Soviet Union was geopolitically rewarded in the post–World War II era and less interested in challenging the status quo and contending for regional hegemony in Europe.

There are fewer power vacuums to fill and less geographical space for China's global interests to expand into. This explains why the US–China rivalry and conflict on the global stage is evolving more gradually, and why China is more likely to focus on safeguarding and expanding its interests in East Asia. The shift from multipolarity to bipolarity in the post–World War II period saw traditional great powers like France and Britain lose their top-ranking positions, opening the way for colonial revolutions, decolonization, civil wars, and power vacuums. The two new post–World War II superpowers embarked on an intense decades-long rivalry to fill the power vacuums and gain influence in the numerous new states that appeared. Colonial revolutions and decolonization created, in the words of Morgenthau, "a moral, military, and political no-man's land neither completely nor irrevocable committed to either side." The faith of the new "uncommitted nations," whether they aligned themselves politically and militarily with the United States or with the Soviet Union, sparked superpower rivalry on the global stage and created the two blocs and Non-Aligned Movement of the Cold War.

Today, no empires are dissolving, and there are no comparable colonial revolutions worldwide, or power vacuums to fill. There are failed states and power vacuums in the contemporary world, but the instability in Africa, the Near and Middle East, Afghanistan, and Latin America is not comparable with the instability in the aftermath of World War II and the decline of the traditional great powers. There is less geopolitical space for the superpowers to be pulled into and fewer newly developed states where the new superpower can compete for influence globally. Stability in Europe and power vacuums globally gave the Soviet Union an opportunity to compete globally with the United States despite the asymmetric power relationship between the Soviet Union and the United States. Instability in East Asia and smaller power vacuums globally prevent China from emulating the Soviet Union's intervention globally.

The competition and rivalry between the superpowers are not only informed by geopolitics and power shifts, but by a new globalized and interconnected world. The new superpowers' rivalry for dominance in the field of fifth-generation networks, artificial intelligence, and robotics contains much broader military, economic, and technological implications than the nuclear and conventional arms race of the previous bipolar system. Globalization, interdependence, and new global supply chains, combined with the technological developments of the fourth industrial revolution, give China a competitive edge in its rivalry with the United States that the Soviet Union never enjoyed. The Soviet Union sought to divide the Western alliance through ideology and coercion, but it was no competitor in terms of trade, investments, and technology.

Conclusion

Despite the economic, technological, and other differences between the superpower rivalry in the twentieth and the twenty-first centuries, the core difference is geopolitics. There would possibly have been more balancing if there had been a strong ideological rivalry, less economic interdependence, and a fragile international institutional order, and the superpowers had not had second-strike nuclear capability. Nonetheless, these additional factors remain secondary and geopolitics primary in explaining why strong balancing has been postponed in the new bipolar system. A new geostructural realist theory combines the distribution of capabilities and geopolitics. Geostructural realism explains and predicts why there is less balancing but a relatively higher risk of a limited war between the two superpowers in the new bipolar system in the twenty-first century compared to the previous bipolar system of the twentieth century.

Notes

1 This chapter draws on Øystein Tunsjø, *The Return of Bipolarity in World Politics: China, the United States and Geostrucutral Realism* (New York: Columbia University Press, 2018).

2 Kenneth N. Waltz, *Theory of International Politics* (New York: McGraw-Hill, 1979, reissued by Waveland Press Inc., Long Grove, IL, 2010).
3 IMF, "World Economic Database, Outlook," 2018, https://www.imf.org/external/pubs/ft/weo/2015/02/weodata/index.aspx
4 Stockholm International Peace Research Institute (SIPRI), "Military Expenditure Database", 2018 https://www.sipri.org/databases/milex
5 Waltz, *Theory*, 131.
6 This is based on IMF numbers in 2018 of a US economy of $20.51 trillion and a Chinese economy of US$13.46 trillion. See https://www.imf.org/external/datamapper/NGDPD@WEO/OEMDC/ADVEC/WEOWORLD/CHN
7 The World Bank, "GDP (current US$, 2019)," http://data.worldbank.org/indicator/NY.GDP.MKTP.CD?page=1
8 Michael Beckley, *Unrivaled: Why America Will Remain the Sole Superpower* (Ithaca, NY: Cornell University Press, 2018).
9 Jim O'Neill, "Building Better Global Economic BRICs." *Goldman Sachs*, Global Economic Paper, no. 66 (2001); Fareed Zakaria, *The Post-American World* (New York: W. W. Norton, 2008); National Intelligence Council (NIC), *Global Trends 2030: Alternative Worlds* (Washington, DC, December 2012); and Donette Murray and David Brown, eds., *Multipolarity in the 21ˢᵗ Century: A New World Order* (London: Routledge, 2012).
10 Waltz, *Theory*, 98.
11 William T. R. Fox, *The Super-Powers: The United States, Britain, and the Soviet Union – Their Responsibility for Peace* (New York: Harcourt, Brace & world, Inc., 1944).
12 Hans J. Morgenthau, *Politics Among Nations: The Struggle for Power and Peace* (New York: Alfred A. Knopf, 1954, reprinted second edition).
13 The United States spent roughly 10 percent on defense as a percentage of its GDP through the Cold War, while the Soviet Union spent more than 20 percent.
14 Avery Goldstein, "First Things First: The Pressing Danger of Crisis Instability in U.S.-China Relations," *International Security*, vol. 37, no. 4 (Spring 2013): 49–89; Thomas J. Christensen, "The Meaning of the Nuclear Evolution: China's Strategic Modernization and US-China Security Relations," *Journal of Strategic Studies*, vol. 35, no. 4 (2012): 447–487.

5

THE CHANGING EAST ASIAN BALANCE OF POWER AND THE REGIONAL SECURITY ORDER

Robert S. Ross

In 2012, China began serial production of modern surface ships and submarines. As China has expanded its capabilities, the US Navy has experienced a decline in its capabilities. The Chinese Navy now possesses a larger fleet than the US Navy, challenging US maritime supremacy in East Asia. The United States retains advantages, especially in technology, but these advantages are eroding, and the trend of China's rise persists.

This changing balance of power is transforming the regional security order. US relative decline has prompted the region's secondary powers to reconsider their alignments within the US–China great power competition, encouraging local powers to move toward equidistance between the great powers.

China's economic growth rate will surely slow, but there is little likelihood that the United States can halt the trend in the US–China maritime balance. Rather, the regional balance of power will continue to evolve over the next decade, contributing to further transformation of the regional security order.

The rise of the Chinese Navy and the evolution of the US–China balance of power

Scholars have long discussed the meaning of the term "balance of power" and how to measure the capabilities of the great powers.[1] This chapter's discussion of the East Asian balance of power refers to the distribution of power between the United States and China. There is also considerable literature that measures relative great power capabilities and the corresponding balance of power though examination of such proxies for power as gross domestic product, steel production, population size, and other quantifiable indices.[2] This chapter examines the East Asian balance of power through an analysis of the trends in US–Chinese war-fighting capabilities, with a primary focus on the naval competition, but also including a consideration of the balance of power on mainland East Asia. Ultimately, the bases of power impact the balance of power when states mobilize the bases of power for war-fighting capabilities.

Over the past ten years, China has significantly expanded naval ship production. Whereas in 2012 China possessed 13 destroyers, by 2019 it had commissioned 30 destroyers. Whereas in 2011 it possessed 25 frigates, in 2019 it had commissioned over 45 frigates. In 2012, it had no corvettes; by 2018 nearly 40 *Jingdao* corvettes had entered service.[3] In 2010 China began production of its *Yuan*-class submarine. By 2018 it had commissioned 18 *Yuan*-class submarines, with 20 projected by 2020.[4] The Chinese Navy now possesses nearly 350 ships and is larger than the US Navy.[5] As China has produced more modern ships, it has decommissioned many of its older ships. In 2010, less than 50 percent of Chinese ships were "modern"; in 2017, over 70 percent were modern. [6]

China's land-based conventional ballistic missiles also challenge the balance of power. The DF21C and DF26 conventional intermediate-range ballistic missiles target maritime facilities throughout East Asia, including in South Korea, Japan, the Philippines, Singapore, Malaysia, and Guam.

The United States retains maritime superiority in East Asia, but the trend is the determined rise of the Chinese Navy. In early 2018, the size of the active US fleet was 289 ships.[7] In its evaluation of the Obama plan for a 308-ship navy, the Congressional Budget Office concluded that if the navy's shipbuilding budget were the average of its budget over the prior 30 years and it maintained its aircraft carrier and ballistic submarine construction schedules, in 2045 the fleet would decline to 237 ships.[8] The Trump administration plans a 355-ship navy. But to reach 355 ships, it will need a budget 80 percent larger than the average shipbuilding budget over the past 30 years and about 50 percent more than the average budget of the past six years.[9]

The United States has technological advantages over China. Nonetheless, its advantage is eroding. Both countries are developing laser weapons, hypersonic missiles, ship-based rail guns, and a broad spectrum of military drones, as well as artificial intelligence for military missions.[10] Moreover, the United States acknowledges that in naval competitions numbers matter, that "quantity has a quality of its own."[11]

The modernization of China's ground forces and its air force shapes the security environment on continental Asia and the security policies of China's immediate neighbors. In East Asia, these developments have had the greatest impact on Vietnam and South Korea. For Vietnam, China's ground-force presence and the proximity of its air bases on the Sino-Vietnamese border are Hanoi's greatest security concern, regardless of developments in the US–China naval competition and in US–Vietnam relations. Similarly, for South Korea, in addition to China's expanding naval presence on South Korea's coastal periphery in the Yellow Sea, the proximity of Chinese ground forces and air power to South Korea and China's dominance throughout mainland Northeast Asia require Seoul to be sensitive to Chinese interests.

As early as 2016, because of the changing balance of power, the US Navy no longer planned to wage war in East Asia's internal seas – the Yellow Sea, the East China Sea, and the South China Sea.[12] The Chinese Navy's numerical advantages, its improved technologies, and its proximity to the region pose excessive risk to US naval operations in East Asian waters. And Chinese land-based ballistic missiles inhibit US wartime use of the port facilities of US regional partners.

The new balance of power and the emerging East Asian security order

The changing East Asian balance of power has transformed strategic alignments in East Asia. Less confident in US ability and resolve to defend them against a rising China, the local powers have increasingly accommodated Chinese security interests.

South Korea

The Obama administration persuaded South Korea to deploy the US terminal high-altitude area (THAAD) missile defense system.[13] China retaliated with economic sanctions against the South Korean company Lotte, which had allowed its property to be used for the deployment. It also canceled South Korean pop music concerts in China.[14] The Chinese people boycotted South Korean automobiles, causing significant losses for the South Korean automobile industry. China also sanctioned South Korean cosmetics, and Chinese tourism to South Korea plummeted.[15] And whereas Seoul had expanded alliance cooperation with Washington, the United States revealed minimal concern for the impact of Chinese economic sanctions on the South Korean economy.

There was also an ominous escalation of the China–South Korean maritime dispute in the Yellow Sea. Chinese fishing boats operating in South Korean–claimed waters increased significantly in 2016. In June 2016, Chinese and South Korean fishing boats clashed and South Korea detained two Chinese fishing boats.[16] In October, when approximately 40 Chinese fishing boats entered South Korean–claimed waters, a South Korean Coast Guard ship sank after a collision with a Chinese fishing boat and the South Korean Coast Guard fired warning shots at Chinese ships.[17]

But in July 2017, South Korean voters elected Moon Jae-in as president. To persuade China to restore cooperation, Seoul assured Beijing that it would not allow any additional deployments of THAAD and that the existing THAAD system would not be integrated into a US–Japan–South Korea missile defense system. It also vowed that South Korea would not join in US–Japan–South Korean alliance coordination.[18] China then lifted its economic sanctions. [19]

Then, in 2018, the Moon administration reached agreement with the United States to transfer in 2022 wartime operational control of South Korean forces to South Korean command, further diminishing South Korean reliance on the

United States for security. South Korea has openly disagreed with US policy toward North Korea. It advocates an incremental approach to denuclearization, eliciting skepticism from the US ambassador to South Korea.[20] Seoul has also promoted unilateral measures toward North Korea to reduce border tension and to advance economic cooperation.[21]

The Philippines

In January 2012, with US encouragement, Manila submitted the Sino-Philippine South China Sea maritime dispute to the UN Permanent Court of Arbitration. The Philippines asked the court to determine the legality of China's EEZ claims.[22] Then, in April 2012, Philippine Navy ships approached Scarborough Shoal to detain Chinese fishing boats in the lagoon. China's ships blocked the lagoon before Philippine ships could detain the Chinese ships. Chinese Vice-Foreign Minister Fu Ying warned that "China has made … preparations to respond to any escalation of the situation."[23] The standoff was resolved when both countries' ships left the area. Chinese ships, however, returned to the shoal and blocked Philippine fishing in the lagoon. China also imposed restrictions on Philippine banana exports to China and Chinese tourism to the Philippines.[24]

In July 2016, the court ruled in favor of the Philippines. But the new Philippine President, Rodrigo Duterte, reversed Philippine policy of cooperation with the United States over the disputed waters. He stated that the court's decision was irrelevant and that the dispute was best ignored, rather than negotiated. China soon restored economic cooperation. It pledged $24 billion in aid and military assistance to the Philippines' battle against its Muslim insurgency, lifted the sanction on Philippine bananas, and allowed Philippine fishing boats to return to disputed waters. From 2016 to 2017, Philippine exports to China grew by 25.81 percent.[25]

In October 2016, Duterte declared in Beijing that in economics and military affairs, "America has lost."[26] In December, Minister of Defense Delfin Lorenzana said that the Philippines would avoid participating in freedom of navigation patrols with the United States to avoid "provocative actions." He also ordered a review of the US–Philippine security treaty. After US Secretary of State Michael Pompeo visited Manila and reaffirmed the US treaty commitment, Lorenzana explained that the purpose of the treaty review was to avoid Philippine involvement in US–China hostilities.[27] Duterte declared that "If I go to war … my Navy will be pulverized in a matter of minutes. … in seven minutes their missiles will reach Manila. …Why would I pick a fight?" He also observed that "China is already in possession" of the South China Sea. Speaking to the United States, he asked "It's now in their hands. So why do you have to create frictions … that will prompt a response from China?"[28] Foreign Minister Teodor Locsin declared that "China's offer of a strategic partnership is a bit more attractive than the current offer of the US strategic confusion."[29]

In many respects, the style of Philippine diplomacy reflects Duterte's unique contribution to Philippine foreign policy. But the substance of Philippine foreign policy under Duterte, in contrast to Aquino's foreign policy, is in line with the foreign policies of South Korea, Singapore, and Malaysia. Aquino's China policy was the exception in regional policies toward rising China; Duterte's policy is the norm.

Vietnam

In 2010 Secretary of State Hillary Clinton twice visited Hanoi and called for a US–Vietnam "strategic partnership" and Secretary of Defense Robert Gates visited Vietnam.[30] Also in 2010, the US Navy held its first engagement with the Vietnamese Navy, the USS George Washington aircraft carrier hosted in disputed waters a Vietnamese civilian–military delegation, and the USS John S. McCain visited Da Nang. In 2012 Secretary of Defense Leon Panetta declared at Cam Ranh Bay that US access to "this facility is a key component of this relationship and we see a tremendous potential."[31]

While improving relations with the United States, Vietnam challenged Chinese territorial claims. But China was confident that Vietnamese cooperation with the United States would not enable Vietnam to challenge Chinese interests: "though Vietnam has asked for help from the United States to counterbalance China, it is fully aware that this is not easy to achieve."[32]

In 2011 and 2102 Vietnamese ships carried out seismic surveys in disputed waters in the South China Sea; Chinese ships cut the cables of the Vietnamese ships.[33] On March 20, 2013, Chinese patrol boats fired a flare at a Vietnamese fishing boat, causing a fire.[34] In early 2014, after negotiations failed to reach agreement on joint exploration in disputed waters, China sent its Haiyang Shiyou 981 oil rig into the Vietnamese-claimed EEZ.[35] When Hanoi sent 29 ships to disrupt Haiyang Shiyou 981's drilling, Chinese ships fired water cannons at the Vietnamese ships and a Vietnamese fishing boat sank after a collision with a Chinese ship.[36] Simultaneously, 1,000 Vietnamese protested at a Taiwanese steel mill in Vietnam. Overall, at least 21 Chinese died during the ant-China protests and over 100 Chinese were injured.[37] Over 4,000 Chinese fled Vietnam and Chinese ships evacuated more than 1,000 Chinese.[38] Moreover, in 2014, border tension escalated when China and Vietnam exchanged military fire, suggesting the possibility of dangerous crisis escalation. [39]

But in August, Vietnam politburo member Le Hong Anh traveled to China "to prevent reoccurrence of the tense incidents." He announced that Vietnam would negotiate bilaterally joint exploration of the South China Sea. Xi Jinping warned that "A neighbor cannot be moved away and it is in the common interests of both sides to be friendly to each other." He further warned Vietnam to "make correct political decisions at critical moments."[40] When Xi then traveled to Hanoi, Vietnam agreed to bilateral negotiations over the dispute, meeting Beijing's demand that Vietnam not cooperate with other countries to internationalize the dispute, and to joint exploration in the South China Sea.[41]

Since the restoration of cooperation, China and Vietnam have carried out joint patrols of the Beibu Gulf.[42] In 2018, they carried out their first joint patrol of the land border.[43] Whereas Vietnamese exports to China stagnated from 2010 to 2014, from late 2014 through 2017, Vietnamese exports to China doubled and its trade surplus with China steadily increased.[44] In 2019, when Vietnam again carried out oil exploration, it restrained its nationalist activists and, after China again threatened escalation, it once again ended its activities.

Elsewhere in East Asia

A January 2019 public opinion poll reported that 60 percent of the respondents from all ten ASEAN countries said that US influence globally had deteriorated over the past year and that two-thirds believed US engagement with Southeast Asia had declined. Approximately one-third of the respondents said they had little or no confidence in the US as a strategic partner and provider of regional security.[45]

Malaysian Prime Minister Mahathir Mohamad observed that "When China was poor, we were frightened of China. When China is rich, we are also frightened of China." Now, however, "I think we have to find some way to deal with China" and Malaysia has to "accept that China is close to us."[46] Since 2015, China and Malaysia have held multiple naval exercises and in 2016 they reached an agreement on naval cooperation and Malaysia made its first significant arms purchase from China.[47]

Singapore held its first bilateral naval exercise with China in 2015 and it will hold a second and larger exercise in 2020. In 2017, it negotiated the first China–ASEAN joint naval exercise.[48] In 2019 Singapore Defense Minister Ng Eng Hen warned that if US terms for trade are "too onerous to bear," countries may "have to choose between the US or China." At an international conference in Singapore, Prime Minister Lee Hsien Loong advised that[49]

> it is well worth the US forging a new understanding that will integrate China's aspirations within the current system of rules and norms. ... China will expect a say in this process, because it sees the present rules as having been created in the past without its participation. This is an entirely reasonable expectation. ... the world ... has to adjust to a larger role for China.

Conclusion

As the East Asian balance of power evolves, a new strategic order is emerging. No longer will the US Navy possess hegemony in East Asia and be able to sustain an alliance system in which local powers are firmly aligned with the United States. But unlike the polarization of Cold War Europe, in twenty-first-century East Asia, the local powers will avoid taking sides in US–China relations. Because they do not fear either US or Chinese occupation of their countries,[50] they do not need tight alliances for security. For most of the local powers, water is an effective buffer against invasion.

The emergence of the new regional order presents a challenge to the United States. As the maritime hegemon, decline is difficult to accept. For China, as the rising power, it must acknowledge that it will not be the next hegemon. If both the United States and China can adjust to this emerging security order, then both great powers will enjoy security and there will be ample opportunities for mutual benefit.

Notes

1 See, for example, Inis L. Claude, Jr., *Power and International Relations* (Ann Arbor, MI: University of Michigan Press, 1962), chapter 2; Ernst B. Haas, "The Balance of Power: Prescription, Concept, or Propaganda," *World Politics*, vol. 5, no. 4 (July 1953), pp. 442–477

2 See, for example, Hans J. Morgenthau, *Politics Among Nations: The Struggle for Power and Peace*, 3rd ed. (New York: Alfred A. Knopf, 1963), chapter 9; Paul Kennedy, *The Rise and Fall of the Great Powers* (New York: Doubleday Publishing Group, 2010).

3 Ronald O'Rourke, *China Naval Modernization: Implications for US Navy Capabilities— Background and Issues for Congress*, August 2018, Congressional Research Service, Report no. RL33153, https://fas.org/sgp/crs/row/RL33153.pdf, 3, 30–39.

4 Office of the Secretary of Defense, US Department of Defense, *Military and Security Developments Involving the People's Republic of China 2019*, https://media.defense.gov /2019/May/02/2002127082/-1/-1/1/2019_CHINA_MILITARY_POWER_RE PORT.pdf, 36.

5 United Nations Conference on Trade and Development, *Trade in Services Annual Bulletin*, https://unctadstat.unctad.org/wds/TableViewer/tableView.aspx

6 Eric Heginbotham, et al., *The US–China Military Scorecard: Forces, Geography, and the Evolving Balance of Power, 1996–2017* (Santa Monica, CA: RAND, 2015).

7 United States Navy, "Status of the Navy," May 31, 2019, https://www.navy.mil/navy data/nav_legacy.asp?id=146

8 Congressional Budget Office, "An Analysis of the Navy's Fiscal Year 2016 Shipbuilding Plan," 2015, https://www.cbo.gov/sites/default/files/114th-congress-2015-2016/ reports/50926-shipbuilding-2.pdf, 20.

9 Congressional Budget Office, "An Analysis of the Navy's Fiscal Year 2019 Shipbuilding Plan," 3.

10 See, for example, Gregory C. Allen, *Understanding China's AI Strategy: Clues to Chinese Strategic Thinking on Artificial Intelligence and National Security*, Center for New American Security, February 6, 2019, https://www.cnas.org/publications/reports/ understanding-chinas-ai-strategy; On China's railgun, see Euan McKirdy, "China Closer to Equipping Warships with Electromagnetic Railguns, State Media Reports," *CNN*, January 4, 2019, https://www.cnn.com/2019/01/04/asia/china-pla-navy-rail gun-intl/index.html; Sydney J. Freedberg, Jr., "US Forces Untrained, Unready For Russian, Chinese Jamming," *BreakingDefense*, October 30, 2019, https://breakin gdefense.com/2019/10/us-forces-untrained-not-ready-for-russian-jamming/

11 Dave Majumdar, "Chief of Naval Operations Richardson: US Navy is Focusing on Enemy Submarine Threat," National Interest, August 30, 2016, at https://nationa linterest.org/blog/the-buzz/chief-naval-operations-richardson-us-navy-focusing-e nemy-17522;

12 Interview, senior US Pacific Fleet officer, September 2016.

13 Kwan Woojun, "US, South Korea to Detail Wartime Military Command Plans," *Wall Street Journal*, October 21, 2014, https://www.wsj.com/articles/u-s-south-k orea-to-detail-wartime-military-command-plans-1413878199; Samuel Songhoon Lee, "Why Wouldn't S. Korea Want US Missile Defenses?," *CBS News*, June 3, 2014,

https://www.cbsnews.com/news/u-s-proposes-advanced-missile-defense-system
-in-south-korea/; Song Sang-ho, "S. Korea Faces Tough Decision on THAAD,"
Korea Herald, November 6, 2014, http://www.koreaherald.com/view.php?ud=201411
06001119

14 Kim Joon-Beom, "Chinese Retaliation Over Antimissile System Has South Korea
Worried," *Wall Street Journal*, March 3, 2017, https://www.wsj.com/articles/in-south
-korea-jitters-grow-that-china-is-punishing-it-1488519202; Laura Zhou, "Chinese
Authorities Seize Equipment from South Korean Retail Giant Lotte as Tensions Over
Missile Defence Shield Continue," *South China Morning Post*, August 22, 2017, https:/
/www.scmp.com/news/china/diplomacy-defence/article/2107827/chinese-author
ities-seize-equipment-south-korean-retail; Celine Ge, "China's Online Boycott Puts
Lotte in Cross Hairs Amid THAAD Row," *South China Morning Post*, March 6, 2017,
https://www.scmp.com/business/companies/article/2076214/chinas-online-boyco
tt-puts-lotte-cross-hairs-amid-thaad-row

15 Song Jung-a, "S Korean Carmakers Feel Impact of China Anti-Thaad Sentiment,"
Financial Times, April 4, 2017, https://www.ft.com/content/ab64d6f0-18fe-11e7
-a53d-df09f373be87.

16 "S. Korea to Urge China for Strong Measures on Illegal Fishing," Arirang, June 10,
2016, http://www.arirang.com/News/News_View.asp?nSeq=192125; Lisa Collins,
"Between a Rock and a Grey Zone: China-Rok Illegal Fishing Disputes," *Asia
Maritime Transparency Initiative*, Center for Strategic and International Studies, July 6,
2016, https://amti.csis.org/rock-grey-zone-china-rok-illegal-fishing-disputes/.

17 "South Korea Vows Armed Crackdown Against Chinese Fishing Boats After Sinking
of Coast Guard Ship," *South China Morning Post*, October 11, 2016, https://www
.scmp.com/news/china/diplomacy-defence/article/2027042/seoul-summons-chine
se-envoy-over-sinking-coast-guard

18 Ankit Panda, "What China Gains with Its Détente with South Korea Over THAAD,"
The Diplomat, November 7, 2017, https://thediplomat.com/2017/11/what-china-ga
ins-with-its-detente-with-south-korea-over-thaad/

19 Christine Kim and Ben Blanchard, "China, South Korea Agree to Mend Ties After
THAAD Standoff," *Reuters*,
October 30, 2017, https://www.reuters.com/article/us-northkorea-missiles/china
-south-korea-agree-to-mend-ties-after-thaad-standoff-idUSKBN1D003G;   Lee
Jeong-ho, "China Ends Sanctions on Lotte Two Years After South Korean Retailer
Cedes Land to US Missile Defences," *South China Morning Post*, May 2, 2019, https
://www.scmp.com/news/china/diplomacy/article/3008576/china-ends-sanctions-l
otte-two-years-after-south-korean

20 Dagyum Ji, "Foreign Minister Admits to Differences Between US, ROK Over
North Korea Policy," *NK News.org*, May 2, 2019, https://www.nknews.org/2019
/05/foreign-minister-admits-to-differences-between-u-s-rok-over-north-korea-po
licy/; Hyonhee Shin, "'All-or-Nothing' US Approach Toward North Korea Won't
Work: Moon Adviser," *Reuters*, March 12, 2019, https://www.reuters.com/article
/us-northkorea-usa-southkorea/all-or-nothing-u-s-approach-toward-north-korea
-wont-work-moon-adviser-idUSKBN1QT0IR; Sarah Kim, "Harris Unsure About
'Middle Step,'" *Korea Joongang Daily*, April 24, 2019, http://koreajoongangdaily.joins
.com/news/article/article.aspx?aid=3062225

21 Hyonhee Shin, "US Opposed to Koreas' Plan for No-Fly Zone Over Border," *Reuters*,
October 18, 2018, https://www.reuters.com/article/us-northkorea-usa-south
korea/u-s-opposed-to-koreas-plan-for-no-fly-zone-over-border-sources-idUSKC
N1MS0OR; "US Pressures Chaebol on North," *Korea Joongang Daily*, October 31,
2018, http://koreajoongangdaily.joins.com/news/article/article.aspx?aid=3054938

22 The Philippines submission is available at file:///C:/Users/Robert/Desktop/Not
ification%20and%20Statement%20of%20Claim%20on%20West%20Philippine
%20Sea.pdf

23 Damian Grammaticas, "China Bangs the War Drum Over South China Sea," *BBC News*, May 10, 2012, http://www.bbc.co.uk/news/world-asia-china-18016901.

24 See James Reilly, "China's Unilateral Sanctions," *Washington Quarterly*, vol. 35, no. 4 (Fall 2012): 129; See Bonnie Glaser, "Trouble in the South China Sea," *Foreign Policy*, September 17, 2012, http://www.foreignpolicy.com/articles/2012/09/17/t rouble_in_the_south_china_sea

25 Jake Maxwell Watts, "China's Xi Woos Philippines as Rivalry with US in Asia Deepens," *Wall Street Journal*, November 20, 2018, https://www.wsj.com/articles /chinas-xi-woos-philippines-as-rivalry-with-u-s-in-asia-deepens-1542722679; Reuters, "China Offers $14 Million Arms Package to Philippines for Free," *South China Morning Post*, December 20, 2016, https://www.scmp.com/news/asia/dipl omacy/article/2056027/china-offers-14-million-arms-package-philippines-free; "China Lifts Import Ban on Philippine Bananas," *Philippine Star*, October 6, 2016, https://www.philstar.com/business/2016/10/07/1630958/china-lifts-import-ban -philippine-bananas;
Simon Denyer, "Duterte's Deal with China Seen by Satellite," *Washington Post*, November 2, 2016, https://www.washingtonpost.com/news/worldviews/wp/2016/ 11/02/dutertes-deal-with-china-seen-by-satellite-fishing-allowed-but-no-change-i n-control-of-disputed-shoal/?utm_term=.6f8e26040461; Bernie Cahiles Magkilat, "China Buying More PH Bananas," *Manila Bulletin*, September 20, 2018, https://bu siness.mb.com.ph/2018/09/20/china-buying-more-ph-bananas/

26 Ron Allen, "Philippine Leader Duterte Ditches US for China, Says 'America Has Lost,'" *NBC News*, October 20, 2016, at https://www.nbcnews.com/news/world/ philippine-leader-duterte-ditches-u-s-china-says-america-has-n670066.

27 Jim Gomez, "Philippines Says it Will not Aid US in Patrolling the South China Sea," *MilitaryTimes*, December 8, 2016, https://www.militarytimes.com/news/penta gon-congress/2016/12/08/philippines-says-it-will-not-aid-u-s-in-patrolling-the-s outh-china-sea/; Jelly Musico "Lorenzana Orders Review of 67-Year-Old US-PH Military Pact," *Philippines News Agency*, December 28, 2018, https://www.pna.gov .ph/articles/1057639; Jason Gutierrez, "Philippine Official, Fearing War with China, Seeks Review of US Treaty," *New York Times*, March 5, 2019, https://www.nytimes. com/2019/03/05/world/asia/philippines-defense-treaty-us.html

28 Christina Mendez and Edith Regalado, "China Just Wants to be Friends with Philippines – Duterte," *Philippine Star*, April 4, 2019, https://www.philstar.com/ headlines/2019/04/04/1907099/china-just-wants-be-friends-philippines-dutert e; Duterte Says "China 'Already in Possession' of South China Sea," *Straits Times*, November 15, 2018, https://www.straitstimes.com/asia/se-asia/duterte-says-china -already-in-possession-of-south-china-sea-tells-us-to-end-military

29 Andreo Calonzo and Claire Jiao, "Philippines Prefers China Loans Over US 'Strategic Confusion' in South China Sea," *Bloomberg*, May 20, 2019, https://www.bloomberg .com/news/articles/2019-05-20/china-has-more-to-offer-than-u-s-top-philippine -diplomat-says

30 See Secretary of State Clinton's October 30, 2010, remarks in Hanoi at http://www .state.gov/secretary/rm/2010/10/150189.htm

31 U.S. Department of Defense, "Transcript", http://www.defense.gov/transcripts/ transcript.aspx?transcriptid=505

32 Li Xiaokun and Zhang Yubin, "Li Underlines Vietnam Ties," *China Daily*, May 13, 2013, http://www.chinadaily.com.cn/china/2013-05/11/content_16491673.htm

33 Edward Wong, "China Navy Reaches Far, Unsettling the Region," *New York Times*, June 14, 2012, http://www.nytimes.com/2011/06/15/world/asia/15china.html?_r=0 Jane Perlez, "Dispute Flares Over Energy in South China Sea," *New York Times*, December 4, 2012, http://www.nytimes.com/2012/12/05/world/asia/china-viet nam-and-india-fight-over-energy-exploration-in-south-china-sea.html; M. Taylor Fravel, "China's Strategy in the South China Sea," *Contemporary Southeast Asia*, vol. 33, no. 3 (December 2011), pp. 292–319

34 Chinese authorities acknowledged that the Chinese vessels had fired, but they called the discharges "warning shots." See Wu Dengfeng, "所谓"中国海军舰艇枪击越渔船"一事纯属捏造" (The so-called "Chinese naval vessels fired on Vietnamese fishing boats" is pure fabrication), *Xinhua*, March 26, 2013, http://news.xinhuanet.com/mil/2013-03/26/c_124506582.htm; The Vietnamese Foreign Ministry Statement is at http://www.mofa.gov.vn/en/tt_baochi/pbnfn/ns1 30326202046/view

35 "China, Vietnam Launch Consultations on Sea-Related Joint Development," Xinhua News Agency, January 9, 2014, http://news.xinhuanet.com/english /china/2014-01/09/c_133032429.htm

36 Associated Press, "Tensions Rise in South China Sea as Vietnamese Boats Come Under Attack", *The Guardian*, May 7, 2014, https://www.theguardian.com/world /2014/may/07/chinese-vietnamese-vessels-clash-south-china-sea; "Vietnam Boat Sinks after Collision with Chinese Vessel," BBC, May 27, 2014, https://www.bbc .com/news/world-asia-27583564

37 Kate Hodal and Jonathan Kaiman, "At Least 21 Dead in Vietnam Anti-China Protests Over Oil Rig," *The Guardian*, May 15, 2014, https://www.theguardian.com/world /2014/may/15/vietnam-anti-china-protests-oil-rig-dead-injured.

38 Kate Hodal, "China Evacuates 3,000 Nationals from Vietnam as Conflict Simmer," *The Guardian*, May 17, 2014, https://www.theguardian.com/world/2014/may/18/ china-evacuates-nationals-vietnam; Agence France-Presse, "Chinese Flee Vietnam as Hanoi Counts Cost of Riots," *The Guardian*, May 19, 2014, https://www.theguard ian.com/world/2014/may/19/chinese-flee-vietnam-hanoi-riots

39 "A China-Vietnam Military Clash," Contingency Planning Memorandum No. 26, *Council on Foreign Relations*, September 23, 2015, at https://www.cfr.org/report/chi na-vietnam-military-clash.

40 "China Welcomes Vietnam's Move to Compensate Victims of Anti-China Protests," *Straits Times*, August 25, 2014, at https://www.straitstimes.com/asia/se-asia/china -welcomes-vietnams-move-to-compensate-victims-of-anti-china-protests

41 The text of the communique is at *Vietnam Plus*, April 8, 2015, at http://en.viet namplus.vn/vietnam-china-issue-joint-communique/74208.vnp

42 "China, Vietnam Wrap Up 23rd Joint Patrol in Beibu Gulf," Huang Panyue, ed., *China Military Online*, December 6, 2017, http://english.pladaily.com.cn/view/2017 -12/06/content_7857752.htm

43 Vietnamk News Agency, "Vietnamese, Chinese Border Guards Hold Joint Patrol," *Vietnam Breaking News*, April 11, 2018, https://www.vietnambreakingnews.com /2018/04/vietnamese-chinese-border-guards-hold-joint-patrol/

44 CEIC Data's Global Database, available at: https://www.ceicdata.com/en/vietnam /exports-by-country-value-annual; https://www.ceicdata.com/en/vietnam/trade -balance-by-country-annual/vn-trade-balance-advanced-economies-china-people -republic-hong-kong

45 "Southeast Asia Wary of China's Belt and Road Project, Skeptical of US," *Reuters*, January 6, 2019, https://www.reuters.com/article/us-asean-singapore-idUSKCN1P 00GP.

46 Bhavan Jaipragas, "I'd Side with Rich China Over Fickle Us: Malaysia's Mahathir Mohamad," *South China Morning Post*, March 8, 2019, https://amp.scmp.com/week -asia/politics/article/2189074/id-side-with-rich-china-over-fickle-us-malaysias-mahat hir?__twitter_impression=true

47 Agencies, "China and Malaysia Agree on Military Cooperation in the South China Sea," *The Guardian*, November 2, 2016, https://www.theguardian.com/world/2 016/nov/02/china-and-malaysia-agree-on-military-cooperation-in-the-south-ch ina-sea; Jason Ou, "China, Malaysia Start Joint Military Exercise," *Straits Times*, September 19, 2015, https://www.straitstimes.com/asia/east-asia/china-malaysia-s tart-joint-military-exercise; Bhavan Jaipragas, "How China is Helping Malaysia's Military Narrow the Gap with Singapore, Indonesia," *South China Morning Post*,

August 20, 2017, https://www.scmp.com/week-asia/geopolitics/article/2107408/how-china-helping-malaysias-military-narrow-gap-singapore

48 Bhavan Jaipragas, "Singapore, China Deepen Defence Ties, Plan Larger Military Exercises Including Joint Navy Drill," *South China Morning Post*, May 29, 2019, https://www.scmp.com/week-asia/geopolitics/article/3012341/singapore-china-deepen-defence-ties-plan-larger-military; Sarah Zheng, "China and Asean to Go Ahead with First Joint Naval Exercise in Sign of Greater Engagement," *South China Morning Post*, October 24, 2017, https://www.scmp.com/news/china/diplomacy-defence/article/2116766/china-and-asean-go-ahead-first-joint-naval-exercise

49 The text of the speech is at "PM Lee Hsien Loong at the IISS Shangri-La Dialogue 2019," Prime Minister's Office Singapore, May 31, 2019, https://www.pmo.gov.sg/Newsroom/PM-Lee-Hsien-Loong-at-the-IISS-Shangri-La-Dialogue-2019

50 See, for example, Jaipragas, "I'd Side with Rich China Over Fickle Us"; Mendez and Regalado, "China Just Wants to be Friends with Philippines."

PART II

Implications for Europe

6

US–CHINA RELATIONS IN THE ERA OF XI AND TRUMP

Implications for Europe

Rosemary Foot

A decade ago Robert Ross, Øystein Tunsjø, and Zhang Tuosheng produced an edited book on US–China–EU relations, and asked me to provide a chapter that compared the US and EU approaches to China.[1] That chapter concluded that the European Union (EU) was predominantly focused on supporting China's regulatory development and on persuading it to accept the benefits of multilateral engagement. The EU was engaged in capacity building, often pushing at issue areas where Beijing's door was already half open. It saw itself in something of a tutelage role. Europe's most ambitious vision was to promote open markets, a democratic political system, and better protection for human rights. It sought in many respects to externalize the policies that operated within the EU itself, and, as others have noted, "envisaged itself as a transformative power whose model of peaceful regional integration and governance based on shared values would radiate outward into its periphery,"[2] and, in the case of China, well beyond its periphery. However, less ambitiously (and more realistically) it tended to circumscribe its actual areas of involvement with China to the largely regulatory, technocratic, and economic.

Somewhat similarly, the US administration, at this point, sought to encourage China in the role of "responsible stake-holder" but engaged rather more than the EU or major European states in a bargaining relationship with Beijing over a large range of strategic and economic issues. The early twenty-first-century era in China–US relations was one where there were elements of cooperation but also serious contention. However, both parties agreed to adopt a formula of strategic dialogues where the two governments could discuss "big picture" issues, and both sides appeared to operate on the basis that they could rely on economic interdependence to smooth over the more contentious issues in the relationship. On the EU–US side of the triangle, their respective efforts in dealing with

Beijing could be seen mainly as complementary. For China, the United States remained its primary interlocutor with European states predominantly in a secondary role, with the hope that Europe might act, on occasion, as a counterweight to America on some issues of concern to Beijing.

A decade later, the relationships are different in tone, more uncertain, and relatively more equal. Most analysts would agree, however, that the US–China prong is generally the most important among the three in the shaping of world order. Whether Europe is essentially in the role of reacting to the "fallout" from the state of bilateral Washington–Beijing ties or can develop a more independent and active role as many have advocated is worth contemplating.[3] But wherever Europe lands in this triangular set of relationships, for many states within the EU, distrust of America and concerns about China's increased global influence have reached a point that suggests a fluidity in policy and positions not seen in earlier periods of discord. In particular, should EU–US tensions continue to deepen, this portends weighty implications for world politics.

This chapter begins first with a brief discussion of what is implied by the phrase "the era of Trump and Xi." Next comes an assessment of the current state of US–China relations, emphasizing some of the major factors that explain the deterioration in ties, in particular since the mid-2010s. This section focuses predominantly on the perceived threat of the new-found nexus between economic and security issues. Finally, the paper considers where this leaves Europe (treating the latter as mostly related to the EU member countries), particularly in light of the difficulties of balancing policies that are responsive to the downsides of China's growing material power and political influence, and Europe's continuing interest in the actual economic benefits that come from a close trading and investment relationship with Beijing. The coincidence of these contradictory imperatives with the turbulence that the Trump era has introduced in US–Europe relations have compounded the EU's problems in determining a coherent and united strategy.

The era of Trump: the United States during the Trump presidency

Undoubtedly, the Trump administration has challenged the deeply rooted notion of the United States as an exceptionalist nation that deserves to be emulated, and as a country that is willing and able to "police the world" as part of a world ordering project. David Kerr, writing in 2007, then described America as a country that "conceives itself as a global state: it cannot tell if there are real boundaries between itself and world order and assumes a congruence of values between the two."[4] President Theodore Roosevelt, as is true of many presidencies that followed his, was sensitive to the notion that increased interdependence in global political and economic relations rendered it "incumbent on all civilized and orderly powers to insist on the proper policing of the world," with the US willing to play a dominant part in that project.[5]

Those statements do not capture the era of Trump – the era of "America First," where the idea of working with others in multilateral or even minilateral institutions holds little or no appeal. Perhaps references to the presidency of Andrew Jackson, as others have noted, are far more appropriate. As Trump put it before the UN General Assembly in September 2018, the world's largest international state-based audience: "We reject the ideology of globalism, and we embrace the doctrine of patriotism."[6] His former director of the National Economic Council, Gary Cohn, and then National Security Advisor, H.R. McMaster, writing in the *Wall Street Journal* in May 2017, noted with some relish that the world is "an arena where nations, non-governmental actors, and businesses engage and compete for advantage." They went on: "Rather than deny this elemental nature of international affairs, we endorse it."[7]

More bruising still, President Trump has argued that the US has, for decades, been cheated by its allies in Asia as well as in Europe and that the free-riding on the US as a security and economic actor – or "world policeman" – has to stop. Removing distinctions between America's "natural" allies in the democratic world and those outside of it, it is well documented that Trump has apparent admiration for "strong men" in world politics. This includes speaking admiringly of Vladimir Putin, Xi Jinping, Kim Jung-un, and Mohammed Bin Salman, to name but a few of his favorites. It underlines too that neither democracy nor human rights promotion is of any urgency for this US president, who swiftly took his administration out of the UN's Human Rights Council. Instead, the priority is economic and military dominance for the United States and the use of trade and fiscal policy to ensure both.

Trump's own perspectives do not necessarily accord neatly with others within his administration, such as Vice President Mike Pence, or Secretary of State Mike Pompeo. And we know that he and ex-National Security Advisor John Bolton differed on most of the major foreign policy issues of our era. Trump's views also did not accord well with earlier administration appointees of note, such as Secretary of Defense Jim Mattis and Secretary of State Rex Tillerson. Neither do they form an entirely close match with the US National Security Strategy of 2017. But those broader views of America's interests and role in the world that are associated with this wider group of policy-makers and with official documents – including sometimes more positive views of the allied contribution to American and global security – are regularly undercut by a presidential perspective that emphasizes "America First," "America Alone," and dominance rather than diplomacy. Dominance in negotiations and in military prowess is viewed as the way to get things done. Success for President Trump is defined in zero-sum rather than positive-sum terms.[8]

The implications of these developments for attempts at aligning US–EU relations are serious. Undoubtedly, the centrality of Europe and of the European allied role in US policy thinking had already receded prior to the advent of the Trump administration, perhaps shown most obviously in the Obama administration's promotion in 2011 of a "pivot to Asia." Nevertheless, future US administrations are going to find it difficult to recover from the more obvious divergence in approach and values that have come in the Trump era, and especially from the perception of US unreliability and unwillingness to consider itself bound by past international agreements.

The era of Xi: China during the Xi presidency

China's resurgence has itself disturbed and disrupted previous patterns of interaction and understandings of the nature of the current era, both because of the consequences (intended and unintended) of that material resurgence, but also because of the social expectations that accompany that rise in material power both outside of China as well as inside China. Beijing expects to provide global public goods, to be accorded the status of "responsible great power," and to acquire leadership and followership in global politics.[9]

However, the ambitious policies that President Xi himself has announced and often enacted have added to this sense of change and challenge to the United States as the hegemonic state in world politics, as well as to the relative standing of other powerful advanced states such as those that make up large parts of the European Union. Like Trump, Xi is also a dominant figure.[10] Unlike Trump, who ignores process and the bureaucracy, Xi seems to be in charge of both. Once in power from late 2012, Xi worked successfully to establish himself as China's "core leader." He also sought greater control over the foreign and domestic policy-making environments, chairing the Central Military Commission, and placing himself in charge of a swathe of policy Leading Groups, including those most important in foreign affairs and national security. In 2018, "Xi Jinping Thought on Socialism with Chinese Characteristics for a New Era" was elevated into China's written constitution, giving Xi a status in CCP history not enjoyed by any leader since Mao Zedong. Xi's hold on power became even further entrenched when he abolished the two-term limit for the state presidency in March 2018.[11]

Xi's world view has been put forward in a series of phrases including the country's commitment to the idea of the "great revival," "renewal," or "rejuvenation" of the Chinese nation. For Xi, China's "rejuvenation" means a return to China's glorious past and its leading role in world affairs. As Xi's speech in 2017 to the Nineteenth Party Congress put it, China "has stood up, grown rich, and is becoming strong." Arguing that China's path could serve as a successful model for other developing countries to follow, Xi stated during that speech that China could offer "Chinese wisdom and a Chinese approach to solving the problems facing mankind."[12] Xi and other senior members of the politburo believe in the power of discourse to shape attitudes and thinking and have put forward a series of new concepts that are not only designed to guide Chinese foreign policy but to shape international reception of that policy. These concepts include: a "new type of international relations", which draws upon China's history, culture, and purportedly unique approach to diplomacy; the "community of shared destiny", which emphasizes the need to integrate China's development with the development of the rest of the world; the idea of "fairness and justice," which advocates an increased role for developing countries in a reformed global governance system; and "win–win cooperation," which highlights the interconnectedness of countries' interests on a range of global challenges. Above all, Beijing has been stressing the notion that economic development is the solution to all the world's ills. Development is projected as the greatest security good; it assists the security of the state and political regime as well as the security of humankind.[13] Beijing has suggested the pathways forward for states of the Global South, urging them to make use of the global goods it has offered as well as the experience it has gained as a result of its own dramatic socio-economic successes since "Reform and Opening" in late 1978.

With respect to relations with Washington, Beijing has sought greater equivalence and reciprocity. Xi has consciously sought peer status with the United States since at least 2013, when, during his first visit to the United States as President, he proposed the idea of a "new model of major country relations" to manage the US–China relationship.[14] From the Chinese leadership's perspective, the United States should respect China's "core interests" especially with regard to its outstanding sovereignty claims to Taiwan and the South and East China Seas.

An era of deteriorating US–China relations

Much of the literature on China–US relations accepts that the relationship began to deteriorate in the second decade of the twenty-first century, and that the Trump administration has accelerated the speed of that deterioration.

A large number of causal factors associated with that deterioration have been put forward in the scholarship on US–China relations. One comprehensive overview, published in 2012, noted the deep-seated distrust between the two states deriving from "different political traditions, value systems and cultures; insufficient comprehension and appreciation of each other's policymaking processes and relations between the government and other entities; and a perception of a narrowing gap in power between the United States and China."[15]

Indeed, shifts in relative power between the two countries particularly after the global financial crisis of 2007–2008 have been critical in changing perceptions and approaches. As is well known, China has the world's second largest economy and defense budget, it is the largest trading nation, the largest exporter, and in 2015 produced about a quarter of the world's manufactures. In a world and region (the Asia-Pacific) where the United States has long enjoyed military predominance, Eric Heginbotham and Richard J. Samuels show the extent to which that lead in Asia is being eroded on the back of a Chinese defense budget that they estimate has grown in real terms some 724 percent between 1996 and 2018.[16] Inevitably, China's expanded range of military equipment has served to complicate the Asian strategic environment for the United States and other major states of the region. Indeed as Robert S. Ross has argued, China is now a "maritime power that competes for influence with the United States from the Korean Peninsula, through mainland Southeast Asia and to the Strait of Malacca," adding that China not only challenges US alliances but also the US navy's "dominance of East Asian waters" thereby transforming the regional balance of power.[17] The Chinese navy has 133 warships over 1,500 tons and is moving away from having a mainly frigate-based navy to one built around destroyers. Beijing now completes an average of two-and-a-half destroyers on an annual basis compared with one destroyer every two years between 2005 and 2011. Similarly rapid increases in production rates have affected China's fighter aircraft inventory: between 2004 and 2010 China was producing 40 fighter aircraft per year; this accelerated to 60 per year between 2011 and 2017.[18]

For a Trump administration focused acutely and proudly on its military dominance and prowess these challenges to US superiority are difficult to digest and have aided the growing prominence within the US national security establishment of those who have long had an antagonistic attitude toward China and depict US engagement strategy as one that has not only failed but has also generated the kinds of material successes that have allowed Beijing to prosper and augment its military capabilities.[19] It is hardly surprising, therefore, that relations have deteriorated over a range of issues in dispute with China, including US policy towards Taiwan, navigation rights in the South China Sea, and the longstanding trading deficit in China's favor.

Trump's own attention to that deficit, to the neglect of the broader economic relationship with China, has also added to the changed perception of the implications of the interdependence of the two economies. The past acceptance that future growth for both parties depended on reasonably smooth relations between the two governments helped to smooth matters over when tensions rose over a range of issues. But this factor is no longer working in the same way; it derives mainly from the strong linkages that have come to be established between economics and security and that have brought Trump's desire to dominate directly up against Xi's more ambitious path for China.[20] This factor is particularly important to explore in any consideration of contemporary US–China relations, not only because it illustrates the competing world views of China and the United States particularly sharply, but also because it highlights the dilemmas that European states have been facing given their predilection for maintaining a broadly productive economic and political relationship with China while policing aspects of those ties that might pose a commercial or strategic threat.

The main issue in this policy area is development in technologies that have both high commercial and military value. Until approximately 2015, the economic–security nexus favored greater rather than lesser economic interdependence between China and the United States, based on the argument that the United States would remain ahead, and US businesses and society would benefit from the two-way trade and investment. However, the perception grew in the United States that China might actually be moving faster than predicted, and probably through illicit means such as cyber-theft; Chinese requirement that

US firms hand over their intellectual property (IP); and failures of protection for IP in China because of weak intellectual property laws. The result has been a growing sense in Washington that China's strengths in these new technologies, and determination to adopt a more forward role in global governance, will allow China to set global standards in these areas and constrain US strategic choices.

Beijing, on the other hand, has signaled its determination to develop a leading role in technological innovation and has put the funding behind it in an attempt to ensure that outcome. Indeed, Xi has been changing the path of China's domestic economic reform: for example, disrupting the trend towards greater market reforms, and putting the Party above the state. In particular, when Beijing announced its "Made in China 2025" policy – an industrial policy designed to enhance China's independent capacity to produce critical advanced technologies – alarm bells sounded in many of the advanced world's capital cities. These areas of Chinese domestic change add an important ideological dimension to US–China rivalry which had largely eroded in the earlier periods of this relationship after its normalization.

Before the onset of this intense rivalry, the basic US policy was to relax export controls on high-tech products destined for China on the understanding that any costs incurred would be offset by benefits enjoyed in other sectors of the US economy.[21] It was also understood that the success of US high-tech firms increasingly depended on Chinese supply chains producing component parts and on Chinese graduate students and skilled workers providing intellectual input in the areas of science and engineering. This generated an important domestic interest group among the US high-tech sector arguing for economic engagement with China. Moreover, this group found allies among some US national security and defense department officials who argued variously that the United States could not prevent China from accessing advanced technologies, and China's indigenous technology capabilities were improving at a fast rate. Alongside this, the Pentagon's own industrial base had become increasingly commercialized and the private sector was driving technological advancement in the military field. Thus, the US Defense Department now had a strong interest in ensuring the US commercial sector remained profitable.

The outcome was that rather than focusing on preventing China from catching up through applying stricter export controls, the US began concentrating on "running faster" than China in developing new technologies. The assumption at that time was that the United States could stay two generations ahead of China; and that the United States could still apply a fence around those technologies particularly important to US military superiority. When those assumptions began to be challenged by the rapidity and comprehensiveness of China's advancement in high technology areas, the China–US relationship began rapidly to deteriorate.

In light of this downturn, what are US larger objectives with respect to its relations with China in this current period? And how do European governments cope with the high levels of tension in those relations and the uncertainties that derive from determining what the Trump administration intends for the future US–China relationship?

US–China hostility: Implications for Europe

Though EU–China relations have never been smooth, there has been much that has been positive, with the EU being China's main trading partner for over a dozen years, and China standing as the EU's second largest trading partner. Chinese investment levels in the EU had, until quite recently, been steadily increasing, with Germany, France, and the UK being particular beneficiaries. European countries moved swiftly to embrace the AIIB, with the UK taking the lead and there has been some interest in the BRI.

However, there is no doubt that most European governments have come to share some of the same concerns associated with the Xi era that have been expressed in the United States, and these concerns have been reflected in a number of European Commission statements and documents. Indeed, a European Commission strategy paper described China as a "systemic rival" with the ambition to lead in future-defining high-tech fields, and a joint European Commission and European Agency for Cybersecurity report – without naming China – warned against dealings with a hostile provider of 5G equipment that had no legal or political checks and balances in place.[22] In addition, Beijing's "Made in China 2025" proposal has led the Commission to set up something equivalent to the Committee on Foreign Investment in the United States, though individual national governments still have the final say over which investments to permit. The assumption is that if China's 2025 strategy is successful this would mean the freezing out of European companies from certain parts of the Chinese market, and an intensification in global economic competition. European governments have also taken a much closer look at firms such as Huawei that play a role, or could play a role, in key European infrastructure, including 5G networks.

There are also concerns about China's continuing ability to exploit the fissures in EU member-state thinking about the future relationship with Beijing. Individual European governments retain considerable leeway when it comes to determining their dealings with China, and often reflect the range of opinion that pertains among the (after Brexit) 27 state members of the EU and the difficulties of speaking with one voice. For example, the European Commission and some EU member states are concerned at Chinese courting of countries in Central and Eastern Europe (originally called the 16+1 policy – now 17+1 with Greece's membership from April 2019), 12 of which are EU members and many of which are open to Chinese investment, and particularly investment associated with China's Belt and Road Initiative (BRI). Poland, Hungary, as well as Serbia initially became prime partners of China in this area, and Italy under its current populist government has also signed on for BRI lending. Other fissiparous tendencies, such as Brexit in January 2020, are also likely to weaken European cohesion on China policy. With Europe as the terminus of both the maritime road and the transcontinental belt, the concern among some Europeans is that China becomes the world politico-economic hub and a politically and economically weakened Europe the outer periphery.

Beijing has additionally made use of its economic leverage to attempt to deflect European criticism of its human rights policies and in one case, in 2016, to stop a strong EU Council declaration on Beijing's approach to the South China Sea. Greece, for example, in 2017 acted to prevent the presentation of a critical joint statement on China's human rights record. More recently, in 2019, some European states issued a letter criticizing Chinese internment policies enacted against Muslim Uighurs in Xinjiang, and certainly raised this as an issue as China underwent its Universal Periodic Review at the Human Rights Council in Geneva in 2018. But key Central and Eastern European states were absent as signatories to that 2019 letter.[23] Thus, these battles inside the EU to maintain a collective stance are often hard-fought, and each future occasion will require vigilance to keep the EU together.

Nevertheless, while the European Commission and some individual European governments have undoubtedly toughened their stances towards China in a number of policy areas, and there is some degree of alignment with US thinking, they generally do not approve of the all-out assault on China being undertaken by the Trump administration. The fixation on the trade deficit, which has led to Trump's focus on tariffs as the main form of punishment, has contributed to a further slowing of the European and world economies, and there is dismay at the way that the Huawei question moved from a point of US pressure on European governments (for example, the United States reportedly threatened that it would no longer share intelligence with Germany if it were to keep Huawei in its networks), to a potential transactional point with China were Beijing to agree to some of the negotiating demands that the United States is making on the country. It is sentiments such as these that encouraged Berlin's announcement in October 2019 that it would not ban Huawei from its 5G network, but would monitor it and subject it to technical evaluations.

Most European governments would subscribe more closely to the world-view and associated China policies that the Obama administration espoused and tried to enact: that is, to be alert and wary of the broader implications of Xi's world view, but also to search for ways of keeping China engaged with the multilateral institutions so prominent and important to the functioning of the current world order. In particular, they have no interest in an all-out trade war with China which would severely damage global growth, and abhor Trump's efforts to weaken the WTO and ignore its rules. Perhaps at the core here is a belief, predominant in Europe, that China has a legitimate role to play in global politics, whereas some in the Trump administration believe it cannot be allowed to challenge current arrangements. As then EU Trade Commissioner Cecilia Malmström stated in 2019: "We expressly do not share Trump's approach. China is an economic rival for us, but not a political enemy."[24]

Moreover, there is a general perception in Europe that not only do Europe and America differ in broad terms on how best to deal with China, they also are no longer together on many other issues of signal importance, at least not with respect to this US presidency whose values appear contrary to many that most Europeans (not the populist or illiberal strain of opinion, of course) associate with liberal democracy. President Macron's decision to cast aside the idea of having a joint communique at the August 2019 G7 meeting is illustrative of this. There will be times, indeed, where China and Europe come closer together than Europe and the United States, as with European state membership of the AIIB, attitudes towards working with Huawei, or the need for continuing engagement with Iran. To quote Malmström again: "An American president who sees Europe as an opponent – we all still have to learn how to deal with this situation. We've often had problems with the US, but at the core, the trans-Atlantic friendship was unbreakable. That appears to be different under Trump, which is disturbing to many Europeans".[25]

Macron, in his annual speech to the country's ambassadors in August 2019, in fact equated the United States and China and argued that neither Washington nor Beijing shared values with France, Paris's presumed ally being decried for its lack of "humanism."[26]

Indeed, Beijing may attempt to cement this European estrangement from America primarily, though not solely, through economic means: for example, by allowing European firms to take majority stakes in Chinese joint ventures; removing the need for companies to operate with a local partner; or stressing China's desire to protect multilateralism and multilateral institutions such as the World Trade Organization and United Nations. Trump himself may further help this evolution were he to keep treating allies in much the same way that he has been treating China, with his particular hostility reserved for the EU's most powerful member – Germany.

* * *

World order is in flux and the implications for China–EU–USA relations are not fully clear, not only because of the inter-relationships among the three sides of this triangle but also because of developments internal to each. What is plain is that levels of distrust on all sides are unusually high, and US–European estrangement is growing in significance. Trust is hard to build, much easier to destroy, as the next US administration is likely to discover were there to be a future US attempt to rebuild more productive and cooperative relations with both China and Europe.

Notes

1 Rosemary Foot, "Strategy, Politics and World Order Perspectives: Comparing the EU and US Approaches to China's Resurgence," in Robert S. Ross, Øystein Tunsjø, and Zhang Tuosheng, eds., *US-China-EU Relations: Managing the New World Order* (Abingdon: Routledge, 2010): 212–234

2 Thorsten Benner, Jan Gaspers, Maareike Ohlberg, et al., *Authoritarian Advance: Responding to China's Growing Political Influence in Europe* (Berlin: Global Public Policy Institute, Report, February 2018): 5.

3 See, for example, Julianne Smith and Torrey Taussig, "The Old World and the Middle Kingdom: Europe Wakes Up to China's Rise," *Foreign Affairs*, vol. 98 (5 September/October 2019): 112–124

4 David Kerr, "Between Regionalism and World Order: Five Structural Factors in China-Europe Relations to 2025," in David Kerr and Liu Fei, eds., *The International Politics of EU-China Relations* (Oxford: Oxford University Press, 2007): 310.

5 Quoted in John Gerard Ruggie, *Constructing the World Polity* (London: Routledge, 1998): 204.

6 Quoted in Ian Schwartz, "Trump Addressed UN: We Reject the Ideology of Globalism, Must Defend Sovereignty," *RealClearPolitics*, September 18, 2008, https ://www.realclearpolitics.com/video/2018/09/25/trump_addresses_un_we_reject_ the_ideology_of_globalism_must_defend_sovereignty.html

7 H. R. McMaster and Gary D. Cohn, "America First Doesn't Mean America Alone," *The Wall Street Journal*, May 30, 2017, https://www.wsj.com/articles/america-first-do esnt-mean-america-alone-1496187426

8 Charlie Laderman and Brendan Simms, *Donald Trump: The Making of a World View* (London: IB Tauris, 2017).

9 Tiang Boon Hoo, *China's Global Identity: Considering the Responsibilities of Great Power* (Washington, DC: Georgetown University Press, 2018).

10 Rosemary Foot and Amy King, "China's World View in the Xi Jinping Era: Where do Japan, Russia and the USA Fit?," *The British Journal of Politics and International Relations* (first published online, March 2020 https://journals.sagepub.com/doi/abs /10.1177/1369148120914467).

11 Elizabeth Economy, *The Third Revolution: Xi Jinping and the New Chinese State* (New York: Oxford University Press, 2018); Weixing Hu, "Xi Jinping's 'Major Country Diplomacy': The Role of Leadership in Foreign Policy Transformation," *Journal of Contemporary China*, vol. 28, no. 115 (2019): 1–14.

12 Xi Jinping, "Secure a Decisive Victory in Building a Moderately Prosperous Society in All Respects and Strive for the Great Success of Socialism with Chinese Characteristics for a New Era", speech delivered at the 19th National Congress of the Communist Party of China, 18 October 2017, http://www.xinhuanet.com/english/ download/Xi_Jinping's_report_at_19th_CPC_National_Congress.pdf

13 Rosemary Foot, *China, the UN, and Human Protection: Beliefs, Power, Image* (Oxford: Oxford University Press, 2020).

14 Ministry of Foreign Affairs, China, "Xi Jinping and US President Obama Hold Joint Press Conference," 8 June, 2013, https://www.fmprc.gov.cn/mfa_eng/topics_66567 8/xjpttcrmux_665688/t1049546.shtml

15 Kenneth Lieberthal and Wang Jisi, "Addressing US-China Distrust," John L. Thornton China Center Monograph Series, (4: March, 2012), www.brookings.edu/ wp-content/uploads/2016/06/0330_china_lieberthal.pdf

16 Eric Heginbotham and Richard J. Samuels, "Active Denial: Redesigning Japan's Response to China's Military Challenge," *International Security*, vol. 42, no. 4 (2018): 132.

17 Robert S. Ross, "Troubled Waters," *The National Interest,* May/June 2018: 53.

18 Heginbotham and Samuels, "Active Denial,": 133–134.

19 Alastair Iain Johnston, "The Failures of the 'Failure of Engagement' with China," *The Washington Quarterly,* vol. 42, no. 2 (2019): 99–114.

20 Rosemary Foot and Amy King, "Assessing the Deterioration in China-US Relations: US Governmental Perspectives on the Economic-Security Nexus," *China International Strategy Review*, vol. 1, no. 1 (June 2019): 39–50.

21 Hugo Meijer, *Trading with the Enemy: The Making of US Export Control Policy Toward the People's Republic of China* (New York: Oxford University Press, 2016); Adam Segal, "Innovation and National Security: Keeping Our Edge," *Independent Task Force Report*, no. 77 (New York: Council on Foreign Relations, September 2019).

22 European Commission. Joint Communication to the European Parliament, The European Council and the Council, *EU-China – A Strategic Outlook* (Brussels: European Commission, March, 2019). For a valuable debate on the Huawei issue see "The Future of Huawei in Europe," *A ChinaFile Conversation,* October 17, 2019, http://www.chinafile.com/conversation/future-of-huawei-europe

23 For a breakdown of the voting see, Catherine Putz, "Which Countries Are for or Against China's Xinjiang Policies?," *The Diplomat,* July 15, 2019. Since the US is no longer a member of the HRC, it did not participate in this activity.

24 C. Malmström, "EU Commissioner on US-China Trade War," *Der Spiegel,* June 26, 2019.

25 Ibid.

26 France Embassy Latvia, "Ambassadors' Conference – Speech by M. Emmanuel Macron, President of the Republic", August 27, 2019, https://lv.ambafrance.org/Ambassadors-conference-Speech-by-M-Emmanuel-Macron-President-of-the-Republic

7

EROSION OF THE AMERICAN PEACE

Europe's strategic dilemma in a world of great power conflict

Gerlinde Groitl

European security under stress: Struggling to keep pace with strategic change

The return of geopolitical rivalry is the defining feature of world politics today. This has altered Europe's strategic environment significantly. Yet despite the need to get serious about security and defense, the EU and European NATO members are struggling to cope with an antagonistic world of great power conflict. Put bluntly, Europe suffers from a two-dimensional strategic dilemma. First, the two established templates for European security, the alliance with the United States as well as European integration and political transformation, have become mired in crisis. Second, Europe has not kept up with the degree of strategic change, and is institutionally ill-suited to play geopolitical hardball.

The argument here is presented in three steps. First, to understand Europe's capacity to deal with a more adversarial international system, it is worthwhile to review past mechanisms of European security provision and their development trajectories. It becomes clear that the United States has for decades parented a highly institutionalized regional order. Second, the paper shows that the return of great power rivalries between Russia, China, and the West from the late 2000s was a rude awakening for Europe. Growing US–China tensions drove the transatlantic partners apart, while it became clear that the US – despite common interest in deterring Russia – would no longer serve as a security manager for Europe. Third, while the US and Europe shared a grand strategic consensus in the past and disagreed primarily over burden-sharing and priorities, the US under Donald J. Trump challenges European (security) interests, in some cases even more bluntly and with more immediate consequence than Moscow or Beijing. Yet substituting a fraying transatlantic partnership with European capacities for an era of great power politics proves difficult in the light of Europe's internal cleavages.

Europe's American peace: Security templates from the Cold War to the post–Cold War era

The degree of security a country or region enjoys is never just a reflection of the external threat level forced upon it. Instead it depends on the capacity to cope. Europe's security to this day is tied to America's power and liberal international-ist grand strategy. This dates back to the early Cold War. After two World Wars and due to fundamental political differences with the Soviet Union, Washington opted for Deep Engagement in Europe and tied its security to Western Europe by setting up NATO in 1949. In addition to deterring Moscow, the United States aided the economic reconstruction and democratic consolidation of Western Europe and alleviated inner-European fears regarding postwar Germany. By taking care of external as well as internal security concerns the US kick-started European integration, allowing it to concentrate on the political and economic realms. The transatlantic partnership as well as European integration and demo-cratic transformation, turned out to be perfect models for Europe's security and well-being during the Cold War.[1]

The end of the East–West conflict improved Europe's security environment significantly. The threat of a devastating, potentially nuclear great-power war on its soil was off the table. In addition, the 1990 Charter of Paris envisioned a Europe characterized by democracy, market economy and freedom without political or ideological cleavages; all states should have the sovereign right to make their own choices. Moscow signed up to it.[2] Nonetheless, challenges remained. First, there was no guarantee that the political transformations in Central and Eastern Europe were successful. Second, inner-European security concerns were far from resolved, as the UK, France, and others feared that a unified Germany might upend the carefully calibrated balance of power and interests. Third, tra-ditional inter-state conflict made way for even more intractable problems, like state failure, inner-state conflicts, or terrorism.

The established templates for European security, American Deep Engagement as well as European integration and political transformation, were adapted for the new era. First, the US continued to provide security assur-ances through NATO, while the newly created European Union tied its mem-bers closer together, all of which were meant to provide stability in an era of rapid change. Second, NATO and EU enlargement emerged as concepts to aid political reforms and export stability into the European neighborhood. To this day, the EU has grown to 27, NATO to 30 members, extending the zones of European peace and transatlantic collective defense. Relatedly, both Europe and the US pursued engagement policies toward illiberal states like Russia or China, hoping for the transformative political effects of economic interde-pendence worldwide. Third, when conflicts erupted in Bosnia and Kosovo, NATO handled these "out of area" missions. As such, the United States helped save European unity by taking the lead, bearing the brunt of the diplomatic and military burden and managing cooperation.[3]

The sustainability of this post–Cold War arrangement had already come into sharp focus in the 1990s. There were concerns the United States might disengage once its global policy priorities shifted. At the same time, European ambitions grew. Both led the European Union to institutionalize a Common Foreign and Security Policy with the Treaty of Maastricht (1993) and initiate an array of follow-on reforms to empower itself in the foreign, security, and defense sectors. Though desiring a more capable Europe, Washington resented any appearance of decoupling, duplication, or discrimination of NATO structures.[4] The Balkans experience affirmed that Europe still lacked the ability to act on its own anyway. NATO and the EU thus agreed on a division of labor of sorts: the EU aspired to develop crisis management capacities to deal with issues when NATO would not act. But the Atlantic Alliance remained the cornerstone for European security.[5]

European and American interests continued to diverge, though. Under the conditions of unipolarity, the US responded to the 9/11 terror attacks with tremendous freedom of action. Determined that this was not the time for cautious diplomacy and frustrated with Europe's failings as a junior partner, the United States marginalized its traditional allies and pushed ahead with "coalitions of the willing" when NATO's collective defense clause was first evoked in 2001. The Bush Administration's unilateral decision for preventive war against Iraq in 2003 divided Europe and challenged the EU's commitment to a rules-based, UN-centric order. On both counts Washington's policies clashed with European needs.[6] Similar concerns arose regarding Russia a few years later. While the Bush Administration forcefully lobbied for Georgia's and Ukraine's accession to NATO regardless of Russia's misgivings, some European states, like Germany and France, feared to provoke Moscow. Missile defense plans led to yet another contentious debate.[7] Increasingly, the US seemed to divide Europe instead of unifying it.

European progress in building up independent capacities remained limited nonetheless. In the early 2000s, the strategic environment was exceptionally benign, as the 2003 EU Security Strategy stated: "Europe has never been so prosperous, so secure nor so free. The violence of the first half of the 20th Century has given way to a period of peace and stability unprecedented in European history."[8] Due to peace dividends and reform efforts focused on stabilization operations, the dependency on US prowess for traditional defense even increased. At the same time, EU initiatives like the creation of battlegroups as rapid response forces after 2004, proved largely irrelevant, while the failure of the constitution in 2005 shattered hopes for a meaningful consolidation of the EU. Its single most important foreign policy concept, namely to inspire transformative change in its neighborhood through integration or association promises, worked in the 1990s and early 2000s, but was a long-term approach which could not be replicated indefinitely. Though the Lisbon Treaty of 2009 eventually strengthened the EU as a global actor, NATO remained indispensable, not least because the EU could not offer a comparable collective defense promise. Capabilities and structures aside, it was policy consensus the EU was often lacking.[9]

In addition, it became evident that expanding European security through engagement and enlargement had limits. There was a natural tension between widening and deepening the Union. Considering the frictions in the transatlantic partnership, the sketchy progress of the EU as an independent actor, and the limitations of its transformative approach, a more adversarial international system promised to be a stress test for European security.

World in flux: Shifting powers and interests from the late 2000s to 2017

By the time Barack Obama assumed office in 2009, the US had lost power, legitimacy, and resolve, while Russia and China increasingly asserted themselves. Both had withstood Western expectations of liberalization and held revisionist ambitions.[10] The return of great power rivalries coincided with acute trends of fragile statehood, civil unrest, and war in the Middle East and North Africa from 2011 onward. In addition, Brussels found itself in the quicksand of perpetual internal crisis management for years on end: it stumbled from a financial into a protracted economic crisis into the Euro-debt-crisis, had to deal with divisive questions of migration and asylum policy, the Brexit referendum, the rise of anti-EU populists, and the roll-back of liberal-democratic norms in some of its member states. The 2016 EU Global Strategy did not sugarcoat the changed strategic environment: "We live in times of existential crisis, within and beyond the European Union. Our Union is under threat."[11] Unlike in earlier years, though, neither the transatlantic partnership nor integration or outward transformation provided easy fixes for Europe's security needs.

It became increasingly clear that the US's global view diverged from Europe's regional interpretation of interests and priorities. The United States sought to rebalance its foreign policy, which had been overextended in wars in Afghanistan and Iraq, and devote due attention to China's rise.[12] Washington's 2009 "reset" with Russia was one step in this regard. It included the review of earlier missile defense plans and the negotiation of the New START treaty. Central and Eastern European states, who had supported George W. Bush's uncompromising stance, opposed Obama's rapprochement. Others, like Germany, saw it as an opportunity for a modernization partnership, still clinging to hopes for Russia's eventual liberalization. Europe was again split on whether US–Russia policy served its interests.[13] Another aspect was to reduce US commitments and get allies to step up. But Europe's deficits in NATO burden-sharing in Afghanistan, its lack of defense investments as well as its overall strategic weakness were corrosive, as then-Secretary of Defense Robert Gates made clear in 2011.[14] Obama later chastised European partners as free-riders.[15] Though the US did not question its collective defense commitment in NATO, Washington's relative restraint made clear that it would not act as a security manager for Europe any longer. While its attention shifted to Asia, European allies feared to be left alone.[16]

Regarding the challenge posed by China, Europe and the US were not on the same page. While the US as a Pacific power viewed China's rise as a holistic strategic challenge early on, Europe had long focused on (national) economic opportunities and hopes of cooperative engagement.[17] Though European states shared concerns about unfair trade practices, the EU struggled to speak with one voice. Beijing adroitly used bilateral (economic) diplomacy, investment promises, and formats like the 16+1 initiative to increase its leverage. Security issues, such as its military build-up or territorial claims in the South China Sea, were rather distant concerns for Europe. While the US lobbied against China's alternative institution building, 14 EU states joined the Asian Infrastructure Investment Bank (AIIB) as founding members in 2015. In its 2016 Global Strategy, the EU acknowledged that its prosperity depended upon stability and a cooperative regional order in Asia.[18] Its leverage was limited though, while its approach was predicated on its own experience of integration and governance. This was out of step with regional dynamics as well as the US's growing frustration with China.[19] Economic interests also increasingly blended with fears of arousing Beijing's anger. When the 2016 ruling from The Hague rejected China's claims in the South China Sea, Europeans had a hard time finding a collective response.[20] Hence, despite commonalities of interest regarding China, there was a potential for transatlantic conflict, and ties loosened.[21]

Russia on the other hand violated Europe's security directly and forced itself on the agenda in 2014. The annexation of Crimea and the war in Eastern Ukraine shattered the European conception of security in the wider region. In addition, hybrid instruments like disinformation campaigns, the mobilization of Russian minorities or cyberattacks were new strategic problems, complicating symmetric deterrence. The challenge posed by Moscow should not have come as a surprise. After all, Russia had undertaken a determined military modernization program since 2008. It had called for a multipolar world order, tried to consolidate a sphere of influence in the post-Soviet space and pursued an anti-Western course that targeted the US, NATO and, increasingly, also the EU. Legitimizing its adventurism, Moscow claimed that the West had used color revolutions to subvert legitimate governments from within. At the end of the day what Russia was up against was the very regional order the EU depended upon, namely one that supports democracy, rule of law, free markets, liberal values and multilateral, process- instead of power-based interaction dynamics.[22]

Russia's aggression against Ukraine was met with Western unity. NATO's collective defense role was reinvigorated and the US stood firmly by its partners. While European unanimity, e.g., over sanctions, was important, it was the US that provided deterrence credibility and compensated for Europe's military weakness.[23] But Washington's regional priorities were not altered: China would remain the prime challenge as a peer competitor, and Obama was increasingly frustrated with and dismissive of Russia.[24] Though ready to help deter Moscow, the US considered Ukraine a European responsibility and prodded Germany to take on a larger role. In addition, there was no firm consensus on how to proceed. The US wanted to punish Russia hard, even more so after 2016 as charges of election meddling and espionage made headlines. European states were torn between a hard-line approach and hopes for de-escalation. Similarly, the future of the Intermediate Range Nuclear Forces (INF) Treaty appeared as a source of friction already under Obama. While the US criticized Russian non-compliance and viewed the INF as a liability with regard to China anyway, Europeans – as highly affected bystanders without leverage – feared for their own security in the case of a collapse.[25]

Europe had to deal with a more complex external environment with a bad hand. Obviously the EU's transformation strategy, the core element of its own foreign-policy-making, had run into trouble with Russia willing to use force to hold on to its sphere of influence.[26] While it depended on the US for credible deterrence, which Washington was willing to provide, it was clear that Europe had to empower itself to bear a larger share of the burden and come to terms with hybrid attacks. NATO members committed to spending 2 percent of their GDP on defense by 2024, but still had live up to it. Meanwhile, the EU, in its 2016 Global Strategy, increased its level of ambition to "strategic autonomy" and focused on the need for "resilience", i.e., the ability to endure and withstand malign interferences.[27] Considering the sketchy development trajectory of EU capacity building as well as the centrifugal forces within the EU, it was an expression of hope disguised as strategy.

End of certainties: The Trump presidency and the erosion of the liberal international order from within and without

By the time US President Barack Obama left office in January 2017, China and Russia had clearly established themselves as geopolitical rivals. The Donald J. Trump Administration's 2017 National Security Strategy (NSS) called Russia and China out as repressive revisionists and promised to stand firm, suggesting a continued intense engagement abroad.[28] The NSS made also clear that economic interdependence was no longer viewed as a stabilizing force, but as a source and realm of strategic conflict. Europe meanwhile shared concerns about the People's Republic, which it labeled a "systemic rival" in 2019,[29] while the policy consensus toward Russia held, despite differing threat perceptions.[30]

Instead of renewing the transatlantic partnership to deal with authoritarian great powers, though, the US under President Trump has since developed into a severe challenge to Europe's (security) interests itself. To a certain degree, this is externally induced. Considering changed power realities and gridlock in international institutions, it is not surprising to see the US act more unilaterally and disrupt the status quo.[31] But the Trump challenge goes far beyond: he set out to destroy the liberal international order his predecessors had cultivated. As such, Trump threatened to upend the political, economic, and normative grand strategic consensus that has tied Europe and the United States together for more than 70 years.

Despite forces of continuity at work in Washington, Trump has emerged as a "disruptor-in-chief." He breaks democratic norms, derides the free press, and disregards alliances, treaties as well as diplomatic procedures. He antagonizes democratic partners and praises authoritarian leaders. Trump pretends that protectionism is a sound economic policy and trade wars are easy to win. He views the world in zero-sum terms, practices a personalized, transactional policy style, and cherishes unpredictability. Washington's readiness to leave treaties like the Paris climate agreement or the Iran nuclear deal and to upend the rules-based economic order of the WTO is deemed irresponsible on this side of the Atlantic. In addition, Trump specifically attacks the two key templates for European security: NATO and European integration.[32]

First, President Trump has undermined the credibility of NATO despite the US's unwavering commitment.[33] It took him half a year to affirm the alliance's collective-defense clause publicly. This was significant, because he had described NATO as obsolete during the election campaign and later suggested that collective defense may be conditioned on members' payment morale. The 2017 NATO summit was remembered for Trump's criticism of allied burden-sharing; at the 2018 summit he demanded a crisis meeting on defense spending, insinuating the US might do its own thing. While expressing his trust in Vladimir Putin at an ensuing meeting in Helsinki and repeatedly suggesting better relations with Russia were in reach, he mused that one of NATO's newest members', Montenegro, might drag the US into a large-scale war. For Europeans who depend on the US security-wise, this is a perpetual stress test.[34] As Gordon and Shapiro put it: "For the first two years of Trump's presidency, European leaders behaved like abused spouses, mistreated but afraid to leave, hoping against hope that things would improve."[35] Pushing back, French president Emmanuel Macron called NATO "brain-dead" before the 2019 London summit, provoking yet another crisis.[36]

Second, President Trump is hostile toward the European Union. He neither views the EU as a peace project nor a partner, but as an economic rival. At the same time, and in line with a general disregard for multilateral governance, the EU is treated as irrelevant politically in a world of sovereign nation-states. Trump openly sympathizes with populist anti-EU voices and applauds Brexit and potential future "exits." Secretary of State Mike Pompeo questioned whether the Union serves the interests of Europeans or bureaucrats in Brussels and suggested the US considered neither the EU nor the UN meaningful institutions.[37] This "hostile ally" is a tough call for the EU at a time when it is struggling with the centrifugal forces of Brexit, domestic illiberalism, and nationalist populism.[38]

Taken together Donald Trump's 'America First' populism has become as much, in some respects even more, of a challenge to European interests and security as illiberal, authoritarian powers like Russia and China. Attacks from Moscow or Beijing on Western values and institutions are something to be reckoned with. Yet the blows are all the more severe if they come from the closest ally. It is hard to calculate how much Russian maneuvering it would have taken to undermine the credibility of NATO as much as President Trump's loose rhetoric has. If Russia or China violate international rules, Western unity can offer a meaningful response. If the United States breaks out of treaties or derides the concept of a rules-based order, Europe has few muscles to flex. Though attempts to cultivate an alliance of multilateralists make sense, blunt great-power defiance all too easily trumps their effects.[39]

Europe's ability to fend for itself without the US or against the US is very limited, despite the EU's determined reform efforts since 2016. First, there is no doubt any longer that Brussels needs to "learn the language of power," as new Commission President Ursula von der Leyen put it.[40] But it has a long way to go. By design, the EU operates slowly and by consensus in foreign affairs, which is a liability. The dependency on the US won't go away anytime soon. All steps to empower the EU have been designed to complement NATO. The key projects of the EU's recent Permanent Structured Cooperation (PESCO) are those that support NATO logistics. The EU still focuses on crisis management scenarios, while member states cling to NATO for hard defense. The political logic of maintaining EU unity additionally slows ambitious progress.[41] Second, while many Europeans are appalled by the Trump Administration, there is no firm policy consensus either. After all, the EU struggles with anti–globalist populism itself. Even when there is agreement on an issue, such as the Iran nuclear deal, the EU has limited means to counteract coercive US policies. Hence the argument that "Europe United" was the solution to "America First" is of limited practical value.[42] Third, it takes unity, strategic wit, and resolve to play geopolitical hardball. At present, a Europe struggling with itself and a changing world lacks all three. Constanze Stelzenmüller's dire warning is accurate: "The challenge Europe faces now is historic. In the simplest terms, the choice before it is to remain a subject of international relations in the 21st century — or to become their object."[43]

Conclusion

European security is at a crossroads. While the democratic, economic, and institutional peace produced by European integration has pacified the continent and given it leverage abroad, the transformative power of the European model is under pressure. In addition, the transatlantic partnership, which has for decades guaranteed Europe's external defense and enabled its institutional integration, is in an existential crisis. This comes exactly at a time when rival powers such as Russia and China assert themselves on the world stage. Though Europe acknowledges it has to become a security provider and stand up for its own interests, it lags behind due to national caveats, collective inertia, and willful dependency on the US – as evident in NATO, within the EU, and at the individual state level. However, muddling through becomes untenable when the closest ally may reconsider its support, as the Trump Administration has suggested.

These developments constitute an erosion of alleged certainties and remind us that future history is yet to be written. Liberals in the 1990s hoped that geopolitical rivalries had vanished for good, because the Western model of democracy, market economy, and individual freedom would change the overall dynamics of world affairs. Realists scolded them for their naivety and warned of the rise of antagonistic peer competitors who would undo the dreams of a US-led liberal international order. The analysis of the state of Europe's security shows that both schools got it wrong. The Western-shaped structures and Europe's regional order erode from within as much as they are challenged from illiberal competitors like Russia or China from without. A European–American failure to reinvigorate the liberal West as a political actor will do lasting damage to the well-being and security of both.

Notes

1 On post–World War II global order building, see for instance G. John Ikenberry, *Liberal Leviathan: The Origins, Crisis, and Transformation of the American World Order* (Princeton, NJ/Oxford: Princeton UP, 2011); on the transatlantic partnership and its development, see Gerlinde Groitl, "Bündnisverteidigung in Europa mit und ohne die USA – Chancen und Risiken," in Uwe Hartmann and Claus von Rosen, eds., *Jahrbuch Innere Führung 2017: Die Wiederkehr der Verteidigung in Europa und die Zukunft der Bundeswehr* (Berlin: Miles Verlag, 2017), 25–40; Gerlinde Groitl, "Ende einer Ära? Die Trump-Präsidentschaft und die transatlantischen Partnerschaften," in Markus Siewert, Christian Lammert, and Boris Vormann, eds., Handbuch Politik USA. Living reference work ed. (Wiesbaden: Springer VS, 2020), 1–10.

2 Charter of Paris for a New Europe, November 21, 1990, www.osce.org/mc/39516.

3 On the post–Cold War continuity of Deep Engagement and NATO transformation, see Stephen G. Brooks and William C. Wohlforth, *America Abroad: Why the Sole Superpower Should Not Pull Back from the World* (Oxford: Oxford UP, 2016), 73–87; Sten Rynning, "The Geography of the Atlantic Peace: NATO 25 Years After the Fall of the Berlin Wall," *International Affairs*, vol. 90, no. 6 (2014): 1383–1401.

4 Jolyon Howorth, *Security and Defence Policy in the European Union.* 2nd ed. (Basingstoke: Macmillan, 2014), 112.

5 European Council, Presidency Conclusions, Helsinki European Council, December 10–11, 1999, www.europarl.europa.eu/summits/hel1_en.htm. On the complexity of European security governance, see Mark Webber et al., "The Governance of European Security," *Review of International Studies*, vol. 30, no. 3 (2004): 3–26.

6 Jeffrey Anderson, G. John Ikenberry, and Thomas Risse, eds., *The End of the West? Crisis and Change in the Atlantic Order* (Ithaca, NY/London: Cornell UP, 2008).

7 Angela Stent, *The Limits of Partnership: U.S.-Russian Relations in the Twenty-First Century* (Princeton, NJ/Oxford: Princeton UP, 2014), 135–158.

8 European Union, *A Secure Europe in a Better World: European Security Strategy*, (2003), www.consilium.europa.eu/de/documents-publications/publications/european-security-strategy-secure-europe-better-world/, 1.

9 Groitl 2017, 32–38.

10 Thomas J. Wright, *All Measures Short of War: The Contest for the 21st Century and the Future of American Power* (New Haven, CT: Yale UP, 2017); Michel J. Boyle, "The Coming Illiberal Order," *Survival*, vol. 58, no. 2 (2016): 35–66.

11 European Union, *Shared Vision, Common Action: A Stronger Europe: A Global Strategy for the European Union's Foreign and Security Policy*, (2016), https://europa.eu/globalstrategy/en/global-strategy-foreign-and-security-policy-european-union, 7.

12 Hillary Clinton, "America's Pacific Century," *Foreign Policy*, October 11, 2011, www .foreignpolicy.com/2011/10/11/americas-pacific-century/.

13 Stent 2014, 211–234.

14 Robert Gates, "The Security and Defense Agenda (Future of NATO)," *Speech*, June 11, 2011, http://archive.defense.gov/Transcripts/Transcript.aspx?TranscriptID=4839

15 Jeffrey Goldberg, "The Obama Doctrine. The U.S. President Talks Through His Hardest Decisions About America's Role in the World," *The Atlantic*, April 2016, www.theatlantic.com/magazine/toc/2016/04/.

16 Sven Bernhard Gareis and Reinhard Wolf, "Home Alone? The US Pivot to Asia and Its Implications for the EU's Common Security and Defense Policy," *European Foreign Affairs Review*, vol. 21, Special Issue (2016): 133–150.

17 Rosemary Foot, "Strategy, Politics, and World Order Perspectives: Comparing the EU and US Approaches to China's Resurgence," in Robert S. Ross, Øystein Tunsjø, and Zhang Tuosheng, eds., *US-China-EU Relations: Managing the New World Order* (London/New York: Routledge, 2010), 221–222.

18 European Union 2016, 37–38.

19 Martin Wagener, "Power Shifts and Tensions in East Asia. Implications for European Security," *European Foreign Affairs Review*, vol. 21, Special Issue (2016): 81–98; Sven Bernhard Gareis and Markus B. Liegl, "Europe in Asia. Policy Options of an Interested Bystander," *European Foreign Affairs Review*, vol. 21, Special Issue (2016): 99–116.

20 Robin Emmott, "EU's Statement on South China Sea Reflects Divisions," *Reuters*, July 15, 2016.

21 Gerlinde Groitl, "Das Ende des Westens? Die Volksrepublik China und die transatlantische Gemeinschaft," in Florian Böller et al., eds., *Die Zukunft der transatlantischen Gemeinschaft: Externe und interne Herausforderungen* (Baden-Baden: Nomos, 2017), 151–174; Philippe Le Corre and Jonathan Pollack, *China's Global Rise: Can the EU and U.S. Pursue a Coordinated Strategy?* Geoeconomics and Global Issues Paper 1/2016 (Washington, DC: Brookings Institution, 2016).

22 Margarete Klein, *Russia's Military Policy in the Post-Soviet Space: Aims, Instruments and Perspectives*. SWP Research Paper 2019/RP 01 (Berlin: SWP, 2019); Stephen Kotkin, "Russia's Perpetual Geopolitics," *Foreign Affairs*, vol. 95, no. 3 (2016): 2–9; Fydor Lukyanov, "Putin's Foreign Policy: The Quest to Restore Russia's Rightful Place," *Foreign Affairs*, vol. 95, no. 3 (2016), 30–37; Magnus Petersson, *NATO and the Crisis in the International Order: The Atlantic Alliance and Its Enemies* (London/New York: Routledge, 2019), 9–19; Wright 2017, 43–52.

23 Petersson 2019, 19–29.

24 Stent 2014, 293, 302.

25 Congressional Research Service, *Transatlantic Relations: U.S. Interests and Key Issues*, CRS Report R45745 (Washington, DC: CRS, 2019), 11–12.

26 John J. Mearsheimer, "Why the Ukraine Crisis is the West's Fault. The Liberal Delusions that Provoked Putin," *Foreign Affairs*, vol. 93, no. 5 (2014): 77–89.

27 European Union 2016; Annegret Bendiek, *A Paradigm Shift in the EU's Common Foreign and Security Policy: From Transformation to Resilience*, SWP Research Paper 2017/RP 11 (Berlin: SWP, 2017).

28 Donald J. Trump, *National Security Strategy of the United States of America*, (2017), www.whitehouse.gov/articles/new-national-security-strategy-new-era

29 European Commission, "Commission Reviews Relations with China, Proposes 10 Actions," *Press Release*, March 12, 2019, https://ec.europa.eu/commission/pre sscorner/detail/en/IP_19_1605; Julianne Smith and Torrey Taussig, "The Old World and the Middle Kingdom: Europe Wakes Up to China's Rise," *Foreign Affairs*, vol. 98, no. 5 (2019): 112–24.

30 Angela Stent, *Putin's World: Russia Against the West and with the Rest* (New York: Twelve, 2019), 44–79.

31 Randall L. Schweller, "Why Trump Now: A Third-Image Explanation," in Robert Jervis et al., eds., *Chaos in the Liberal Order: The Trump Presidency and International Politics in the Twenty-First Century* (New York: Columbia UP, 2018), 22–39.

32 Groitl 2020, 5-8.

33 Michael O'Hanlon, "Can America Still Protect Its Allies: How to Make Deterrence Work," *Foreign Affairs*, vol. 98, no. 5 (2019): 193–203; Marco Overhaus, *A Matter of Credibility: Conventional and Nuclear Security Commitments of the United States in Europe*, SWP Research Paper 2019/RP10 (Berlin: SWP, 2019).

34 Petersson 2019, 30–48; Overhaus 2019.

35 Philip H. Gordon and Jeremy Shapiro, "How Trump Killed the Atlantic Alliance. And How the Next President Can Restore It," *Foreign Affairs*, February 26, 2019, www.foreignaffairs.com/articles/2019-02-26/how-trump-killed-atlantic-alliance

36 The Economist, "Emmanuel Macron Warns Europe: NATO is Becoming Brain-Dead," *The Economist*, November 7, 2019.

37 Gardiner Harris, "Pompeo Questions the Value of International Groups like U.N. and E.U.," *New York Times*, December 4, 2018.

38 Constanze Stelzenmüller, *Hostile Ally: The Trump Challenge and Europe's Inadequate Response*, Brookings Institution, August 2019, www.brookings.edu/research/hostile-ally-the-trump-challenge-and-europes-inadequate-response/

39 Richard Gowan and Anthony Dworkin, *Three Crises and an Opportunity: Europe's Stake in Multilateralism*, Policy Brief ECFR 299 (Brussels: ECFR, 2019).

40 Ursula Von der Leyen, *Europe Address* (Berlin), November 8, 2019, https://ec.europa.eu/commission/presscorner/detail/en/SPEECH_19_6248.

41 Groitl 2017, 36–38; Simon Duke, "The Competing Logics of EU Security and Defense," *Survival*, vol. 61, no. 2 (2019): 123–142.

42 Heiko Maas, "Wir lassen nicht zu, dass die USA über unsere Köpfe hinweg handeln." Handelsblatt, August 21, 2018.

43 Stelzenmüller 2019, 18.

8

CHINA'S BRI

Implications for Europe

Philippe Le Corre

China released key details of its Belt and Road Initiative (originally termed "One Belt, One Road"), during President Xi Jinping's visits to Kazakhstan and Indonesia in the Fall of 2013. Initially billed as a network of regional infrastructure projects, encompassing road and rail routes, as well as oil and gas pipelines and facilities (the "Belt"), the scope of the BRI has continued to expand over the past few years. The "Road" component of China's plan, the twenty-first-century Maritime Silk Road, envisaged a network of new port facilities and other coastal infrastructure extending from China through South and Southeast Asia all the way to Africa and the Mediterranean. The initiative featured prominently in China's 13th Five-Year Plan, guiding national investment strategy from 2015 to 2020, and enhancing the coordination of all China's policies across the Asian continent, including financial integration, trade liberalization, people-to-people connectivity, and a "digital silk road." Although the geographical coverage of the BRI has repeatedly expanded, there is one long-lasting trend. Both the overland Silk Road Economic Belt and the Maritime Silk road have fundamentally been linking China with the European continent and its 500-million consumer market.

From a Chinese viewpoint, there are many benefits to multiple interactions with the European Union, which is now China's largest trading partner, but also with countries at the periphery of the EU such as Norway, Iceland, Switzerland, or the West Balkan states.

First of all, on the economic front, Beijing is attempting to alleviate its chronic overcapacity by investing in infrastructure along the trade routes to the European continent.

Second, it helps Chinese companies, mainly state-owned enterprises, to develop their experience abroad in fields that are important to China's future: construction, telecommunication, transport, digital technologies.

Third, it allows Beijing to increase its influence in regions where it was relatively weak, including Central Asia and the Middle East while targeting the largest non-US component of "the West," the European Union, a potential partner for a country which officially declared its interest in taking "center stage" in international relations.[1] Under the current US administration of Donald Trump, Sino-American relations reached one of their lowest points 2020 during the Covid-19 crisis, allowing proponents of a rapprochement between Europe and China to take their chance. In Beijing, the current period is considered extremely favorable to reinforcing Sino-European ties, especially on the economic front. But while US–China relations appear strained, it may also be risky to assume that the Chinese leadership has put aside its fascination/obsession with America, the only remaining superpower it may compare with.

From Chinese FDI to BRI projects: a new era of competition in Europe?

From the early 2000s, China's "going global" policy encouraged Chinese companies, both state-owned and private, to pursue opportunities abroad in order to acquire technologies and expand their footprint, using Chinese state-aid to develop.

Both Europe and the United States attracted major Chinese FDI projects in recent years (overall 90 percent of total FDI between 2000 and 2018). China's annual FDI into the EU skyrocketed from $840 million in 2008 to $42 billion in 2017, covering a wide range of geographic areas and industrial sectors, including automobile, energy, robotics, port and airport infrastructures, telecommunications, hospitality, finance, retail, fashion.[2] The count about doubles when including Switzerland, a non-EU country, which has captured the lion's share of Chinese FDI with ChemChina's acquisition of the agri-business giant Syngenta for $43 billion – the world's single largest acquisition by a Chinese company. However, data from the last two years indicates that in aggregate terms Chinese FDI into Europe is slowing down from its 2016 peak. In 2018, Chinese FDI in Europe declined by 40 percent compared to 2017, for a total of $22.5 billion.[3] The 2017–2018 decline in FDI in Europe is largely the outcome of the Chinese government's recently introduced controls on private capital outflows.

From 2016, the Chinese official language started describing more and more FDI as BRI-related.

In Greece, the acquisition of a Piraeus Port Authority control stake by China Ocean Shipping (Group) Company (COSCO) in 2016 was the result of a long negotiation, which started under the Conservative government which leased two terminals to COSCO for a 35-year period, immediately after the financial crisis. Piraeus – now the world's thirty-sixth commercial port in the world, and with a 51 percent control stake by COSCO – has been described as a successful project "which gives a snapshot of the immense business potential possible through growing trade and connectivity between China and Europe, highlighted by the

Belt and Road Initiative" according to a Chinese official report [4]. President Xi Jinping toured the Greek harbor during his state visit in November 2019. Some €395 billion of Chinese goods were transshipped through the Greek port in 2019, and COSCO's investment has been successful both "in operational and management terms," according to a well-informed local analyst, Plamen Tonchev. On a less positive note, the Chinese investment has not produced a lot of jobs, although it may have saved some. Looking at the distribution of benefits, one should also add that "economic gains are overwhelmingly in favour of China",[5] the same analyst wrote. Meanwhile, some further expansion projects by COSCO have been slowed by local conditions.[6]

Other BRI-related investments in Europe include the "Friendship Bridge" in Belgrade, the Hålogaland Bridge in Norway (built-in cooperation with a Serbian firm, VNG),[7] and the €357-million Croatian bridge across the Mali Ston Bay, which is 85 percent financed by EU structural funds.[8] Meanwhile, the upgrading by Chinese firms of an existing railway line between Belgrade and Budapest appears to have stalled ever since the Hungarian government failed to comply with EU competition rules. The European Commission has been investigating the matter. Although the BRI-enthusiast Serbian government appears willing to start the construction, Chinese contractors have adopted a wait-and-see attitude.[9]

China's BRI support through other means

First and foremost, China has been targeting Central and Eastern European countries through the so-called 16+1 mechanism, a process initiated by Beijing in 2012 to encourage links between China and the region.[10] Many of the countries involved in this project felt chastised by the EU and Germany during the financial crisis and chose to engage with China in order to attract fresh investments (which in fact have not always materialized). From the Chinese side, there are also old ties to be revived between the PRC and some of the former members of the socialist block. The creation of the 16+1 group is a lot more about initiating a network than about actual investments in those countries.

Since Greece officially joined the forum in 2019, the group now has 17 members, including 12 EU member-states, all willing to meet once a year with China's prime minister Li Keqiang and to be part of a coalition of nations friendly to China. China announced the establishment of a €3 billion fund to encourage Chinese investors to engage in public–private partnerships for infrastructure development in the region, as well as in the privatization of a range of industrial enterprises. In conjunction with these efforts, China is exploring investment in maritime port and airport facilities in Bulgaria, Slovenia, and Croatia.

All of these activities are seen as integral parts of the BRI. Twelve members of this 17+1 platform have signed the formal BRI Memorandum of Understanding, although these countries have no correlation with where the growth in volume of Chinese FDI has been happening, nor with the largest destinations of

Chinese capital. In March 2019, during President Xi Jinping's state visit, Italy became the first G7 country to formally endorse the BRI. Luxembourg and Switzerland followed suit in April. Despite the 16+1 initiative, the Central and Eastern European countries made up only 1.5 percent of all the Chinese FDI in the EU in 2018.[11] Overall, it is too early to see many of the promised investments linked to adherence to the BRI, since European countries have only been "joining" the initiative recently.

In Italy, China is working to develop trade hubs on the Adriatic side (to reach Central Europe) and on the western coastline of Italy (to reach France and Spain). The port of Trieste, one of the new investment projects announced during Xi's visit, is part of the EU–China-sanctioned "Trihub" project aimed at increasing reciprocal infrastructure investments, and China Merchants Group began talks in late 2018 to take over shares of the port from its Italian operators (but according to a recent report, talks to acquire shares in the logistics platform of Trieste port are still going on without any official agreement[12]). CCCC, which signed an agreement with the port of Trieste as part of Italy's MoU[13], is similarly exploring a €1.3 billion investment in the port of Venice. In 2018 China Merchants Group had already invested €10 million in the port of Ravenna. But China's largest existing stake in Italy is the Vado Ligure port near Genova, where it owns a 49.9 percent stake (owned by COSCO and Qingdao Port) with a 2016 investment that was planned to be operational at the end of 2019.[14]

Second, China has tried to rally support by organizing thematic conferences and events as part of its "forum diplomacy." That includes the Council Meeting of the Belt and Road News Network (BRNN) which met this year in order to promote "Belt and Road cooperation." [15] China also organized two major Belt and Road Forums (BRF) in Beijing, in 2017 and 2019, in the presence of many foreign dignitaries. In both cases, a number of European leaders attended, including no fewer than ten in 2019 (Italy, Portugal, Austria, Greece, the Czech Republic, Cyprus, Hungary, Luxembourg, Switzerland, Serbia). The European Commission was also represented by one of its commissioners and, in 2017, EC vice-president Jyrki Katainen pointed out that, although China and Europe were at "both ends of the BRI," a number of prerequisites were necessary for the EU to engage further, including "openness, transparency, interoperability, sustainability, and complementarity with other networks."[16]

Policy orientation and European interest in China trade deals and investment

Beijing's new initiatives, including the BRI, have increased competition in Europe as countries appeared to have rushed to sign new trade and investment deals with China.

Western European Countries, in particular, who first competed for a share of China's market in the 1990s, have started competing for a share of its outbound investments.

Until recently, the United Kingdom's attitude towards China underscored this point. In the 22 years since the British returned Hong Kong to China, London has courted China in a way that has surprised even Beijing. In December 2013, former British Prime Minister David Cameron, accompanied by six ministers, led an impressive 120-member business delegation to China. In September 2014, during a visit to China that took him across the country as far as the western Xinjiang autonomous region, former British Chancellor of the Exchequer George Osborne proclaimed a "golden decade" in the Sino-British relationship. The United Kingdom then became the first European country to join the AIIB as a founding member – paving the way for France, Germany, Italy, Poland, and other close US allies to join. The UK is already Europe's top destination for Chinese foreign direct investment, with stocks totaling $55.3 billion in 2018, across sectors from banking, property, and retail, to telecommunications, energy, and utilities. With Brexit looming, London's China policy has become more uncertain. Although he had declared at first that his government would be "pro-China", Prime Minister Boris Johnson reversed course by opening the door to Hong Kong citizens in 2020 following the introduction by China of a new national security law in the former British colony. He also questioned Huawei's role into the UK's 5G network."[17]

Since the start of its open-door policy 41 years ago, China has shown an astute grasp of European politics and an aptitude for playing one European country off against another. The 16+1 initiative is a case in point, but large European countries follow suit. While London has now proclaimed its desire to serve as a bridge between Europe and China[18], Beijing has continued to court other European countries. France was the first Western country to establish full diplomatic relations with the People's Republic of China in 1964. As a permanent member of the UN Security Council and one of the world's top defense spenders, Paris is trying to build a long-term global partnership with Beijing. In order to build a long-term alliance with Xi (and also attract Chinese tourists and investors to France), President Emmanuel Macron made visible gestures to please the Chinese leadership during his November 2019. He was rewarded with some contracts, but Xi then flew to Athens the week after, displaying a message of "deepening cooperation" with the newly-elected Greek government. China understands it is dealing with a divided Europe with diverging interests.[19]

Germany is the second-largest recipient of Chinese FDI in the EU, including machine-tools, semi-conductors, robotics, automobiles, and financial services. In September 2019, the Chinese President welcomed German Chancellor Angela Merkel to China for her 12th official visit since 2005, accompanied by a substantial business delegation focused on concluding large investment and trade deals. Merkel has been hoping to crown her 12 years at the German Chancellery by finalizing an EU–China bilateral investment treaty by the end of 2020, but things appear far from certain due to opposition with the German establishment itself.[20]

Other examples of countries courting China at various times include Portugal, which has attracted substantial and diversified Chinese investments;[21] the Czech Republic;[22] and most West Balkan countries.[23] Under Prime Minister Viktor Orban, Hungary has been welcoming Chinese investments even before the BRI launch and made headlines by blocking an EU statement criticizing China's human rights record in 2017, withdrawing from a 2018 joint letter by all 28 EU ambassadors to China questioning the BRI as running "counter to the EU agenda for liberalizing trade", and by "pushing the balance of power in favor of subsidized Chinese companies."[24] In 2016, Greece and Hungary blocked direct criticism by the European Union External Action Service (EEAS) of China's role in the South China Sea following the decision by an international arbitration court in The Hague to strike down Beijing's legal argument.

FDI or BRI?

While the Chinese government has been promoting the BRI towards European countries, the reality is that most Chinese FDI, including by state-owned enterprises[25] has been targeting countries that did not officially join the BRI. Between 2000-2018, the biggest recipients of cumulative Chinese investments were the UK ($55.3billion), Germany ($26.3 billion), Italy ($18billion), and France ($17.5 billion).[26] Of these four, only Italy recently "joined" the BRI.

Figure 8.1 shows that several countries, including Germany, the UK, and France, have continued to attract Chinese FDI despite not being included in the BRI.

There is a long list of European countries who have signed on to the BRI through the formal Memorandum of Understanding, but these countries do not correlate with where the growth in volume of Chinese FDI has been happening, nor with the largest destinations for Chinese capital.

Behind the big picture of an aggregate fall in FDI, there are shaper increases in a more diverse pool of EU countries: Spain, Sweden, Luxembourg, Denmark, as well as Hungary, Croatia, Poland, and Slovenia all saw growing investments, as did two of the more established FDI markets Germany and France.[27] Overall,

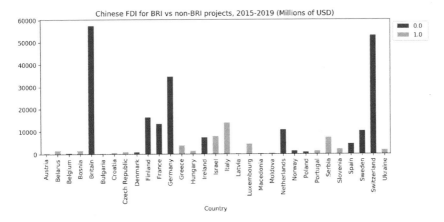

FIGURE 8.1   Chinese FDI for BRI vs. non-BRI projects, 2015–2019 (source: AEI, Chinese FDI tracker, 2019).

Chinese FDI, especially state-backed, has tended to target the strong industries in advanced economies. In Europe, this has been advanced manufacturing industries, with automotive, chemical, agribusiness, energy, and machinery taking a significant share of non-infrastructure (non-greenfield) investment. It is mainly in those countries where infrastructure is weaker and who have a connection to the BRI that China has focused on building up railways and ports to connect its commerce routes. Recently, there were fewer 'mega-deals' and a shift away from infrastructure and real estate projects in favor of more consumer-facing sectors.[28] Investment in utilities and infrastructure went from €13.9 billion in 2017 to €0.5 billion in 2018. The €9 billion takeover bid by China Three Gorges (CTG) for Energias de Portugal SA (EdP) has so far encountered regulatory complications and stalled, but would have otherwise changed this outlook.[29]

Overall, it is fair to say that most European countries do not have strong positive feelings with regard to the BRI.[30] Those which signed MoUs or 16+1 documents labeled as such have done so pragmatically in order to attract more Chinese FDI. It is particularly the case with Greece and Balkan countries, which have attracted most "BRI-labeled investments."

Europe's responses to the BRI

Nevertheless, the continuing expansion of the BRI has created a new set of challenges for Europe. Besides the noticeable intra-European divisions (South/North, East/West), several massive infrastructure projects carry risks of exposing vulnerable economies to potentially unsustainable debt levels. In Europe, the most controversial case has been Montenegro's highway project[31], which has sent the country's debt soaring. Similar questions have been raised about BRI-related investments in Serbia or Albania; in Portugal, a country member of both the EU and NATO, it could be argued that the government's sale of wide-range state assets to Chinese state-owned entities since 2010 has been somewhat overzealous[32] and risked compromising the country's energetic autonomy.[33]

Unlike developing countries, most European states have enough domestic expertise to build or revamp their infrastructure. In addition to European structural funds, institutions such as the European Investment Bank or the European Bank for Reconstruction and Development can provide the funding. In 2015, when former European Commission President Juncker announced a €315bn plan for revamping infrastructure, China expressed some interest but in the end, Brussels and Beijing could not agree on an appropriate frame. Still, unlike most EU countries, West Balkan states – who also happen to have more favorable regulatory environments – are happy to welcome China's help for infrastructure.

How does the BRI impact Europe's economy, internal situation, and foreign relations? The EU has established trade deals with Japan, Canada, South Korea, Vietnam, and Singapore while remaining, at a political level, a close US ally. This explains the cautious approach taken by Brussels when dealing with China's ambitious plan.

Perhaps the most efficient response so far has been the launch by the EU in September 2018 of a new connectivity strategy with the aim of increasing links between Europe and Asia.[34] The strategy seeks to build on and expand existing EU connectivity initiatives by establishing three broad objectives: creating transport links, energy and digital networks, and human connections; offering connectivity partnerships to countries in Asia; and promoting sustainable finance through the use of diverse financial tools. The strategy received unanimous support from European leaders, sending a clear message about the EU's intentions.[35] Early 2019, the EEAS also appointed its ambassador-at-large for connectivity, Romana Vlahutin, who has started promoting related projects. The European Parliament will have to decide how to allocate adequate funding in the upcoming multiannual budget, taping onto the European Fund for Strategic Investments. For its part, the European External Action Service is expected to guarantee €60 billion towards investments in connectivity[36] over 2021–2027, with the expectation that this will help mobilize additional funding from multilateral development banks and the private financial institutions.[37]

Beyond these actions, the EU had started in 2019 to re-evaluate its relationship with China, favoring a coordinated EU approach that can effectively stand up to China as an equal power. France's President Emmanuel Macron summoned German Chancellor Angela Merkel and former European Commission President Jean-Claude Juncker to Paris on the occasion of Xi Jinping's state visit in March. For the first time, China's leader faced not just one European counterpart, but three, including the EU representative. Germany's Economy Minister insisted later that large EU member states had "agreed" not to sign similar deals on a bilateral basis, but as a European bloc.[38]

Also in March 2019, the European Commission issued an EU–China "Strategic Outlook" in which it labels China as a "systemic rival" and "strategic competitor" and set out a number of intended steps to contrast the lack of reciprocity and violation of international rules.[39]

> China is, simultaneously, in different policy areas, a cooperation partner with whom the EU has closely aligned objectives, a negotiating partner with whom the EU needs to find a balance of interests, an economic competitor in pursuit of technological leadership, and a systemic rival promoting alternative models of governance,

it says. Such language is unusually bold for the EU and captures the concerns of EU institutions and several member states with an increasingly felt Chinese presence on its soil and periphery.

In addition, the EU concluded the process to introduce a centralized (non-binding) FDI screening mechanism, instructing those eleven EU member-states (out of 28) that still lacked equivalent domestic measures to introduce such provisions aiming at sharing information across the union. Although it specifically targets FDI in infrastructure and technology, this investment screening mechanism is a relatively loose cooperation-and-oversight system. The rapid passing of this new EU measure in just 18 months is indicative of heightened concerns over the terms of China's economic expansion, and the impact it may have on the European economy and social environment.

The 2019 annual EU–China summit, which took place in Beijing in April just before the second Belt and Road Forum and shortly after the announcement of the EU's FDI screening measure, concluded with a stern communiqué and an overall tone not as optimistic as in the past. Issues such as protecting WTO rules including IP protection, avoiding forced transfers of technology, and improving reciprocity with European companies were mentioned. Although these are not directly connected to the BRI, they have a lot to do with China's rise and increasing presence on the European continent. In June 2020, the EU-China summit –the first under the Covid-19 global crisis- ended with no joint communiqué at all. Although Europe's response to China's initiative took some time to develop, it is now gradually taking shape. Between a gradually disengaged US Administration under Donald Trump and an ambitious China with a plan to connect Eurasia as a continent, Europe has no choice but to be more offensive.

Notes

1 "It will be an era that sees *China* moving closer to *center stage*," in Xi Jinping's policy speech to the 19th Party Congress, http://www.xinhuanet.com/english/special/2017-11/03/c_136725942.htm
2 Thilo Hanemann, Mikko Huotari, and Agatha Kratz, *Chinese FDI in Europe: 2018 Trends and Impact of New Screening Policies* (Berlin: Mercator Institute for China Studies, February 2019).
3 "Chinese FDI into North America and Europe in 2018 Falls 73% to Six-Year Low of $30 Billion Baker McKenzie," July 11, 2019, https://www.bakermckenzie.com/en/newsroom/2019/07/chinese-fdi-into-europe-new-low
4 Belt and Road Portal, "Report Reveals Benefits and Concerns of BRI Port Project," April 4, 2019,
https://eng.yidaiyilu.gov.cn/qwyw/rdxw/85877.htm
5 Plamen Tonchev, "Xi's Visit to Greece: Four Questions Waiting to Be Answered," *Chinaobservers*, November 20, 2019, https://chinaobservers.eu/xis-visit-to-greece-four-questions-waiting-to-be-answered/
6 Nektaria Stamouli, "China's Biggest Investment in Greece Blocked by Archeological Authority," *Wall Street Journal*, April 3, 2009, https://www.wsj.com/articles/chinas-biggest-investment-in-greece-blocked-by-archaeological-authority-11554317046
7 OBOReurope, "A Belt, a Road and a Bridge," December 18, 2018, https://www.oboreurope.com/en/belt-road-bridge-norway/
8 Jens Bastian, "China's Expanding Presence in Southeast Europe – Taking Stock in 2018," *Reconnecting Asia*, December 19, 2018, https://reconnectingasia.csis.org/analysis/entries/chinas-expanding-presence-southeast-europe/
9 Philippe Le Corre, *China's Rise as a Geoeconomic Influencer. Four European Case Studies*, Carnegie Endowment for International Peace, October 15, 2018, https://carnegieendowment.org/2018/10/15/china-s-rise-as-geoeconomic-influencer-four-european-case-studies-pub-77462

10 Members include Bulgaria, Romania, Poland, the Czech Republic, Hungary, Latvia, Lithuania, Estonia, Slovakia, Slovenia, Greece, Croatia, Bosnia-Herzegovina, Albania, Serbia, Montenegro, Northern Macedonia.

11 Hanneman, Huotari, and Kratz, *Chinese FDI in Europe: 2018 Trends and Impact of New Screening Policies.*

12 Il Sole 24 ORE, "Il porto di Trieste ai cinesi, sbocco per il made in Italy a Est," *Il Sole 24 ORE*, accessed September 12, 2019, https://www.ilsole24ore.com/art/il-porto-trieste-cinesi-sbocco-il-made-italy-est-ACt6Fce

13 "Il porto di Trieste ai cinesi, sbocco per il made in Italy a Est."

14 Alessia Amighini, "Fact Checking: BRI, la nuova via della seta," *Istituto per gli Studi di Politica Internazionale*, August 9, 2019, https://www.ispionline.it/it/pubblicazione/fact-checking-bri-la-nuova-della-seta-23784

15 People's Daily, "People's Daily President Praises Media Cooperation Among BRI Countries,"
People's Daily Online, April 23, 2019,
http://en.people.cn/n3/2019/0423/c90000-9571232.html

16 European Commission Vice-President Jyrki Katainen speech at Belt and Road Forum Leaders' Round Table Beijing, May 16, 2017, https://eeas.europa.eu/delegations/china/26154/european-commission-vice-president-jyrki-katainen-speech-belt-and-road-forum-leaders-round_en

17 Zhenhua Lu, "Pro-China' Boris Johnson 'Enthusiastic' About Belt and Road Plan," *South China Morning Post*, July 24, 2019, https://www.scmp.com/news/china/diplomacy/article/3019884/pro-china-boris-johnson-enthusiastic-about-belt-and-road-plan

18 A claim also made by others, such as Hungary, Bulgaria, and Serbia.

19 Philippe Le Corre, "A Divided Europe's China Challenge," *East Asia Forum*, November 26, 2019, https://www.eastasiaforum.org/2019/11/26/a-divided-europes-china-challenge/

20 Noah Barkin, "Europe's Backlash Against Huawei Has Arrived," *Foreign Policy*, November 27, 2019, https://foreignpolicy.com/2019/11/27/europe-huawei-backlash-merkel-germany-summit/

21 Portugal: A former superpower cosying up to an aspiring one, in *China's Rise as a Geoeconomic Influencer. Four European Case Studies*, op. cit.

22 The Czech Republic: Buying influence?, in *China's Rise as a Geoeconomic Influencer. Four European Case Studies*, op. cit.

23 Serbia: The Open door Balkan space, in *China's Rise as a Geoeconomic Influencer. Four European Case Studies*, op. cit.

24 Dana Heide, Till Hoppe, Stephan Scheuer, and Klaus Stratmann, "EU Ambassadors Band Together Against Silk Road," *Handelsblatt*, April 14, 2018, https://www.handelsblatt.com/today/politics/china-first-eu-ambassadors-band-together-against-silk-road/23581860.html?ticket=ST-32629711-lOOsjthSDF1yaEw27BJh-ap1

25 Sixty-three percent of Chinese FDI in the EU are by SOEs, see Hanemann, Huotari, and Kratz, *Chinese FDI in Europe: 2018 Trends and Impact of New Screening Policies.*

26 Thilo Hanemann, Mikko Huotari, and Agatha Kratz, *Chinese FDI in Europe: 2018 Trends and Impact of New Screening Policies.* MERICS, March 6, 2019, https://www.merics.org/en/report/chinese-fdi-europe-2018-trends-and-impact-new-screening-policies.

27 Baker McKenzie, "Chinese FDI into North America and Europe in 2018 Falls 73% to Six-Year Low of $30 Billion," *Baker McKenzie*, January 14, 2019, April 16, 2019, https://www.bakermckenzie.com/en/newsroom/2019/01/chinese-fdi

28 Hanemann, Huotari, and Kratz, *Chinese FDI in Europe: 2018 Trends and Impact of New Screening Policies.*

29 Hanemann, Huotari, and Kratz, *Chinese FDI in Europe: 2018 Trends and Impact of New Screening Policies*, 11.

30 Pew Research, "Few Europeans Confident in Xi as He Seeks to Extend Chinese Economic Influence in the Region," *Pew Research*, March 2019, https://www.pew research.org/fact-tank/2019/03/22/few-europeans-confident-in-xi-as-he-seeks-to -extend-chinese-economic-influence-in-the-region/

31 Financial Times, "Montenegro Fears China-Backed Highway Will Put It on Road to Ruin," *Financial Times*, April 10, 2019, https://www.ft.com/content/d3d56d20 -5a8d-11e9-9dde-7aedca0a081a

32 Due to the aftermath of the 2008 financial crisis, the Lisbon government was asked by the "Troika", made of the European Central Bank, European Commission and International Monetary Fund, to privatize state assets for up to €5.5billion

33 Philippe Le Corre, "China's Golden Era in Portugal," *The Diplomat*, November 24, 2018, https://thediplomat.com/2018/11/chinas-golden-era-in-portugal/Portugal.

34 European Union External Action, "The European Way to Connectivity – A New Strategy on How to Better Connect Europe and Asia," *EEAS*, September 19, 2018, https://eeas.europa.eu/headquarters/headquarters-Homepage/50752/european -way-connectivity-%E2%80%93-new-strategy-how-better-connect-europe-and -asia_en

35 Erik Brattberg and Etienne Soula, "Europe's Emerging Approach to the BRI," *Carnegie Endowment for International Peace*, October 19, 2018, https://carnegieendo wment.org/2018/10/19/europe-s-emerging-approach-to-china-s-belt-and-road-in itiative-pub-77536

36 European Commission, "Explaining the European Union's Approach to Connecting Europe and Asia," September 19, 2018, https://europa.eu/rapid/press-release_ME MO-18-5804_en.htm

37 Brattberg and Soula, "Europe's Emerging Approach to the BRI," *op. cit.*

38 US House of Representatives, Committee on Foreign Affairs, "China's Expanding Influence in Europe and Eurasia," May 9, 2019, https://foreignaffairs.house.gov/20 19/5/china-s-expanding-influence-in-europe-and-eurasia

39 European Commission, *EU-China – A Strategic Outlook* (2019), https://ec.europa. eu/commission/sites/beta-political/files/communication-eu-china-a-strategic- outlook.pdf

PART III

The US, China, and Europe: Toward new strategies?

9

EUROPE AND ASIA (AND CHINA) IN US GRAND STRATEGY

Joshua Shifrinson

Introduction

The United States is undergoing its most intense grand strategy debate since after the Cold War.[1] For the first time in a generation, scholars and policymakers are debating the scope and content of the United States' engagement in world affairs.[2] It remains unclear how the debate will resolve. Amid the noise, however, it is increasingly clear that secular trends in world politics – particularly the rise of China – are spurring a substantial change in US priorities. Regardless of what emerges, American grand strategy – its foundational "theory" over how to create security for itself using the political, economic, and military tools at its disposal – will be substantially different than over preceding years.

This trend becomes clear when considering the respective roles of Europe and Asia in US grand strategy. As Eurasia's primary cluster of economic and military potential, Europe traditionally enjoyed priority in US policy. Motivated to contain the Soviet Union and Germany – and later with ensuring that the United States could shape European affairs – the US invested vast economic (e.g., the Marshall Plan), military (e.g., stationed military forces), and political resources (e.g., creating and expanding, NATO) in the region after World War II.[3] China's rise, however, is pulling American strategy toward East Asia.[4] Having previously sought to "engage" China, a growing chorus now holds that the US should prepare to repeat the post-1945 European experience and contain a rising PRC.[5] Of course, not everyone is yet sold on a hawkish stance, with many analysts in the academy and think-tank worlds questioning the necessity of Chinese–American competition.[6] Still, even these alternatives allow that China and East Asia will take precedence in future decades.

Building on this debate, this chapter investigates four questions. First, what are the main divides on the respective roles of Europe and China/Asia in US grand strategy? Second, how significant are the envisioned adjustments to US policy in each region? Third, to what extent are the proposed strategies strategically coherent: to what degree do they represent a coherent approach to international relations that accords with what scholars know of international behavior while knitting US ends and means together in an integrated fashion? Finally, what circumstances would favor one strategy over another?

Paralleling existing research, I identify four main positions of argument in the grand strategy debate. I refer to these as Second Generation Primacy; Deep Engagement; Offshore Balancing; and Restraint. Except for Second Generation Primacy, these labels should be familiar to those following US security discussions.[7] Further in keeping with existing research, I argue that each option envisions some adjustments to US strategy, though Restraint and Offshore Balancing propose more fundamental changes. The regional focus adopted in this chapter, however, also highlights underappreciated elements of overlap in several of the strategies. Most importantly, Second Generational Primacy and Offshore Balancing embrace similar recommendations for East Asia and China. A regional approach, moreover, showcases internal contradictions and potential problems for each option. These problems loom largest for Second Generation Primacy, which loses coherence when its implications are considered in detail but each of the others also confronts problems. I return to these points later.

The remainder of this chapter proceeds in five sections. Following this Introduction, I briefly describe the evolution of the United States' postwar grand strategy. Next, I identify the main contours in the strategy debate. I subsequently classify the scope of the envisioned adjustments and use international relations theory and current US policy debates to evaluate the coherence of the envisioned strategies. Finally, I conclude by identifying the strategic conditions that would aid or undermine each strategy's appeal.

Postwar US grand strategy: a brief review

Since 1945, the United States has effectively had two grand strategies. During the Cold War, US policy centered on containing the Soviet Union.[8] Owing to its economic and military potential, Europe – especially *Western* Europe – was central to this struggle. Indeed, despite occasional excursions in Asia, Latin America, and Africa, US policy focused on the security of Western Europe to foreclose the possibility of Soviet gains in a region that (so the argument went) might shift the balance of power against the United States.

This strategy changed after the Cold War. Following a brief debate inside the H.W. Bush and Clinton administrations, American policymakers quickly embraced a primacist grand strategy.[9] Different policymakers pursued primacy using different means: members of the Clinton and Obama administrations, for instance, were more willing to seek US dominance by working with multilateral organizations, whereas the George W. Bush administration sought a muscular unilateralism.[10] Regardless, American leaders resolved to sustain the US as the world's sole great power.

The scope of American efforts expanded accordingly. Western Europe remained important, but the US increased its footprint by enlarging NATO while variously engaging or isolating Russia.[11] It also devoted additional attention to Asia, driven by the region's mounting importance with − first − its economic growth and − subsequently − China's rise as a near-peer competitor. To this end, the 1990s−2010s saw the United States expand regional ties via revamped alliances with Japan and South Korea, alignment with India, and attempts to engage China.[12] The US then backed these commitments with an expanded military presence as policymakers aimed to cap the US presence in Europe for the sake of East Asia.[13] This trend continues today: despite efforts following the 2014 Russian intervention in Ukraine to revitalize the US presence in Europe, Asia continues to receive the lion's share of new equipment, funding, and attention.[14]

The contemporary strategy debate

As suggested earlier, the primacist consensus has proven remarkably resilient.[15] Even recognition starting around 2015 that US efforts had largely failed and the country faced ostensible "revisionist" great powers in China and (to a lesser extent) Russia has not affected the impulse, as strategists call for confronting said challengers to sustain US preeminence.[16] Still, the growing mismatch between the ends sought in US policy and the means available to do so − coupled with costly wars in Iraq and Afghanistan and growing domestic demands − has spurred a debate over the future of US grand strategy. Four positions are present in this conversation; I refer to these as Second Generation Primacy, Deep Engagement, Offshore Balancing, and Restraint. Each envisions different roles for Europe and Asia in US policy, but consistent across all is the acknowledgment that East Asia should take precedence over Europe.

Second Generation Primacy

Second Generation Primacy derives from the United States' post−Cold War efforts. However, where post−Cold War primacy sought (and failed) to simply *maintain* American unipolarity, Second Generation Primacy looks to *reclaim* American preeminence.[17] The effort thus contains aspirational elements that post−Cold War primacy lacked. To achieve these ends, proponents argue the US must (1) prevent further losses to its power position, and (2) compete with Russia and China by building up and containing them to the point of their surrender or collapse;[18] some also advocate utilizing international institutions and diplomacy to legitimate US efforts, curtailing Russian and Chinese growth, and/or seeking regime change.[19]

Although often framed as a strategy aimed at both China and Russia, most analysts agree that China presents the larger problem.[20] As the 2018 National Defense Strategy declared, China "seeks Indo-Pacific regional hegemony in the near-term and displacement of the United States to achieve global preeminence in the future," whereas Russia primarily challenges Europe's periphery.[21] Reflecting this emphasis, the United States is redeploying air and naval forces from Europe to Asia, developing new military platforms and operational concepts optimized for the Asia-Pacific region, courting new allies, and attempting to coordinate the activities of existing partners such as South Korea and Japan.[22] The objective seems to be to erect a sufficiently robust containment perimeter that China is hemmed in and either overawed or exhausted. This is not to argue Europe is ignored by Second Generation Primacy.[23] Rather, proponents call for deploying infantry and armor units to Eastern European states threatened by Russia. The calculation seems to be that the US can allocate *ground* forces to Europe, while otherwise sending *air and naval* power to Asia.[24] Reflecting the inversion of Europe and Asia in US priorities, however, strategists are also exploring ways for the United States' European allies to assist against China.[25] Combined, Second Generation Primacy thus blends Cold War-era containment with post-Cold War primacy, leveraging existing US military capabilities and political ties in an attempt to reclaim unipolarity.

Deep Engagement

Where Second Generation Primacy seeks to overcome Russia and China to dominate Europe and Asia, Deep Engagement calls for a more limited exercise in maintaining "stability" in those regions. Put differently, where Primacists look to garner US preeminence, Deep Engagement focuses more on preventing crises and major power conflict in geopolitically important regions.[26] The strategy therefore implicitly accepts that US power may erode, but does not view these losses as inherently problematic. To do so – as Stephen Brooks and William Wohlforth offer – the United States is advised to maintain existing alliances, forward deploy military forces to reassure partners and deter adversaries, and use the resulting security ties to craft institutional and economic relationships that reinforce US oversight.[27]

What does this mean at the regional level? As US goals are primarily defensive, Deep Engagers suggest that Europe is basically secure: with Russia a shadow of the former Soviet Union, the United States can focus on sustaining ties to the area via NATO, deploy rotational military assets to backstop states immediately threatened by Russia, and invest limited sums in acquiring additional military assets to deter Russia in peacetime and which could aid in wartime resupply.[28]

China, in contrast, merits additional attention. For sure, Deep Engagers break with Primacists in arguing that unipolarity is not yet dead; hence, competing with China loses its urgency. Nevertheless, Deep Engagement proposes a gradual military buildup to (1) contain China within its existing security perimeter while reassuring nervous regional actors like Japan, and (2) deter any Chinese efforts at military expansion.[29] And, where Second Generation Primacists view such efforts as a way of winnowing down China's position, Deep Engagers present these steps as maintaining a status quo that is only slowly changing. Hence, where Second Generation Primacists often marry their political-military plans with calls for strategic competition, Deep Engagement implies sustaining existing economic and institutions relationships even if they disproportionally benefit China (and/or Russia).[30] In sum, Deep Engagement accepts the potential loss of US dominance provided world politics remain free of major conflicts in the interim.

Offshore Balancing

Despite differences, Second Generation Primacy and Deep Engagement advocate an activist US grand strategy. In contrast, Offshore Balancing represents a less forward-leaning approach. Offshore Balancing shares with Deep Engagement the argument that the United States should prevent great power threats to Europe or Asia. Unlike Deep Engagement, however, it proposes that the US should first rely on local actors to check potential threats, only intervening if local efforts fail.[31]

In Europe, this represents broadly good news for the United States since – as John Mearsheimer and Stephen Walt write – "no potential hegemon" is around.[32] That said, Asia is a potential problem owing to China's economic and military growth. Mearsheimer and Walt, for instance, argue that "if China continues its impressive rise, it is likely to seek hegemony in Asia"; Sebastian Rosato and John Schuessler allow that "if China were to continue to grow economically, convert its wealth into military power, and show any sign of wanting to use that power [...] we would recommend that the United States balance against it";[33] Christopher Layne argues that China's rise is pushing the United States to counterbalance.[34] After all (as Walt separately explains) China may be poised to surpass other Asian actors in power potential and swamp local counterbalancing options. Likewise, organizing a regional alliance against China may be difficult as potential counterbalancers "do not always get along." It therefore falls to the United States to offset China's rise.[35]

Accordingly, Offshore Balancing advocates an American exit from Europe to free up resources for use against China and an expanded US presence through Asia.[36] This does not mean abandoning Europe entirely: Offshore Balancing recognizes the importance of retaining a residual diplomatic presence to monitor developments and ensure that local actors indeed uphold regional balances. Still, the locus of American activities would move east. In particular, the United States may need to undertake a military buildup in Asia to reassure partners, contain further Chinese expansion, and ultimately prevent China from dominating the region.[37] The net effect could be an open-ended American commitment to the region, potentially resulting in a Cold Waresque standoff that might continue until if and when a regional balance was restored.

Restraint

The last grand strategy discussed is Restraint.[38] Although often conflated with Offshore Balancing, Restraint actually represents a separate approach built on distinct assumptions regarding world politics and judgments of the contemporary security environment.[39] In particular, while Restraint advocates acknowledge China's rise in line with Offshore Balancers, they differ in concluding that local states threatened by China's rise can go a long ways toward providing for their – and, by extension, regional – security even without American assistance; in a phrase, the system is defense-dominant. Hence, as Posen writes, "a very great shift in China's regional and global influence is necessary to affect the United States," in large part because local actors can and will balance any Chinese threat.[40] As for Europe, Restrainers recognize tensions with Russia, but counter that a rough balance exists among Russia, Germany, Britain, and France. None is poised to dominate the continent, just as defense dominance – combined with the presence of nuclear weapons – mean deterrence and stability should be viable indefinitely.[41]

Restraint thus calls for the United States to draw down in both Europe and Asia.[42] In Europe, the United States would winnow down its commitment to little more than a vestigial pledge to consult in a crisis while empowering the European Union to handle hard security tasks. As for Asia, the United States would encourage states like India and Japan to act in line with their natural interest and balance China's rise. American alliances would therefore be reduced, and their terms adjusted to give local actors primary responsibility for regional developments. The United States might pair this with limited military commitments to, for instance, maintain the sea lines of communication, but would stop far short of the military effort envisioned even by Offshore Balancers.[43] Restraint, in other words, is just that: a plan for the United States to curtail engagement in Europe and Asia, relying on and incentivizing regional actors to craft local balances of power.

Continuity and change in US grand strategy

Again, it remains unclear whether and which of these grand strategies will triumph in the contemporary debate. Nevertheless, one overarching theme is clear: across the debate, the respective roles of Europe and Asia have inverted in terms of US priorities. Offshore Balancers and Second Generation Primacists are most explicit on this point, but even Restraint acknowledges the issue in recommending East Asia as the one region where a limited US security presence continues.

The primary driver of this trend is also clear: although the gradual shift of economic power from Europe to Asia would have reoriented US priorities to some degree, China's economic-military growth makes it the most likely candidate to seek regional hegemony and so the most sustained threat to US security.[44] Europe, in contrast, lacks a comparable threat. Baldly stated, China's rise means that, for the first time in modern history, American efforts are moving away from Europe and toward East Asia.

Still, the strategies under discussion suggest different degrees of policy change and continuity. For sure, classifying strategic adjustment is difficult: as Colin Dueck observes, the best one can often do is make rough judgments over the relative degree of change on issues such as defense spending and strategic commitments.[45] Building on Dueck's insight, the envisioned adjustments can be compared by asking three questions of the proposed US course in both across Europe and Asia. First, are alliances expanded or contracted? Second, are military forces added to or withdrawn from different regions? Finally, does the United States seek to maintain, increase, or decrease the influence it exerts over key geopolitical actors? However, where Dueck assesses changes qualitatively, I evaluate and classify the envisioned adjustments on a four-value scale ranging from "minimal/none" (i.e., maintaining current US efforts), "moderate" (seeking mid-range changes to extant policies), "substantial" (calling for substantial shifts in US policy), and "foundational" (advocating novel or seminal adjustments to US strategy).

Table 9.1 reports the results. Overall, Deep Engagement seeks the least change to existing policies: although proposing a moderate military buildup against China, it otherwise accepts current commitments and military balances. Conversely, other options suggest significant strategic adjustments. Insofar as post–Cold War primacy failed to maintain unipolarity, Second Generation Primacy paradoxically demands substantial shifts in US military, alliance, and political efforts in both Europe and Asia; in pursuing dominance, the United States would commit itself to even costlier and more expansive policies. Strikingly, Offshore Balancing shares some similarities with Second Generation Primacy as, in advocating reorienting US policy from Europe towards Asia, both camps advocate foundational increases in US efforts in the Asia-Pacific. Where Offshore Balancers and Second Generation Primacists differ, however, is Offshore Balancers' call for limiting US efforts in Europe. In this, they dovetail with Restrainers – who, however, additionally call for fundamentally reducing US activities in Asia. Indeed, by these metrics, Restraint is the most radical of all the grand strategies as it seeks foundational changes to US policy in both Europe and Asia.

Assessing the options

To what extent do the strategies present coherent, logical, and well-integrated approaches to guide US policy? At root, grand strategy attempts to knit together the ends and means of a state's security efforts. This requires not only setting objectives, but working within fiscal, military, diplomatic, and strategic limitations.[46] Any judgment of the respective coherence of the strategic options is necessarily speculative. Still, a combination of international relations theory and the terms of the strategies themselves highlights problems – though they vary in scope and extent – with each option.

TABLE 9.1 Comparing Envisioned Adjustments per US Grand Strategy Options

Categories	Second Generation Primacy		Deep Engagement		Offshore Balancing		Restraint	
	Europe	Asia	Europe	Asia	Europe	Asia	Europe	Asia
Alliances	Minimal–Moderate: maintain NATO and continue its expansion	Moderate–Substantial: accelerate and expand efforts at creating anti-China coalition	Minimal: maintain existing NATO alliance	Minimal: maintain and consider expanding alliances in Asia	Foundational: eliminate existing alliances in Europe	Moderate–Substantial: accelerate and expand efforts at creating anti-China coalition	Foundational: eliminate existing alliances	Substantial: reduce and adjust to encourage local states to provide for security
Military presence	Substantial: deploy significant forces into Europe to overmatch Russia	Substantial: accelerate military buildup against the PRC	Minimal: maintain limited military presence	Moderate: begin gradual military buildup against China	Foundational: withdraw US forces from Europe	Substantial–Moderate: accelerate military buildup against the PRC using resources reallocated from Europe	Foundational: withdraw US forces	Foundational: withdraw most US military forces, keeping at most residual presence
Control	Minimal: maintain US efforts to shape behavior of European partners and allies; isolate Russia	Moderate: maintain efforts to shape behavior of Asian allies and partners; continue efforts to prevent Chinese aggrandizement; increasing European presence in Asia to augment US capabilities	Minimal: continue present efforts to act as organizer of European security	Minimal: maintain efforts to shape behavior of Asian allies; continue efforts to prevent Chinese aggrandizement	Foundational: turn European security over to local actors	Moderate: direct activities of anti-China coalition to assuage intra-coalition tensions and maximize US oversight	Foundational: turn European security over to local actors	Foundational–Substantial: minimize US involvement in regional politics

Second Generation Primacy

Second Generation Primacy is the least coherent of the options. The strategy is poised to be very expensive, requiring the United States to spend substantially more on defense than at present. Considering the United States already runs large budget deficits – with the military constituting the largest portion of discretionary spending – it is unclear where the needed funds should come from.[47] As importantly, the strategy risks generating severe geopolitical problems. The competitive policies at the strategy's core are largely aspirational, with advocates lacking a logic explaining how US pressure will lead targeted states to decline or surrender. Indeed, states tend to balance when facing threats, and the United States – in seeking to reclaim its unipolar position – would effectively declare itself a threat to highly capable countries: Russia and China for sure, and potentially even American allies worried about being dragged into conflicts of limited interest.[48] In response, Russia and China may adopt competitive policies of their own, just as allies may loosen the bonds tethering them to the United States and so hinder the United States' ability to mobilize for action in Europe or Asia.[49] Ultimately, the prospective tensions inherent in this approach would put American security at risk. It is a recipe for open-ended competition for unclear ends, using contradictory means, and which is likely to undermine the security the United States already enjoys.

Deep Engagement

Deep Engagement performs better than Second Generation Primacy but also contains potential problems. Unlike Second Generation Primacy, the strategy may be fiscally sustainable.[50] As it essentially calls for cooperation among states favoring the status quo in Europe and Asia, it also has a natural constituency. That said, Deep Engagement confronts three potential dilemmas. First, despite the strategy's emphasis on "stability," this focus elides that one state's stability is another state's revisionism.[51] Consider contemporary Asia: despite linking Japan to the United States to limit a China–Japan security spiral, the result joins US power to Japan's and requires the United States to take many Japanese interests as its own.[52] As a result, it changes regional conditions and can appear threatening to actors such as China. Stability seeking, in other words, is not value-neutral. Along the way – second – US policy gives allies leverage over the United States' behavior, potentially entrapping it in disputes that the United States might otherwise avoid.[53]

Finally, there is a question over long-term viability. Although Deep Engagement rejects that China is soon to be an American peer competitor, even supporters of the strategy acknowledge that China's rise is real and ongoing.[54] If so, however, then American efforts to "stabilize" Asia by reassuring allies and dampening local security spirals may become increasingly expensive and politically risky. This problem also interacts with the first issue noted above: insofar as Deep Engagement injects the United States into regional politics in ways that threaten China, it encourages counterbalancing that makes these risks more likely to be realized. Combined, Deep Engagement may be effective in the near term, yet lose coherence as the distribution of power shifts.

Offshore Balancing

What of Offshore Balancing? Although advocating a military buildup against China, the strategy is likely affordable given the calls for drawing down in Europe. In doing so, it also reduces the likelihood of competition with Russia, thus avoiding one of the problems with Second Generation Primacy. Still, problems come from two directions. First, the risks involved in a large-scale military buildup against China noted in the discussion of Second Generation Primacy apply to Offshore Balancing as well. Second, although the strategy's proposal for withdrawal from Europe assumes the region will remain stable, stability is not guaranteed. To be sure, there are reasons for optimism: a rough balance of power holds in the area, key states have nuclear weapons, and economic and institutional ties are robust. Still, multipolarity – as is likely to obtain following an American withdrawal – often generates miscalculation.[55] Crises may be less likely in Europe even without the United States than at any time before the postwar era, but there is some risk it will be greater than Offshore Balancers allow.

Restraint

Finally, by drawing down in Europe and Asia, Restraint has the advantage of minimizing the United States' economic costs and political risks. A second advantage follows: by removing the US from Europe and Asia, it reduces bilateral tensions with notional adversaries like China and Russia, opening up the possibility of more or less explicit bargains to advance US security. Moreover, by building on the proposition that states tend to balance proximate threats, and the empirical observation that many capable states have incentives to balance Russia and (especially) China, Restraint is anchored in both theory and practice.[56]

Despite these advantages, Restraint – like Offshore Balancing – carries the risk that its expectations regarding local behavior may be off-base. After all, states may balance inefficiently: internal buildups may lag threats, and coalitions may be hard to form. This can be a particular problem in East Asia, where water barriers may increase states' incentives to buck pass, and historical tensions impede alignment.[57] Furthermore, although Restraint expects the defense to dominate, defense may still prove inadequate if the distribution of power sharply favors one side over another;[58] in context, China may eventually be able to seek regional dominance despite local efforts. How the United States could position itself to hedge against such possibilities is unclear.

Conclusion: paths and prospects

In sum, none of the envisioned strategies is unproblematic – each contains internal contradictions and/or may confront difficulties when applied to contemporary world affairs. This raises one final question: if none makes a dispositive case, what might cause the United States to adopt one strategy over another?

Any strategy ultimately emerges from a combination of domestic and international compromises and bargains. Within this, however, the international security environment tends to play a decisive role.[59] It is no accident, for instance, that the United States embraced containment when Cold War bipolarity presented the US with an obvious threat, nor surprising that post–Cold War unipolarity allowed American ambitions to expand; shifts in the international environment did not *cause* containment or primacy, but they made the results far more likely.

This logic suggests that shifts in the security environment are likely to take center stage in shaping US strategy. The implication of this, however, is less than clear-cut given that analysts remain divided over the shape of the contemporary international environment: given China's rise, some predict the return of bipolarity, some multipolarity, and others – irrespective of arguments that unipolarity is over – continued US dominance.[60] Indeed, the absence of agreement may help to explain why, despite acknowledging China's rise, US grand strategy has largely continued along the same primacist course that has guided American efforts since the 1990s.[61] Still, as the security environment clarifies, we can expect certain grand strategies to become more or less likely to be adopted.

Table 9.2 summarizes the basic expectations. All things being equal, Second Generation Primacy is poised to gain traction the longer proponents can plausibly argue American unipolarity (or something close to) it endures. After all, only with American dominance at hand or nearby can analysts make a credible case that the strategy's benefits outweigh the risks. Conversely, the strategy is poised to lose salience in bipolar or multipolar conditions: the more China and/or other actors can impose costs on ambitious US policies, the more likely US strategists are to decide that game is not worth the quid.

An analogous situation holds for Deep Engagement. In aiming for stability in key geopolitical locales, Deep Engagement assumes US power is able to foster the stability sought. This assumption, however, is less plausible if bipolarity and/

TABLE 9.2 International Conditions Affecting US Grand Strategic Options

	Strategy			
	Second Generation	Deep Engagement	Offshore Balancing	Restraint
Conditions favoring the argument	Unipolarity or near-unipolarity	Unipolarity or near-unipolarity	Bipolarity or offense-dominant multipolarity	Unipolarity or mulipolarity
Conditions challenging the argument	Multipolarity or bipolarity	Multipolarity or bipolarity	Unipolarity or defense-dominant multipolarity	Bipolarity or offense-dominant multipolarity

or multipolarity return in full force: facing real external challengers, US power may prove insufficient to create stability in all desired theaters. Like the Cold War, policymakers may need to pick and choose their regional contests (e.g., retrenching in Europe for the sake of Asia). On the other hand, the longer it takes multipolarity or bipolarity to emerge – and/or the more defenders have strategic advantages over aggressors – the longer Deep Engagement can appeal.

Offshore Balancing and Restraint, in contrast, gain traction the more the world shifts from unipolarity. However, each's appeal is greatest under distinct conditions. Designed to draw down in stable regions to balance a looming regional hegemon, Offshore Balancing becomes more plausible the more the world moves toward bipolarity and/or China appears poised to dominate East Asia. The inverse is also true: the more we see continued US dominance, multipolarity, and/or regional actors able to offset the PRC, the less compelling the argument. In contrast, Restraint gains salience under those conditions: continued American dominance despite China's rise would justify less American strategic activism (as some proposed in the early to mid-1990s), just as the return of multipolarity and/or an Asia with actors capable of containing China would justify greater American buck-passing and retrenchment. If, however, China's rise precipitates true bipolarity and China's emergence as a potential hegemon – or if states prove unable or unwilling to balance China – then Restraint arguments would suffer accordingly.

In short, just as the US grand strategy debate is itself in flux, so too are the international conditions that will drive the appeal of the different options. Still, the bottom line is clear: China and Asia are increasingly the focus of US strategy debates. As international conditions change, analysts therefore need to proceed judiciously to accurately assess strategic circumstances and tailor the tools and solutions embraced in response. Given the stakes involved, only clear-eyed analysis of current and expected future developments can chart a path forward in a changing world.

Notes

1 An overview of the debate can be found in Paul C. Avey, Jonathan Markowitz, and Robert J. Reardon, "Disentangling Grand Strategy," *Texas National Security Review*, vol. 2, no. 1 (November 2018): 29–50.

2 For a range of strategies, see Loren Schulman, ed., *New Voices in Grand Strategy* (Washington, DC: Center for a New American Security, April 2019).

3 Marc Trachtenberg, *A Constructed Peace: The Making of the European Settlement, 1945–1963* (Princeton, NJ: Princeton University Press, 1999).

4 Thomas J. Christensen, "Obama and Asia," *Foreign Affairs*, vol. 94, no. 5 (October 2015): 28–36.

5 On the turn from engagement see Kurt M. Campbell and Ely Ratner, "The China Reckoning: How Beijing Defied American Expectations," *Foreign Affairs*, vol. 97, no. 2 (April 2018): 60–70; Peter Mattis, "From Engagement to Rivalry: Tools to Compete with China," *Texas National Security Review*, vol. 1, no. 4 (August 2018): 81–94.

6 For overviews, see Barry R. Posen, "The Rise of Illiberal Hegemony: Trump's Surprising Grand Strategy Letting Go," *Foreign Affairs*, vol. 97, no. 2 (April 2018): 20–27; John Glaser, Christopher Preble, and A. Trevor Thrall, *Fuel to the Fire: How*

Trump Made America's Broken Foreign Policy Even Worse (Washington, DC: Cato Institute, 2019), conclusion.

7 For use of these terms, see Alexander Kirss, et al., "Does Grand Strategy Matter?," *Strategic Studies Quarterly*, vol. 12, no. 4 (2018): 116–132; Hal Brands, "Choosing Primacy: US Strategy and Global Order at the Dawn of the Post-Cold War Era (February 2018)," *Texas National Security Review*, vol. 1, no. 2 (February 2018): 7–33.

8 John L. Gaddis, *Strategies of Containment: A Critical Appraisal of American National Security Policy During the Cold War*, Rev. and expanded ed. (New York: Oxford University Press, 2005).

9 On the post-Cold War debate, see Barry R. Posen and Andrew L. Ross, "Competing Visions for US Grand Strategy," *International Security*, vol. 21, no. 3 (Winter, 1997 1996): 5–53.

10 Barry R. Posen, "Stability and Change in US Grand Strategy," *Orbis*, vol. 51, no. 4 (October 2007): 561–67; Brands, "Choosing Primacy."

11 An overview of these efforts is in William Hill, *No Place for Russia: European Security Institutions Since 1989* (New York: Columbia University Press, 2018).

12 See, e.g., Joseph S. Nye, "The Case for Deep Engagement," *Foreign Affairs*, vol. 74, no. 4 (1995); Ashley J. Tellis, "Unity in Difference: Overcoming the US-India Divide," *Carnegie Endowment for International Peace*, January 21, 2015, http://carnegie endowment.org/2015/01/21/unity-in-difference-overcoming-US-india-divide

13 Nina Silove, "The Pivot Before the Pivot: US Strategy to Preserve the Power Balance in Asia," *International Security*, vol. 40, no. 4 (April 2016): 45–88; Robert S. Ross, "The Problem with the Pivot," *Foreign Affairs*, vol. 91, no. 6 (December 2012): 70–82.

14 Thanks go to Elbridge Colby for assistance on this point.

15 Patrick Porter, "Why America's Grand Strategy Has Not Changed: Power, Habit, and the US Foreign Policy Establishment," *International Security*, vol. 42, no. 4 (May 2018): 9–46.

16 Donald Trump, *National Security Strategy of the United States of America* (Washington, DC: The White House, 2017), 27, https://www.whitehouse.gov/wp-content/up loads/2017/12/NSS-Final-12-18-2017-0905.pdf For broader recognition, see Emma Ashford and Joshua R. Itzkowitz Shifrinson, "Trump's National Security Strategy: A Critics Dream," *Texas National Security Review*, vol. 1, no. 2 (February 2018): 138–144.

17 As a group of policy analysts and former policymakers recently argued, the United States must focus on regaining the ability to "reverse its rivals' momentum across [... a] spectrum of competition"; National Defense Strategy Commission (NDSC), *Providing for the Common Defense: The Assessments and Recommendations of the National Defense Strategy Commission* (Washington, DC: US Institute of Peace, 2018), vii.

18 Analysts use different terms to capture the trend, but the basic idea is the same. Thus, Zach Cooper and Hal Brands argue the US should "build a coalition of allies and partners strong enough to deter or simply hold the line against Chinese revisionism until such a time as the Chinese Communist Party modifies its objectives or loses its grip on power [...] It would lead the coalition in efforts to reduce China's geopolitical, economic, and ideological influence; weaken its power potential; and exacerbate the strains under which Beijing operates"; Hal Brands and Zack Cooper, "After the Responsible Stakeholder, What? Debating America's China Strategy," *Texas National Security Review*, vol. 2, no. 2 (February 2019): 80. Similarly, Thomas Wright proposes that the United States "is in a competition with Russia and China for the future of the international order" in which "it is not possible to fashion win-win outcomes": defending US interests means triumphing over Russia and China; Thomas Wright, *All Measures Short of War* (New Haven, CT: Yale University Press, 2017), 189. Meanwhile, the US National Defense Strategy echoes these proposals in asserting that the US will compete with Russia and China until the states are ready to cooperate on the basis of "a [US] position of strength and based on our national interests;" Department of Defense, "*National Defense Strategy 2018*, https://dod.def

ense.gov/Portals/1/Documents/pubs/2018-National-Defense-Strategy-Summary
.pdf, 4. See also Aaron Friedberg, "Competing with China," *Survival*, vol. 60, no. 3
(2018): 38; Wright, *All Measures*, chap. 7; NDSC, *Providing for the Common Defense*, ix.

19 See, e.g., Friedberg, "Competing with China," 26–27; Wright, *All Measures*, 206.

20 See, e.g., Hal Brands, "The Lost Art of Long-Term Competition," *The Washington
Quarterly*, vol. 41, no. 4 (Winter 2019): 47; NDSC, *Providing*, 7.

21 *National Defense Strategy*, 2.

22 Congressional Research Service, "China Naval Modernization: Implications for US
Navy Capabilities – Background and Issues for Congress," August 30, 2019, RL33153,
19; Sam LaGrone, "Work: Sixty Percent of US Navy and Air Force Will Be Based
in Pacific by 2020," *USNI News*, September 30, 2014; Department of Defense, *Asia-
Pacific Maritime Security Strategy* (Washington, DC: Department of Defense, 2015),
20–29.

23 As Wright argues, East Asia and China should be given equal weight to Europe and
Russia; see Wright's comments in Sergey Aleksashenko et al., *Restoring Equilibrium:
US Policy Options for Countering and Engaging Russia* (Washington, DC: Brookings
Institution, 2018), 7.

24 Aleksashenko et al., *Restoring Equilibrium*, 8; Alexander Lanoszka and Michael
Hunzeker, *Conventional Deterrence and Landpower in Northeastern Europe* (Carlisle
Barracks, PA: Strategic Studies Institute, 2019); NDSC, *Providing*, ix, 3n1.

25 Matthew Karnitsching, "For NATO, China is the New Russia," *Politico*, April 5,
2019.

26 The canonical statement on Deep Engagement remains Stephen Brooks and William
Wohlforth, *America Abroad: The United States' Global Role in the 21st Century* (New
York: Oxford University Press, 2016); for earlier treatment, see Robert J. Art,
"Geopolitics Updated: The Strategy of Selective Engagement," *International Security*,
vol. 23, no. 3 (1999): 79–113.

27 Brooks and Wohlforth, *America Abroad*, chap. 5; see also Stephen G. Brooks, G. John
Ikenberry, and William C. Wohlforth, "Lean Forward," *Foreign Affairs*, vol. 92, no.
1 (February 2013): 136–39; Bryan McGrath and Ryan Evans, "American Strategy
and Offshore Balancing by Default," *War on the Rocks*, August 27, 2013, https://wa
rontherocks.com/2013/08/the-balance-is-not-in-our-favor-american-strategy-and
-offshore-balancing-by-default/

28 Stephen G. Brooks, G. John Ikenberry, and William C. Wohlforth, "Don't Come
Home, America: The Case Against Retrenchment," *International Security*, vol. 37, no.
3 (December 2012): 35; for related discussion, see Michael Beckley, *Unrivaled: Why
America Will Remain the World's Sole Superpower* (Ithaca, NY: Cornell University Press,
2018), 138–52.

29 In addition to the sources above, see Kurt Campbell and Jake Sullivan, "Competition
with Catastrophe," *Foreign Affairs*, vol. 98, no. 5 (September/October 2019): 96–110.

30 Along similar lines, see Paula Dobriansky, Andrzej Olechowski, Yukio Satoh, and
Igor Yurgens, "Engaging Russia: A Return to Containment?," *Trilateral Commission
Task Force Report 2013-2014*, May 15, 2014, http://www.trilateral.org/download/
doc/TF_Russia_for_WEBSITE_final_15_May_2014.pdf, 17.

31 John J. Mearsheimer and Stephen M. Walt, "The Case for Offshore Balancing,"
Foreign Affairs, vol. 95, no. 4 (August 2016): 70–83; Christopher Layne, "Offshore
Balancing Revisited," *The Washington Quarterly*, vol. 25, no. 2 (June 2002): 233–248;
Reginald McClam, *Balancing on the Pivot: How China's Rise and Offshore Balancing
Affect Japan's and India's Roles as Balancers in the Twenty-First Century* (Montgomery,
AL: School of Advanced Air and Space Studies, 2017).

32 Mearsheimer and Walt, "The Case for Offshore Balancing," 81.

33 Mearsheimer and Walt, "The Case for Offshore Balancing," 81; Sebastian Rosato
and John Schuessler, "A Realist Foreign Policy for the United States," *Perspectives on
Politics*, vol. 9, no. 4 (December 2011): 813.

34 Christopher Layne, "The (Almost) Triumph of Offshore Balancing," *The National Interest*, January 27, 2012, https://nationalinterest.org/commentary/almost-triumph-offshore-balancing-6405

35 Stephen M. Walt, *The Hell of Good Intentions: America's Foreign Policy Elite and the Decline of US Primacy* (New York: Farrar, Straus and Giroux, 2018), 269.

36 Walt, *Hell of Good Intentions*, 269; Layne, "(Almost) Triumph."

37 Drawing down in Europe might indirectly help this policy by dividing Russia from China and potentially enabling US-Russian partnership against the PRC; Rosato and Schuessler, "Realist Foreign Policy," 813.

38 See Barry R. Posen, *Restraint: A New Foundation for US Grand Strategy* (Ithaca: Cornell University Press, 2014); Eugene Gholz, Daryl G. Press, and Harvey M. Sapolsky, "Come Home, America: The Strategy of Restraint in the Face of Temptation," *International Security*, vol. 21, no. 4 (Spring 1997): 5–48.

39 Among works conflating the strategies are James Holmes, "Why Offshore Balancing Won't Work," *The National Interest*, July 18, 2016, https://nationalinterest.org/featur e/why-offshore-balancing-wont-work-17025?page=0%2C1; Evan Montgomery, "Contested Primacy in the Western Pacific," *International Security* , vol. 38, no. 4 (Spring 2014): 118–121; Brands, *Limits of Offshore*, 1–2.

40 Posen, *Restraint*, 96.

41 Joseph Parent and Paul MacDonald, "The Wisdom of Retrenchment: America Must Cut Back to Move Forward," *Foreign Affairs*, vol. 90, no. 6 (December 2011): 42; Posen, *Restraint*.

42 Glaser, Preble, and Thrall, *Fuel to the Fire*, 174–175.

43 Posen, *Restraint*, 98–100; Parent and MacDonald, "The Wisdom of Retrenchment," 42–43; Joshua R. Itzkowitz Shifrinson, and Sameer Lalwani, "It's a Commons Misunderstanding: The Limited Threat to American Command of the Commons," in Christopher A. Preble and John Mueller, eds., *A Dangerous World?: Threat Perception and US National Security* (Cato Institute, 2014), 223–244.

44 Even analysts skeptical of China's rise acknowledge this potential Stephen G. Brooks and William C. Wohlforth, "The Rise and Fall of the Great Powers in the Twenty-First Century: China's Rise and the Fate of America's Global Position," *International Security*, vol. 40, no. 3 (Winter 2015–2016): 7–53.

45 Colin Dueck, *Reluctant Crusaders: Power, Culture, and Change in American Grand Strategy* (Princeton, NJ: Princeton University Press, 2006), 11–12.

46 Barry R. Posen, *The Sources of Military Doctrine: France, Britain, and Germany Between the World Wars* (Ithaca, NY: Cornell University Press, 1984), chap. 1; Hal Brands, *What Good Is Grand Strategy?: Power and Purpose in American Statecraft from Harry S. Truman to George W. Bush* (Ithaca, NY: Cornell University Press, 2014).

47 As the Government Accountability Office notes, already "by 2028 the government will spend more on net interest than it will spend on either defense or nondefense discretionary outlays." Increasing defense spending will only exacerbate this problem, ironically creating long-term pressure to cut spending overall; Government Accountability Office, *The Nation's Fiscal Health: Action is Needed to Address the Federal Government's Fiscal Future*, June 2018, GAO-18-299SP, 24.

48 Kenneth N. Waltz, *Theory of International Politics* (Reading, MA: Addison-Wesley Pub. Co, 1979); Eric J. Labs, "Do Weak States Bandwagon?," *Security Studies*, vol. 1, no. 3 (1992): 383–416.

49 On efforts by American allies to limit their exposure to US actions, see Christopher Layne, "The Unipolar Illusion Revisited: The Coming End of the United States' Unipolar Moment," *International Security*, vol. 31, no. 2 (Autumn 2006): 7–41.

50 Again, though, long-term deficits may limit what the US can spend on security.

51 Robert Jervis, "Unipolarity: A Structural Perspective," *World Politics* 61, no. 1 (January 2009): 200.

52 See, e.g., Justin McCurry and Tania Branigan, "Obama Says US Will Defend Japan in Island Dispute with China," *The Guardian*, April 24, 2014, https://www.theguard

ian.com/world/2014/apr/24/obama-in-japan-backs-status-quo-in-island-dispute
-with-china

53 On entrapment, see Glenn H. Snyder, "The Security Dilemma in Alliance Politics," *World Politics*, vol. 36, no. 4 (July 1984): 461–495.

54 Brooks and Wohlforth, "The Rise and Fall of the Great Powers in the Twenty-First Century."

55 On miscalculation in multipolarity, see Thomas J. Christensen and Jack Snyder, "Chain Gangs and Passed Bucks: Predicting Alliance Patterns in Multipolarity," *International Organization*, vol. 44, no. 2 (Spring 1990): 137–168.

56 On the tendency to balance proximate threats, see Stephen Walt, *The Origins of Alliances* (Ithaca, NY: Cornell University Press, 1987); on local tensions in the China case, see M. Taylor Fravel, *Strong Borders, Secure Nation: Cooperation and Conflict in China's Territorial Disputes* (Princeton: Princeton University Press, 2008).

57 For illustration, see Jennifer Lind, "The Japan-South Korea Dispute Isn't Just About the Past," *Washington Post (The Monkey Cage)*, August 30, 2019, https://beta.washing tonpost.com/politics/2019/08/30/japan-south-korea-dispute-isnt-just-about-past/

58 Still, even analysts skeptical of Restraint allow that local actors should be able to obtain substantial security on their own; see Michael Beckley, "The Emerging Military Balance in East Asia: How China's Neighbors Can Check Chinese Naval Expansion," *International Security*, vol. 42, no. 2 (Fall 2017): 78–119; Lanoszka and Hunzeker, *Conventional Deterrence*.

59 Posen, *Sources*; Brendan Rittenhouse Green, "Two Concepts of Liberty: US Cold War Grand Strategies and the Liberal Tradition," *International Security*, vol. 37, no. 2 (October 2012): 9–43; Rosato and Schuessler, "A Realist Foreign Policy."

60 Illustrating the disagreement are Barry Posen, "From Unipolarity to Multipolarity: Transition in Sight?," in G. John Ikenberry, Michael Mastanduno, and William C. Wohlforth, eds., *International Relations Theory and the Consequences of Unipolarity* (New York: Cambridge, 2011); Layne, "The Unipolar Illusion Revisited"; Øystein Tunsjø, *The Return of Bipolarity in World Politics: China, the United States, and Geostructural Realism* (New York: Columbia University Press, 2018); Joshua Shifrinson, "The Rise of China, Balance of Power Theory and US National Security: Reasons for Optimism?," *Journal of Strategic Studies* (online first view): 1–42; Beckley, *Unrivaled*.

61 To return to an earlier point, hence why the US may be building up military forces in both Europe and Asia.

10

CHINA–US RIVALRY IN THE RECENT PAST, PRESENT, AND FUTURE

Implications for China's grand strategy in a new era

Shi Yinhong

Introduction

This chapter argues that the current escalation in China–US tensions is a result of certain fundamental developments that accelerated through the past decade, stemming from the dynamic interactions between Washington and Beijing. In the context of relative Western decline and malfunction since the 2008 global financial crisis and economic recession, and China's more than 15 years of drastic economic growth, China began transforming its national aspirations to become a major power on the world stage. The decisive moment came at the end of 2012 when, during a change in top Chinese leadership, *ingenuity* became a decisive national objective. China mobilized its sudden boost in national strength and resources to meet this objective, supported by an ideological belief in China's national greatness and strengthened by the Communist State's pervasive command.

On the strategic front, between 2008 and the end of Barack Obama's presidency in 2016, the basic trend was the starting and intensification of a strategic rivalry between Beijing and Washington. To simplify the rivalry during these years, it was first "Hu Jintao vs. Barack Obama" and then "Xi Jinping vs. Barack Obama." Structurally speaking, the primary dynamics for the escalating rivalry came from the side of the Chinese, while the United States saw the steady erosion of its long-standing major global position in various areas to China – or increasingly *by* China. On the trade front, all the major elements for the upcoming China–US confrontation were already in place, increasing in prominence from 2008. The story for a while was "Hu Jintao *and* Xi Jinping vs. Barack Obama." The American (and EU) complaints against China were becoming more severe, focusing on several critical areas that have become so prominent in the China–US trade war since July 2018. However, apart from certain slow, piecemeal responsive measures, China made little or no revision to its trade and business practices, having focused instead on rhetorical adjustments and on the presentation of vague, nonspecific promises.

Since being elected president in 2016, Donald Trump has proven to be a brutal strategist and tactician in his dealings with China. President Trump has deliberately focused on one major issue at a time, imposing terrible pressure and threats (with the occasional cajoling) to squeeze as much as possible from the opposite side. Largely because of this, since early 2018, when the 19th CCP National Congress confidently defined China's New Era under Xi Jinping, we suddenly find an extraordinary picture of extreme rivalry, even confrontation, between Beijing and Washington, first on the trade and strategic fronts and then on the political and ideological fronts. In its short-term and its long-term strategic planning, the United States, headed by Trump and based on American domestic consensus at large, is mobilizing against China as its Number One Rival.

What should China's overall strategic objectives be, both now and in the future? This chapter argues that, for the next five to six years (or longer, depending on rational strategic planning), China's imperative could be defined as conducting a new type of "taking a low profile while doing something," borrowing the words of Deng Xiaoping. This means that China could make sufficient strategic retrenchments while conducting a sort of new "Great Leap Forward" in improving its trade and business practices based on broadening, deepening, and expediting domestic economic reform. A major strategic purpose in doing so would be to demobilize its antagonists, namely the United States, before making any new advances. China's strategic vision and stamina will be tested through this.

The chapter is divided into eight sections. Section One gives a general survey of China's international posture, emphasizing the decisive significance of Xi Jinping's ascendancy to power and his overall strategic objectives. Section Two traces back through the Obama years, observing the development of the China–US trade rivalry conducted by each of their top leaders. In the third, fourth, and fifth sections, the China–US relationship since the inauguration of Donald Trump is presented and analyzed, with the North Korea problem and the trade war being prominent topics respectively in 2017 and between 2018 and 2019, followed by the current tensions between the two countries, and touching on China's recent campaign against the coronavirus epidemic. Section Six gives a contextual framework for the China–US trade war and China's related vulnerability on the economic and financial strategic front, and why this has been generally demoted to a secondary status. In Section Seven, China's overall strategy is advocated as an imperative, together with a demonstration of the emerging dangers of a selective, expanding "decoupling." Finally, Section Eight concludes the entire chapter with a presentation of more than four decades of China–US relations, in light of a nostalgic past, then in the context of the stark realities of the present situation, and finally, in light of a desired future.

I

The China–US relationship of the past decade has been generally characterized by rivalry rather than accommodation, first on the strategic front, and then even more so on the trade front. Though the relationship in a situational sense has had its ups and downs with oft-dramatic vicissitudes, and "offensive" or "defensive" postures adopted by both sides at different times, in a structural sense the primary dynamics for the escalating rivalry have come mostly from the Chinese side. The United States, historically conditioned to take a "defensive" posture, has found its long-standing, dominant position in certain areas on the global scene either gradually lost to China or increasingly eroded by China.

First under the remarkably weak leadership of Hu Jintao and then under the all-powerful leadership of Xi Jinping, over the past decade China has risen to become a formidable power, boosted onto the international stage by a booming national economy and surging military strength. China's expanding national strength (that at times has not always been compatible with Beijing's domestic and international rhetoric on its long-term goals in the Asian Pacific and elsewhere) has brought a transformation in China's national intentions and aspirations, however ambiguous, self-conscious, or insufficiently these have been communicated at times. However, Xi Jinping's ascension to China's top position (and with extraordinary speed, power was concentrated in his hands and his hands alone) was a decisive factor in the transformation of national intention.[1] Xi Jinping believes that his Chinese and Communist values (however they are perceived) will work to achieve his oft-declared "Resurgence of the Chinese National Greatness" and intends to realize these aspirations during the indefinite tenure given him in early 2018 through a revision of the Constitution. He is fully aware of the domestic popular support he would win by presenting and leading an aggressive foreign policy agenda.[2]

Since taking power at the 18th Party Congress held in November 2012, Xi Jinping has, more than any of his predecessors, committed to exerting China's strength and power, to (1) widen and deepen China's involvement in the world political economy and global governance, striving for a leading role in some particular issue or important area thereof; to (2) realize China's economic and diplomatic superiority on the Asian continent and (with a somewhat softer commitment and with greater flexibility in retrenchment if needed) in other regions of the developing world – a dominance not necessarily over particular countries and societies, but rather over other great powers, with the United States at the top of the list; (3) during his extremely long tenure, to obtain Chinese strategic and military dominance over the United States in the western part of the western Pacific, extending from China's sea coast to whatever island archipelago one comes to first.[3] President Donald Trump's international behavior, including his policy of para-isolationism and greater retrenchment from America's role as "world leader" (which Trump never refers to – he seems to be disgusted at the possibility), while alienating the US in varying degrees from most of its allies and strategic partners, these global conditions encourage China to exert its power by providing it with something of a "power vacuum." The same Trump, however, because of his pro-military mindset and vigorous launching of technological renewal nearly across the entire range of American strategic forces (including its latest development, in June 2018, to establish a separate military "space force" branch), suddenly poses a formidable challenge to Xi's aspirations.

II

The China–US rivalry can be categorized by two primary fronts of contention, which are strategy and trade; however, these have been supplemented with a new contentious front, a front that is ideological in nature but bears a certain striving for international power and influence. Since 2008, when the global financial crisis and economic recession broke out, and up to when Donald Trump was elected US President, a strategic rivalry carried on between Beijing and Washington. The situation can be simplified as, first, "Hu Jintao vs. Obama" and then, "Xi Jinping vs. Obama." The China–US arms race over the western Pacific (and beyond) increasingly intensified during these years, and then broadened, especially after Xi's ascendancy to power. This race has been conducted by both powers and has transpired at sea, in the air, in cyberspace – even in outer space. The maritime rivalry in both the South China Sea and the East China Sea has played out in the world's limelight, with Beijing and Washington declaring diametrically opposed legal positions over the conflict.[4] The rivalry has been intensified by the occasional naval squabble, by China's massive warship construction program and immense land reclamation projects (greatly strengthening Beijing's position of military strength in the South China Sea), and from the American side with its US Freedom of Navigation Operations (FONOPs), which deny Beijing's claimed territorial rights through the potential use of military action. There have also been severe disputes between China and most of the Southeast Asian maritime countries over maritime territory and EEZ; China was under threat of a potentially dangerous armed confrontation with Japan, Japan being the single most important military ally (besides Israel?) of the US in the world. As a vital part of President Obama's "re-balancing," diplomatic competition against China's influence along its periphery was remarkably advantageous to the US at the time, with Obama relying on his Administration's diligence and "smart power" – and benefiting from China's faults in foreign policy.[5] Moreover, closely connected with all of the above, China–Russia strategic/military cooperation escalated simultaneously with intensification in both Russia–US and China–US strategic antagonisms.

On the trade front, though the situation was better before the sudden emergence of the trade war initiated by President Trump in mid-2018, the major structural elements for the confrontation were already in place and have only increased in prominence since 2008. At this point, the story was "Hu Jintao *and* Xi Jinping vs. Barack Obama." Of course, China has held complaints against the

US in terms of trade, especially the US's non-recognition (non-grant) of China's status as a market economy nation and its severe restrictions on American high-tech exports to China (and the EU); however, US complaints against China, while severe, have been plausible to most international audiences.[6] The US has focused on four areas, regarded by a growing number of American politicians and by the American public as important or even vital to economic security and societal welfare: (1) the enormous Chinese trade surplus (or American trade deficit with China); (2) China's largely static – or narrowing – market access to American (and other advanced industrial countries) capital; (3) state control of China's domestic economy and foreign economic activities, which under Xi Jinping has been regarded as a stain on the remarkable Chinese economy, with its so-called "theft" of intellectual property, the "forced transfer" of technology from American manufacturing firms in China, and the emerging "Made in China 2025" program regarded as disturbing, even threatening, to American interests; (4) also in terms of China's robust economy, China's favoring its own State-owned Enterprises (SOEs) with massive subsidies, placing foreign enterprises in China – and Chinese private enterprises – at an economic disadvantage.

China had been enjoying the benefits of liberal economic globalization too much to heed to the words emerging on the wall: ENOUGH IS ENOUGH! Liberal economic globalization has become increasingly unpopular, even distasteful, to increasing numbers of voters, both in the US and in many other advanced industrial nations; they have perceived China as exploitative, even destructive, to their jobs and welfare. At the same time, more American strategists are foreseeing the demise of American strategic world dominance, since the US has been losing ground on both economic and technological fronts. Speaking somewhat hyperbolically, the complaining and anger of the American people against China haven't convinced China to change. Except for its slow and piecemeal responsive measures, China had made almost no substantial revisions to its trade practices – making instead only largely rhetorical and nonspecific promises, with Xi's Seattle speech in September 2015 as the most notable example.[7] In other words, China has been slow to realize that time is running out, that liberal economic globalization – something that China has benefited so greatly from since it joined the WTO – is losing much of its domestic, social, and political basis, both in the US and in most other advanced industrial nations. President Obama's (limited) politeness in these areas, backed by his liberal beliefs, together with China's slow downturn in its GDP growth rate and increase in financial risks, only aggravated the potential severity of the problem.

III

Politeness and liberal beliefs mattered, however. Despite his engaging in strategic rivalry with China with his strategic, diplomatic, and economic "re-balancing," President Obama made three major, even historic agreements with President Xi: (1) agreement for addressing climate change, which constituted the basis for the global Paris Climate Change Accord; (2) agreement to prevent clashes between Chinese and American warships and warplanes, an urgently necessary result of the intensifying China–US strategic/military rivalry; (3) agreement on cybersecurity, also a result of the intensifying strategic/economic competition. One cannot be blamed for feeling a bit nostalgic when looking at the current China–US relationship under Donald Trump!

Throughout 2017, the situation on the strategic front received the greatest attention when Xi and Trump dealt with China–US relations; the trade front was only a secondary (for Trump) accessory. Trump's strategy toward China throughout that year was to make China–US relations, which had up to then been based on a broad range of issues, a prisoner of a single issue: namely, that of North Korean nuclear and missile development, an issue that had been one of the most difficult in the world to solve – or even to influence. In addition to Trump's notoriously wild, volatile, and Machiavellian personality, the seemingly wonderful atmosphere of China–US relations since the Xi–Trump Mar-a-Lago Summit was almost doomed to fail less than three months later.[8] At the same time, Chinese influence on North Korea had been reduced to virtually nothing, while North Korea's hostility toward China continued to escalate.

China seemed to be "tamed," largely through Trump's extraordinary threats of military strikes against North Korea and of "secondary sanctions" against China. From Trump's election as President to the end of 2017, China endorsed, with reduced limitations, six or seven successive escalating sanctions over the North Korea nuclear problem, almost to the point of North Korean economic strangulation. Beijing had been close to completely exhausting its means of pressure against Pyongyang, while the corresponding political and strategic costs (including the possibility of making North Korea a permanent enemy of China) would be excessively high; it would also be an action that could easily give the world the impression that China had succumbed to American pressure. Throughout 2017 in the South China Sea, the Trump Administration's FONOPs surpassed Obama's both in frequency and intensity, in addition to the highly publicized initiative for a quadrilateral Indo-Pacific strategic coalition (US, Japan, India, and Australia) to keep China in check, both in the South China Sea and in other regions. On top of this, the word "predatory" had become the Trump Administration's standard adjective to define China's economic practices in the developing world (China's "Belt and Road Initiative" in the first place).[9] Moreover, the concept of "sharp power" and an accusation against China's ideological drive within the advanced countries emerged, reflecting a new dimension in the China–US rivalry. [10]

On the trade front, throughout 2017 the situation was surprisingly quiet, "surprisingly" because of the countless threatening words issued by Trump while touting an "America First" flag during his election campaign. A trade truce was won by Xi's numerously large concessions made to Trump over North Korea, constituting the only earning China gained through those yields. Structural problems still exist, including China's enormous trade surplus, a static or narrowing market access, and state control of economic and technological activities – issues that are still on Trump's agenda to target on China (and as a way to gain widespread congressional and public sympathy for his dealings with China). What is also remarkable is that, through his behavior on the North Korea problem in his relations with Beijing, Trump has used pressure and threats to compel maximum concessions from the opposite side.

IV

Since early 2018, we have seen an extraordinary picture of a severe rivalry, even confrontation, between Beijing and Washington on both trade and strategic fronts. Having depleted China's utility on North Korea, President Trump began to apply the same general strategy and tactics to the China–US trade front. Successive threats to impose higher tariffs on China's exports to the US, raising maximum demands to squeeze concessions as much as possible, tough negotiation positions alternated with slightly softer tones, showing last-minute "mercy" to Beijing on destructive ZTE sanctions as a way to cajole: all of these tactics are familiar Machiavellian approaches Trump employed in his dealings with the North Korea problem. China seems to have no other option than to make huge concessions on trade surplus (after a possible period of trade revenge) and to create broader market access, as a way of adhering to the Trump-labeled "structural changes" and "industrial policies." If not, China might have to conduct a real, protracted trade war, causing great suffering to China's economy. Moreover, this would only result in a temporary truce, with round after round of threatening trade wars initiated by Trump in the name of his "America First" ideology. Time is running out, and the later the adjustments become, the more expensive they also become, even though they would fall in line with President Xi's own overall national objectives and work toward China's own "high-quality development."

At the same time, Trump has intensified the rivalry against China on the strategic front. In mid-December 2018, the *National Security Strategy of the United States of America* was published by the White House. Along with Russia, China is defined as a rival to the US, challenging

> American power, influence, and interests, attempting to erode American security and prosperity … determined to make economies less free and less fair, to grow their militaries, and to control information and data to repress their societies and expand their influence.[11]

One month later, the Pentagon published *2018 National Defense Strategy of the United States of America*, stipulating from a military angle the strategy of "retaining the US strategic competitive edge relative to China and Russia."[12] In mid-March 2018, President Trump signed the Taiwan Travel Act, the second major legal statute following the Taiwan Relations Act enacted in 1979, unleashing "legitimate" high-level official visits and direct consultations between US and Taiwan, should the US President deem them necessary, on any occasion, on a case-by-case basis. Public or secret military ties with Taiwan were already strong, but have become even stronger under Trump. Arms sales to Taiwan have surpassed 10 billion USDs in value under the Trump Administration, adding numerous F16V advanced fighters to Taiwan's arsenal, together with some dramatic diplomatic support given to Taiwan, repaid by Taiwan by giving permission to US naval warships to pass through the Taiwan Strait in an increased frequency of nearly once a month – all for the benefit of supporting Taiwan's opposition to China, or the blackmailing of China, encouraging the DPP Administration in its confrontation against the Chinese Mainland.[13] Moreover, Trump has launched more frequent, intensive, and ally-supported FONOPs while advocating for an Indo-Pacific quadrilateral strategic coalition, and supporting the technological renewal of US strategic armed forces nearly across the entire range. There is also a real potential of Trump adding new measures in the foreseeable future.

V

Donald Trump's first round of tariffs in a US-imposed trade war on China, initiated on July 6, 2018 (25 percent higher tariffs on 16 billion USD on Chinese exports, with another 34 billion soon after) was quickly followed by a second, even more severe round of tariffs (10 percent; then, since May 10, 2019, 25 percent higher tariffs on an additional 200 billion), and then followed by a third (15 percent higher tariffs on an additional 122 billion since September 1, 2019, which was reduced to 7.5 percent due to Phase 1 of the Trade Agreement reached on January 15, 2020), all accompanied by the higher tariffs imposed on American exports by China as revenge. Along with this escalating conflict over high tariffs, there has also been a "high tech warfare" launched by the Trump Administration since its executive order issued on May 15, 2019, revealing an increase in numbers and strictness in measures to restrain China's high-tech trade and development, with Huawei's 5G program as the first target and victim. According to many observers this "high tech warfare" is important to the US policy agenda, and has in fact been "immune" to China–US trade negotiations with little hope of being substantially mitigated.

During the trade war, one theme or objective of the Trump Administration has been prominent, which is the forced "structural changes" to China's economic mode and "industrial policies," with constant demands by the US for China to cease doing the following: (1) "stealing" American intellectual property rights; (2) "forcing" the transfer of technology by American firms in China; (3) giving special preferences with massive subsidies to China's SOEs by the Chinese state; (4) revising and retrenching China's "Made in China 2025." American high tariff leverage and strict "enforcement mechanisms" are in place to force China's hand in implementing the promised changes.

Through the course of certain vicissitudes, Beijing and Washington finally reached a Phase I Trade Agreement in January 2020. This can only be regarded as a delicate de-escalation. China's commitment to doubling imports from the US by the end of 2021 has the following negative characteristics: (1) it goes beyond China's domestic requirements at a time when its economic growth has remarkably diminished; (2) it potentially raises the base of reference for US imports after 2021; (3) it burdens Beijing's already shrinking foreign-exchange reserves; and (4) it dramatically reduces the demands and capacities by which Beijing could increase imports from both advanced industrial nations and primary developing nations, which undermines China's strategic and diplomatic imperative when facing the US as its Number One antagonist. In short, the Phase I Trade Agreement will be tough for China to implement.

There is no real truce in sight for the trade war between China and the US. It is still unclear which fundamental concessions one side might be willing to make to the other, whether in terms of Trump-forced "structural changes" or in terms of China's demand for high tariff cancellation. The Trump administration has no current plans to lift the 25 percent tariffs, worth 250 billion USD, it has levied against China since 2018. Many of the thornier structural issues lying at the heart of the US–China trade dispute have yet to be tackled, such as China's massive subsidies extended to its SOEs, and issues with its "Made in China 2025" initiative. Phase II of the trade agreement between the two nations is certain to be more complicated.[14]

The forceful purchase of enormous amounts of US products that characterizes the Phase I Agreement and will surely characterize Phase II negotiations, along with the forceful squeeze for "structural changes," has already surpassed China's real requirements. In other words, any incentive for the talks to progress on either side is quite limited. The Chinese leaders seem to show no strong desire to completely acquiesce to US demands, particularly those demands viewed by China that would reverse China's development model and restrict China's further economic rise.

VI

In the context of China's pre-existing economic vulnerabilities, the China–US trade war is truly an historic event. It has forced China to prioritize its foreign policy agenda that became somewhat diffused after the 18th CCP National Congress six years ago. The priority of China has unquestionably become to deal with the trade war in a way that protects China's vulnerable domestic economy from being damaged so much as to destabilize China socially. Beijing has recently made "stability maintenance" to China's domestic economy its top priority. Therefore, China's strategic front (including the North Korea problem, operations on the Taiwan Strait and on the South and East China Seas, the arms race with the US over the western Pacific, strategic/military cooperation with Russia, the Belt and Road Initiative, etc.) has been demoted to secondary strategic status, due to the development of its trade war with the US, its economic vulnerability, and its decrease in available state resources.

For the same reason, China's strategic front will be dramatically retrenched in comparison to the situation of the past six or seven years. Only operations on the Taiwan Strait and the arms race with the US would be prioritized above other strategic affairs and might indeed be milder than before. This new prioritizing will be a definite blessing to China's diplomacy, for themes such as accommodation, rapprochement, mutual consultation, and winning as many friends in the world as possible would surely be put at a premium. Any relational improvements recently made with its neighbors (including such an important one as Japan), will continue to be maintained and developed.

Before we move toward the last sections of this chapter, China's most recent campaign against the coronavirus epidemic should be briefly discussed. This campaign, defined by Xi Jinping as a "People's War and Total War" after the coronavirus had raised its ugly head in the epidemic's epicenter, Wuhan, demonstrates both a strength and weakness of the "totalistic" Chinese national system.[15] The strength of the Chinese system is revealed in its extraordinarily swift and complete mobilization against the virus, with a top-down implementation one could not image occurring in most other countries in the world, something that most likely prevented the epidemic from spreading wider and becoming even more severe. However, as a weakness, the rigidity of the system led to a para-lockdown of almost all cities (if not towns) outside of Hubei Province, areas where the threat of the coronavirus had been much lighter, leading to excessive and unnecessary economic and social cost in much of China.

The total lockdown of Wuhan and the whole of Hubei Province has proven to be not as completely positive in terms of its effectiveness in the campaign against the virus. There is some truth in what Dr. Amesh Adalja, a senior scholar at Johns Hopkins Center for Health Security, said: "Authoritarian, free-speech restricting, individual rights-violating policies can panic populations, make conditions in an outbreak zone worse, and still fail to contain … the spread of a virus of this nature."[16] When the coronavirus is eventually behind us, it would be unfortunate if China's "totalistic" system was remembered much more for its strength than for its weakness.

There is still one problem remaining to be addressed, that of the self-proud, self-reinforcing totalistic Chinese system. Because of the enormous economic and financial costs accrued during its "total war" against COVID-19 and with few alternatives available to deal with these costs, China must now rely heavily on "command finance" at a time when its financial resources are depleted and when the external economic environment is becoming uglier. China is therefore facing dire challenges.

VII

What should be China's overall strategic imperative from this point forward? To find an answer we might want to review the recent past. In retrospect, though

China attained extraordinary achievements in its foreign relations in the past six or seven years, there were also certain faults, even regrets: China jumped too high and too quickly on the strategic front to increase its own gains, while doing little on the trade front to reduce the losses of other nations. This resulted in China aiding its antagonists to mobilize against China.

China's imperative for the next five or six years (or even longer, should China wisely choose to combine times of tension with times of restraint) could be defined as conducting a new type of "taking a low profile while doing something," in Deng Xiaoping's words, or alternatively, "taking a two steps forward and one step back." This means that China should make strategic retrenchment to a sufficient degree while continuing its "Great Leap Forward" in a manner that improves its trade and business practices while at the same time broadens, deepens, and expedites domestic economic reform. A strategy to accomplish this, while having a balanced "liberalization" of some aspects of domestic, political, and social lives, is to strive to demobilize its antagonists, before making any new advances. China's strategic vision and stamina will be tested in this way.

Since early 2018, a dangerous trend of expanding selective "decoupling" began to emerge in the dramatically shifting world political economy.[17] The US has already begun to decouple from China in the following fields: (1) strategic high-tech and various related exchanges; (2) strategic armed forces and associated military-to-military exchanges; (3) cyberspace telecommunications important to strategic military capability and national security; (4) the attractiveness of one's institutional regime, political culture, and ideology to the rest of the world. Through various bilateral negotiations, the US government is reaching out to other advanced industrial economies and their close partners through free trade or para–free trade agreements. Moreover, after directly or indirectly demolishing the global WTO regime, the US would probably build a new set of trade rules which would generally only cover the developed world and its close partners. In this context, China, with its severe aggravation of rivalries with the US and, having worked to build its own "Belt and Road System" in the form of an international para-bloc under its own leadership, might have no option but to increase its dependence on the friendly developing countries to conduct its primary foreign economic activities. However, such a dependence would yield little or no financial profit, either for China or for its developing partners, as China's capital would flow out with little or no pay-off. China's swiftly expansive involvement in the different areas of the developing world inherently comes with the potential for increased risk, without the assurance of China acquiring what it really needs – a broad-based high-tech capability.

China must do its utmost to reduce this trend of dichotomy in the world political economy, otherwise its national long-term prospects could be damaged to a historic degree. From such a perspective, protracted and essential improvements to its relations with Europe, Japan, South Korea, Australia, Canada, to name a few, would be greater in historic significance.

VIII

It would be best that the concluding notes of this chapter to go further back into the history of China–US relations than the point in history with which we began our first section, the 2008 global financial crisis and economic recession. We would find that China and the United States have a relationship with *a nostalgic past*, dating from when the China–US cold war ended with the visit of President Nixon to Beijing in 1972. China, still deeply carrying a keen memory of Mao's disastrous radicalism in governance, focused on domestic development and liberal economic reform with "diluted" (as it were) political reform; however, these reforms were largely compatible with American liberal expectations of China at a time when the US strongly believed in liberal values in domestic and international affairs. Moreover, China, with its weakness in national strength and thus limited aspirations to attain the status of a global power, focused instead on "local politics and the local political economy" on the international stage prior to 2008; and, combined with a prudent foreign policy and (decreasing) conservative military build-up policy, gave the US no reason to be concerned about economic, geo-strategic, or ideological "Chinese expansionism."

Since the 2008 global financial crisis and economic recession, in the important context of relative Western decline and malfunction that encouraged China to question liberalism in its "original form," and since the launching of Chinese liberal economic reform that stimulated China's economic triumphalism, there has been a keen awareness of the ongoing power transition between the US and China. In its early phase, this power transition was somewhat overestimated by the Chinese elite, as it still is by an increasing number of elites in China. National aspiration followed this transformation, aspirations that increasingly reflected the brave imaginations and willingness to strive for overseas economic presence, "new mercantilist" advantages, diplomatic preponderance, and ultimately strategic power.

The decisive moment came toward the end of 2012 when a change in top leadership occurred in China. Chinese aspirations were broadened to the point of almost becoming a national objective; a booming economy allowed national strength and resources to be mobilized and expended for China to reach these aspirations. An ideological belief in China's national greatness and in the Communist State's commanding leadership role worked to strengthen the resolve to achieve this new national objective.

Together with the profound and dramatic changes that have occurred in the US since the 2016 presidential election campaign, we have arrived at the point of a *critical present*. By 2018 the China–US rivalry was being fought on all three major fronts: the strategic front, the trade front, and the ideological front. In comparison to the Anglo–German rivalry of 1907, one could surmise that the current situation is even more critical.[18]

The overall strategy China should have in the current "new era" was advocated for in the previous section, an era that has been in part defined by the dramatic changes occurring in Beijing–Washington relations since 2018 and, to a lesser degree, by the changes occurring in China's domestic economy. Finally, we will now discuss Beijing's desired future. at least in the short-term, based on policy facts currently emerging here in China.

A fundamental fact should be made prominent, that strategy on China's part is just beginning to advance in the direction of strategic retrenchment and improvements in the practice of trade and business. Why is this happening now? There are three primary reasons: (1) a new assessment of China's current situation has just been made, drafted and declared by China's top leadership and presented in official government discourse in such phrases as "China's economy is facing new pressure of a downturn" and that its "external environment has profoundly changed" in an ominous direction;[19] (2) the likelihood of a new assessment being made, specifically on Chinese national resources and available capability, based on the scenario of a prolonged reduction of national revenue combined with a prolonged stagnation of GDP growth accompanied by a sharp increase in essential state expenses in various major fields; (3) the likelihood of a review of ongoing major national projects in terms of cost-effectiveness, based on work already completed on these projects, with one exception: an unquestionable, positive outcome is projected *only* in the field of strategic military build-up. In summary, a change in strategy has already become a reality, with concrete indications of this change, both factual and potential, already appearing here and there in different national enterprises and on various strategic fronts, including the Belt and Road Initiative, an alteration in Chinese behavior on the South China Sea issue, changes in peripheral diplomacy, extraordinary concessions promised by China to the US in bilateral trade negotiations, and emphases of conduct on the Taiwan issue, to name a few.[20]

One more, vital question must be addressed: what should the United States *do*? If there are real retrenchments and improvements happening on the Chinese side, the US government should recognize them without taking a perfectionist approach toward them, a mistaken approach that previously led to the collapse of the Hanoi US–DPRK summit and to a breakdown in China–US trade talks in May 2019. The US government should instead approach any Chinese improvement measures with a reciprocal, complementary, and encouraging response, engaging in genuine dialogue, or honest negotiations with China to secure at least a temporary truce, followed by a partial solution based on clarifying the vital interests of each side, and thereby respecting each other's interests as much as possible. Though the prospect of such conduct on the part of Washington has been far from hopeful, what the United States should do must still be pointed out – at least for the sake of China's moral conscience – and offered as a remedial guide for bilateral negotiations through future, possibly greater, bilateral tensions.

Notes

1 Elizabeth C. Economy, the C. V. Starr senior fellow and director for Asia studies at the Council on Foreign Relations, discusses this in some comprehensiveness in her *The Third Revolution: Xi Jinping and the New Chinese State* (Oxford: Oxford University Press, 2018).
2 Cf. James Fallows, "China's Great Leap Backward," *The Atlantic Monthly*, December 2016.

3 An example of a previous realization of this point in the Western world is Hugh White, "America's China Consensus Slowly unravels," *The World Post*, April 20, 2015.

4 See especially Mark Landler, "US Challengers China on Island Chain," *The New York Times*, July 23, 2010; "Obama Urges China to Accept the Judgment of Arbitration on South China Sea," *Kyodonews*, August 2, 2016 (in Chinese); "Statement by the Government of the People's Republic of China on the Territorial Sovereignty and Maritime Rights in South China Sea," (in Chinese), www.gov.cn, July 12, 2016.

5 Shi Yinhong, "Trouble in the Backyard," *China Economic Quarterly*, March 2012.

6 Cf. David Lynch, "Tensions Push Congress to Get Even with China," *USA Today*, June 13, 2007; Andrea Hopkins, "Trade Jitters, Anti-China Sentiment Rouse Voters," *Reuters*, November 15, 2007; Kevin Johnson and Donna Leinwand Leger, "US Accuses China of Hacking Westinghouse, US Steel," *USA Today*, May 19, 204; Ellen Nakashima, "Indictment of PLA Hackers is Part of Broad U.S. Strategy to Curb Chinese Cyberspying," *The Washington Post*, May 23, 2014.

7 Cf. David Nakamura, "China's Xi to Get a Pomp-Heavy U.S. Welcome Friday, but Maybe Not a Warm One," *The Washington Post*, September 24, 2015.

8 John Pomfret, "Trump and China: The Honeymoon is Over," *The Washington Post*, June 25, 2017; Paul Gewirtz, "How China Misread Donald Trump," *Politico Magazine*, July 6, 2017.

9 Nicole Gaouette, "Tillerson Raps China as 'Predatory' Rule Breaker," *CNN*, October 19, 2017.

10 For an earlier American action in this aspect, see Josh Rogin, "University Rejects Chinese Communist Party-Linked Influence Efforts on Campus," *The Washington Post*, January 14, 2018.

11 *National Security Strategy of the United States of America* (Washington, DC: The White House, December 2017), p. 46, http://nssarchive.us/wp-content/uploads/2017/12/2017.pdf [2019-03-10].

12 Summary of 2018 National Defense Strategy of the United States of America: Sharping the American Military's Competitive Edge, https://dod.defense.gov/Portals/1/Documents/pubs/2018-National-Defense-Strategy-Summary.pdf

13 For the major strategic developments on the issue of Taiwan, cf. Scott B. MacDonald, "Taiwan is Back on the Geopolitical Menu," *The National Interest*, July 5, 2018.

14 Cf. Kevin Freking, "White House Adviser Compares China Trade Talks to Cold War," *Associate Press*, September 7, 2019.

15 For a report with some analysis, see Raymond Zhong and Paul Mozur, "What the 'Total War', Mao-Style Social Control Blankets China," *The New York Times*, February 16, 2020.

16 Lindsey Tanner, "China's Virus Slowdown Offers Hope for Global Containment," *Associate Press*, March 5, 2020.

17 For the formal and prominent beginning of this trend, see David J. Lynch, "Are the U.S. and China Heading for A Deal—or A Divorce?" *CNN*, May 16, 2019.

18 Shi Yinhong, "China–US Competition in 2018 *vs.* Anglo–German Rivalry in 1907," *China-US Focus*, January 31, 2019. https://www.chinausfocus.com/foreign-policy/china-us-competition-in-2018-vs-the-anglo-german-rivalry-of-1907

19 The first major expression by the Chinese government of this new definition of the situation, which was repeated again and again officially thereafter, is 'The Report on the Work of the Government' delivered at the Second Session of the 13th National People's Congress on March 5, 2019, https://mp.weixin.qq.com/s?src=11&timestamp=1583419177&ver=2198&signature=aUGr7*cQgbm72DdAxOF5vE6Noa2rH7AkKZ-x6tHgAfgi4LCGkKH5XLG5Qi1IUkL6DRZB38

CLUlEJqHdndOBmp778HzoXRm6TOUN8wLtt4LxOeOXSt92SYFmbxXaUt
kYc&new=1

20 The retrenchment of the Belt and Road Initiative is paid particularly more attention by the Western media, along with extraordinary concessions promised to the
US in trade talks. For the former, a well-written example is Sheridan Prasso, "One
of China's Most Ambitious Projects Becomes a Corridor to Nowhere," *Bloomberg*,
March 3, 2020.

11

EUROPE'S ROLE IN ASIA

European strategies for an Asia-centered world and US-China rivalry[1]

May-Britt U. Stumbaum

Introduction

The power shift toward Asia and the ensuing power competition in the region and beyond, epitomized by the United States' once proclaimed "pivot" to Asia and the current ongoing trade war been the United States and the People's Republic of China, is forcing the Europeans to invest more – more into strategic thinking with a traditional strategic ally United States that can no longer be taken for granted under a Trump administration and interests that had been diverging already before Donald Trump got into power; but also more in capabilities, given that Europeans are now forced to look more after their interests themselves and hence provide also the facilities to do so.

On the other hand, the impact of a Trump Administration with its deal-oriented policy lines in constant flux remains hardly predictable for the US' traditional allies in the region. As they can also not be sure as to how long the alliances will hold on, Asian countries such as Japan, Korea, India, and China as well as ASEAN and its member states have concurrently increased their interest into working with the European Union – ranging from trade issues to climate change and cooperative security. The new Commission President Ursula von der Leyen, the former German Defense Minister, claims that she will be heading a "geopolitical Commission" that needs to develop a new relationship about power, and exercising power.[2] Asia is the most important trade and production region for the EU, so any conflicts in the region will have direct impacts on the EU's economy.

Yet, defense spending is still hesitant among EU Member States that are ailing from the financial crisis that started in 2008/2009, structural changes, and demographic challenges while facing a globalized competition and the necessity for restructuring amidst increasing automatization of production. Challenges ranging from youth unemployment to high national debt rates and increasing populism, feeding off from a perceived influx of migrants, have intensified divisions among EU Member States and aggravate creating and implementing a strong and unified EU policy toward Asia. On the other hand, rising challenges and constrained resources at home have spurred further calls for spending more wisely while focusing more on cooperation with other partners, combining resources and deploying means with a clearer strategic base that focuses on EU interests (and potential job growth) and have been shaping EU policymaking globally, but towards Asia specifically, since the peak of the refugee crisis in 2015 and the publication of the EU's Global Strategy (EUGS) in 2016.[3]

Key challenges and priorities as set out in the EUGS resonate with the EU's strategic partners in principle as well as in detail, i.e., broken down to the tactical level, including policy recommendations, of Humanitarian Assistance Disaster Relief (HADR), the upholding of global common goods (such as keeping maritime routes open for everybody), and finding ways to deradicalize foreign fighters returning home. The focus thereby is to exchange lessons learned, best practices, but also to identify where the EU can work with its partners on a global level and continent-to-continent on common security challenges – and particular on troubling areas in-between, such as the Middle East. The focus today thereby is on "what can we do together" instead of the traditional "what can we do for you" approach that the EU used to take towards the Asia-Pacific. EU policies are more and more interest-driven, i.e., finding ways to addressing security interests together, security interests that affect both sides significantly.

Additionally, the EU side oversees an array of new tools and papers to add new momentum to the existing frameworks of the EU's Common Security and Defense Policy and its Development Cooperation (DevCo), ranging from strategies including the EU–Asia Connectivity Strategy and new country strategies toward e.g., India to programs such as CRIMARIO, increasing collaboration between EU and EU Member States in the Council Working Groups COASI, COAFR, and specific initiatives and tools provided by the Commission's Partnership Instrument (PI) that supports e.g. the EU's activities around the Asia–Europe Meeting (ASEM), ASEAN, and the ASEAN Regional Forum (ARF).

Given that the relationship between the EU and the United States used to be the most substantial strategic relationship, while the relations with Asia had a tendency to be more words than deeds when touching upon strategic/security-related issues, the following chapter focuses on the EU's policies toward Asia, the impact of its strained relationship with the United States and China, which the EU faces as much as other Asian partner countries, and the EU's new strategies and instruments and its opportunities for cooperation in Asia.

A new set of strategies and new tools

Analysts often criticize and dismiss EU strategies as being too vague, too watered-down by the interplay of EU institutions and EU Member States, as not presenting realities as they are. However, with a closer look at the reality of EU policymaking, these strategies serve two central goals beyond presenting the EU's position in a certain area to the outside world: first, the work leading toward the publication of a strategy entails countless exchanges between the European External Action Service (EEAS)'s different units involved, the EU Member States, and EC Services. With an EU foreign policy-related strategy consisting of two parts – the Joint Communication by the European Commission and the EEAS and the subsequent Council Conclusions by the EU Member States – the strategy-writing and adoption process hence already provides momentum to more communication, convergence, and, in the end, compromise to come up with a joint position. So, while the debate on the necessary capabilities needed to fulfill the strategy is neither solved nor finished, the strategy itself presents the outcome of a joint formation of will. Second, the adopted strategy does present a reference framework for EEAS diplomats in their future policy work on areas that are covered in the strategy and thereby indicates the direction in which initiatives will be geared.

Given this systematic approach toward foreign policy that characterized the tenure of then High Representative for Foreign and Security Policy/Vice President of the Commission (HRVP) Federica Mogherini, the following part of the chapter first takes a look at strategies and tools before subsequently assessing both.

The EU acknowledges the centrality of Asia in its most recent strategy papers ranging from the 2016 Global Strategy to the EU's 2018 Connectivity strategy and country-specific strategies alike, such as the EU's Strategy on China 2016, the Joint Communication on EU–China relations 2019, the EU's new India strategy from 2018, and new agreements such as the EU–Japan Connectivity Partnership signed in September 2019 at the first European Connectivity Forum.[4] The EU has also reached out to partners to create joint papers – be it a close exchange with India in the drafting of the EU strategy on India, or in joint documents such as the EU–China 2020 Strategic Agenda for Cooperation.[5] Striving to avoid taking sides in the US–China rivalry and trying to walk a third path between these major actors while staying engaged with both countries, the European Union aims to collaborate with the EU's Asia-Pacific partners including the Strategic Partners China, Japan, India, and Korea in the region and beyond in order to address challenges together.

The 2016 EU Global Strategy addresses the EU's role, aims, and ambitions in a "more connected, contested and complex world"[6] and lays out five "key priorities," i.e., Security of the Union, State and Societal Resilience, an Integrated Approach to Conflicts and Crises, Cooperative Regional Orders, and Global Governance for the Twenty-First Century. The EUGS further acknowledges that

> There is a direct connection between European prosperity and Asian security. In light of the economic weight that Asia represents for the

EU — and vice versa — peace and stability in Asia are a prerequisite for our prosperity. We will deepen economic diplomacy and scale up our security role in Asia.[7]

Building on this and two years of striving for mainstreaming Asia into the EU's foreign policy (EEAS and the EU Member States), working for increasing convergence and a more concrete take — including taking stock of the individual EU Member States' defense and security policy assets in the region — the Council of the European Union acknowledges in its Council Conclusion of May 28, 2018, the necessity for security cooperation in and with Asian partners to become more operational — to put more deeds to the words. The Council hence calls for tailor-made cooperation that draws on accumulated EU security-related efforts by the EU Member States and the EU with those of priority Asian partners such as the EU's Strategic Partners in the region, China, India, Japan, and South Korea, as well as with other partners, first and foremost ASEAN and its member states, in order to enhance visibility and collective impact. Policy areas that are specifically singled out for this cooperation include maritime security, cybersecurity, counterterrorism, hybrid threats, conflict prevention, the proliferation of chemical, biological, radiological, and nuclear weapons (CBRN), and the development of regional cooperative orders.[8]

In its Conclusions, and thereby adding more details to the bird's-eye view perspective of the EU's Global Strategy, the Council

> reaffirms that the EU has a fundamental interest in co-operating with partners worldwide, including in Asia, to safeguard its citizens, defend the fundamental values upon which the Union is founded, including the protection of human rights, uphold the international rules based system, promote multilateralism, contribute to regional stability, prevent violent conflicts and secure the Union's economic interests.[9] [It explicitly] recognises the increasing importance of Asian security for European interests and emphasise that Asian countries, regional organisations and platforms, such as the Asia Europe Meeting (ASEM), are crucial to help secure a more stable and peaceful world. The Council stresses that efforts to enhance EU-Asian security cooperation and Euro-Asia connectivity should be mutually reinforcing.[10]

The Conclusions thereby take the trend of EU policies post-EUGS further to focus on reciprocity, common efforts, and ensuring that policies support EU interests — gone is the traditional rather "altruistically" framed policy approach of "what can the EU do for you," that used to shape EU policies toward Asia. Furthermore, the Conclusions underscore that for an EU that is riddled with refugee and legitimacy crises, policies have to achieve tangible results, in cooperation with partners that have joint interests *and* joint ownership of policy actions being taken:

Here are important possibilities to deepen EU security cooperation with its Asian Strategic Partners: China, India, Japan and the Republic of Korea. It also underlines the importance of deepening co-operation with other partners, along with ASEAN and its member states. In each case, the emphasis should be on achieving tangible results in addressing shared security challenges, both in Asia and elsewhere (notably Africa and the Middle East), including on the full implementation of UN Security Council resolutions, making cooperation a two-way street.[11]

These shared security challenges affect the European Union and its partners in the Asia-Pacific, alike: natural catastrophes, internal turmoil, and violent conflicts in the near neighborhood force ever-increasing numbers of people to leave their livelihoods and regions and turn into flows of refugees at ever-higher levels, demanding responses in regulation as well as integration, and, first and foremost, coping with basic needs. New challenges such as cybersecurity as well as international terrorism – with foreign fighters returning from Syria to their home countries in Europe and Asia-Pacific alike – put governments to the test everywhere. Responding to global challenges by regional integration to form more effective associations remains a task for the EU, ASEAN, and other multilateral entities.

Drawing on the May 2018 Council Conclusions on Asia, the June 2018 Council Conclusions on CSDP and ESDP capabilities and the basic tenets of the 2016 EUGS, the EU is increasingly looking into possibilities to cooperate with its Asian partners – through bilateral Strategic Partnerships (India, China, Japan, and South Korea), inter-institutional cooperation (such as EU-ASEAN), and within multilateral fora such as the Asia–Europe Meeting (ASEM) and the ASEAN Regional Forum (ARF) – within Asia and beyond on global challenges that concern both sides, and that are not necessarily geographically bound to the Asia-Pacific region.

Given its ambitions, it is interesting to see that the EU is viewed in a much better way externally than is often assumed within Europe. A 2015 major public policy baseline study on the perception of the EU's Strategic Partners of the EU and its policies abroad conducted by the author as part of a major consortium for the European Commission showed a surprising majority of respondents in favor of a strong leadership for the EU in world affairs as well as in desirability for this role for the EU (see Table 11.1 and Table 11.2).

Building upon strategies and amidst perception in target countries, the EU has in recent times received new instruments under the 2009 Lisbon Treaty and the EU Global Strategy in order to pursue its foreign policy goals to promote security cooperation in and with Asia.

On the framework side, the EU has put out several new country papers, including an EU Strategy on China,[12] one on Myanmar,[13] a new India Strategy,[14] and an EU Strategy on Connecting EU and Asia.[15] The EU has also concluded several agreements with its Strategic Partners: South Korea signed the "Framework for

TABLE 11.1 Question: How Desirable Is it that the European Union Take a Strong Leadership Role in World Affairs?

Responses from:	Very desirable	Somewhat desirable	Neither/nor	Somewhat undesirable	Very undesirable	n/a	Total (N)
All 10 SP	18,9%	34,9%	27,2%	7,1%	4,1%	7,8%	11621
USA	23,9%	28,8%	24,3%	4,0%	2,9%	16,2%	1007
Japan	5,9%	31,4%	37,9%	6,7%	2,8%	15,2%	1024
China	9,6%	46,1%	35,6%	5,0%	0,6%	3,0%	1410
S. Korea	9,8%	38,8%	37,5%	6,3%	1,5%	6,1%	1238
India	29,5%	37,5%	23,0%	2,6%	1,7%	5,7%	1056

TABLE 11.2 Question: How Likely Is it That the EU Will Take a Strong Leadership Role in World Affairs in Five Years?

Responses from:	Very likely	Rather likely	Neither/nor	Rather unlikely	Very unlikely	n/a	Total (N)
All 10 SP	22,7%	36,7%	24,2%	6,2%	2,2%	8,0%	11621
USA	20,8%	29,4%	24,5%	4,6%	3,6%	17,2%	1007
Japan	8,4%	30,9%	35,3%	7,7%	3,4%	14,2%	1024
China	17,2%	50,8%	25,9%	3,1%	0,3%	2,6%	1410
S. Korea	12,7%	40,8%	34,8%	5,9%	0,7%	5,1%	1238
India	31,2%	37,8%	21,5%	3,1%	0,9%	5,6%	1056

(EU; PPMI; NCRE, 2016)

Participation of the Republic of Korea in EU Crisis Management Operations" agreement in 2014[16] as the first Asian–EU Partner country, thereby establishing the scope of cooperation and participation of South Korea in EU crisis management operations, both civilian and military. The EU–Japan Economic Partnership Agreement entered into force in February 2019, the joint EU–Japan adequacy decision in January 2019 created the world's largest area of safe data flows, and on September 27, 2019, Juncker and Abe signed the EU–Japan Connectivity Partnership. The unpredictability of the US administration's policy toward Asia and its Asian allies under US President Trump has been adding a huge momentum to the new interest in cooperating with the EU and consolidating the cooperation in signed frameworks.

Discussions on how to collaborate with the Asia-Pacific on topics ranging from North Korea to China's Belt and Road Initiative now happen frequently on all levels, beyond the Council's Asia-Pacific Working Group (COASI – with a first-of-its-kind joint session between COASI and COAFR); discussions are also going on in the Political and Security Committee and other fora.

On the other hand, the European External Action Service also has more tools to hand now: The Commission's Partnership Instrument (PI) strategically supports the EEAS's work in a most flexible way with external resources. While the EU's Asia-Pacific Research and Advice Network (#APRAN) supports the Asia-Pacific Department and the respective EU Delegations in the region internally, ASIAFORA actively advances "the EU's role in multilateral fora in Asia" including ARF, ASEM, and ASEAN. A planned merger of PI with the Neighbourhood Policy in a single instrument, the Neighborhood, Development, and International Cooperation Instrument (NDICI), will also open the way for new PI projects directly implementing the ambitions of the May 2018 Conclusions, in a new joint approach by EEAS, the Commission, and EU Member States.

In sum, in a time when the transatlantic relations are getting weaker and the EU–Asian ones are getting stronger, the EU's foreign and security policy toward Asia aims to be more focused on finding joint interests that drive cooperation in Asia-Pacific and beyond, addressing common challenges jointly, in and with Asia.

Common challenges: From maritime security to foreign fighters

In an attempt to translate strategies into initiatives and to let deeds follow words, the EU's paper on Asia looks at challenges that Asian countries face as well as those Europeans do. The following provides background to three of them – maritime security, mass migration flows due to conflict, disaster, and displaced persons, and dealing with foreign fighters in Syria and elsewhere, returning to their home countries in Europe and Asia-Pacific – before turning to possible cooperation opportunities.

Maritime security

Maritime security has become a central topic in EU–Asian exchanges, particularly with India, despite the lack of naval capabilities among EU Member States: with 90% of European trade being seaborne, potential conflicts or piracy in the region impact major sea-lanes of communication (SLOC) and thereby disrupt crucial trade and energy sea-routes for Europe. Trade and, increasingly, FDI are the backbone of relations between the EU and the Asia-Pacific. Exceeding trade with North America substantially, the Asia-Pacific presents the biggest trading partner for the EU totaling almost €1.7 trillion in 2018.[17]

Maritime security developments in the region also have the potential to challenge the current global rules-based order and for the general provision of international public goods. Particularly given the different perceptions of the interpretations of UNCLOS – with Asian partners, first and foremost China, defining Economic Exclusive Zones (EEZ) as quasi-territorial borders, while Western countries, first and foremost the United States, see EEZ as a right for the concerned country to exploit the resources such as fishing, yet see the high seas as international waters that are open to everybody – closer exchange and cooperation by the EU with its partners to work toward a common understanding and upholding of the global common good is demanded. Joint workshops on maritime security, like the two sessions that the EU held with India in 2019, feed into the buildup of a common view here.

So far, however, the general impression among the EU's Strategic Partners is that the EU is not playing a very important role outside of anti-piracy operations in the Gulf of Aden. While member states and traditional maritime powers like the United Kingdom (UK) and France are heavily involved in maritime security arrangements, the EU is not so visible in comparison. Ongoing cooperation with India as well as a more active engagement toward the Indian Ocean Rim Association might change that impression over time.

Mass migration and refugee flows

Most visible on the agenda in 2015 with record numbers of over 1.2 million first-time asylum seekers,[18] managing irregular and unprecedented migration flows has remained a demanding issue for the EU and its Strategic Partners alike, concurrently presenting opportunities for closer exchange and cooperation. Asia-Pacific is hit most by natural disasters, while Europe faces most people fleeing from conflicts in the neighborhood: 74 percent of people displaced by natural disasters in 2018 were in Asia – 9.3 million in East Asia and 3.3 million in South Asia. Disaster-induced displaced persons amounted in China up to 3.8 million in 2018, up to 2.7 million in India, and 3.8 million in the typhoon-struck Philippines.[19] Since 2017, ASEAN has been facing the Rohingya refugee crisis at an unprecedented level, negatively impacting the ASEAN community and putting its principles of consensus and non-interference once more to the test – not only among ASEAN member states, but also between ASEAN members and EU members in the ASEM context. Borders between states remain porous, making migration and border management, including undocumented workers, a core issue for ASEAN. But also, countries like China are concerned about refugee flows, particularly from North Korea.

Europe saw most people displaced due to conflicts in the almost immediate neighborhood: in 2018, 7.4 million were displaced in sub-Saharan Africa and 2.1million in the Middle East/North Africa (MENA) region, with Syria and the Democratic Republic of Congo being the prime origin for refugees.[20] These mass migration flows are expected to mount up to 200 million people on the move in the future due to the impact of climate change: a massive challenge that calls for concerted action.

Counterterrorism and returning foreign fighters

Counterterrorism (CT) is high on the agenda on both sides – the European and the Asia-Pacific – exemplifying the shared threat perception of international terrorism as a core security threat of our time. In particular, the mass escape from prison camps of "Islamic State of IRQ and SYR" (ISIS/IS) fighters in the Kurdish-dominated part of Syria in the wake of the 2019 Turkey invasion of Northern Syria, has magnified the challenge with several hundreds of IS combatants on the run. Indonesia alone expected 50 fighters to have escaped from the camps with their families and to be on their way home to link up with local IS-minded terrorist groups, with the number of foreign fighters in Indonesia assessed to be around 350 in November 2019. The tropical island group of the Maldives has the highest number of foreign fighters per capita, aiming to return to their homeland, threatening the fragile peace there. Particularly Southeast and South Asia are targeted, with the Easter Bombings in Sri Lanka and further terrorist attacks in 2019 in Balochistan and Kashmir being atrocious cases in point. On the European side, the horrific terrorist attacks in Paris, Brussels, London, Berlin, and elsewhere underlined the challenge these returning foreign fighters and their impact on local terrorist groups pose.[21] The EU and its Strategic Partners face a joint challenge, where exchange on intelligence sharing and Asian experiences with de-radicalization programs – as in the case of India – are a promising area for cooperation.

Avenues for cooperation

With the EU's focus on promoting a rules-based international order, its center of attention is on shaping rules together, sharing lessons learned, on policy dialogues, and actual capacity building, thereby connecting EU security interests with those of its Asia partners.

The EU's involvement in the Asia-Pacific addresses thereby a broad portfolio: it ranges from high-level dialogues with Strategic Partners, pursuing regular exchange with all countries in the region through Joint Commissions, participating in regional capacity building in lesser developed countries all the way to cooperation on the ground in Asia and with Asian partners in international missions elsewhere, such as the Gulf of Aden or peacekeeping operations in the Middle East and on the African continent.

Within the respective strategic partnerships, regular summits entail security dialogues that focus on a broad range of issues from cybersecurity to humanitarian assistance and disaster relief (HADR); these EU–Strategic Partner state summits and their dialogues complement defense-related dialogues between individual EU Member States with the Asia-Pacific countries such as Japan, Korea, Australia, and New Zealand and their dialogues with France, the United Kingdom, Germany, and others.

In the area of military policy as pursued by the European Military Staff and within the framework of the Common Foreign and Security Policy and its Common Security and Defense Policy, these summits are underpinned by high-level visits such as those of the Chairman of the EU Military Committee

(CEUMC) to the region. Visits included, for example, Pakistan and Vietnam in 2019 (for the signing of the EU–Vietnam Framework Participation Agreement for EU missions); Singapore, Myanmar, Vietnam, and China in 2016; South Korea in 2015; China and Japan in 2014; as well as exchanges in Brussels, such as with the South Korean Vice Chief of Defense (CHOD) in January 2017 and participation in the East Asian Summit as a guest since 2017.

The EU participates in the ASEAN Regional Forum's Defense Officials Dialogue twice a year and is an active member of the ASEAN Regional Forum (ARF). Since 2017, the EU attends the East Asia Summit as an observer; yet the EU is still striving to become a full member of the East Asian Summit[22] against reservations on the part of such countries as Singapore and Australia.

The EU has also rediscovered the Asia–Europe Meeting (ASEM) – although still with less enthusiasm for action than for words. ASEM is the biggest exclusively Europe–Asia forum encompassing 53 partners (51 countries and 2 regional organizations), yet not the United States. For examples in the efforts of the EU to work toward joint global norms, the ASEM Pathfinder Group on Connectivity, coming together during the ASEM Senior Officials' Meeting (SOM) in June of 2017, is a good example for the European External Action Service aiming to use these multilateral fora to push for internationally accepted norms, also in new fields like connectivity (connectivity is the overall term used for large infrastructure initiatives connecting states in the Eurasian region, with the most known initiative being the Chinese Belt and Road initiative BRI). The Brussels-based ASEM Summit in 2018 was used to introduce the EU's new Strategy on Connecting the EU and Asia as well as the EU-funded and operationalized ASEM Sustainable Connectivity Portal.

On the capacity-building side, in the maritime security realm, among other projects, EU CRIMARIO aims to strengthen maritime safety and security in the wider IO region by supporting coastal countries in enhancing maritime situational awareness (MSA). Responding to the challenge that critical maritime routes in the Indian Ocean face – among others, piracy – the EU supports the implementation of a regional mechanism, the Djibouti Code of Conduct, agreed by 21 littoral states of the Western Indian Ocean, and the initiative, the Critical Maritime Routes (CMR) program. A key tool of CRIMARIO is the IORIS (Indian Ocean Regional Information Sharing) platform, a web-based communications tool for regional and national multiagency use that allows (a) information-sharing in a secure and flexible environment; (b) real-time management of incidents at sea; (c) secure communications between users (national agencies, regional centers); allowing each to control members and access rights for their designated areas. The first phase was funded with €5.5mn (2015–2019), the next phase will be budgeted with about €7mn, again managed by Expertise France. The EU is furthermore the main development partner of the Indian Ocean Commission; individual EU Member States participate in organizations including the Indian Ocean Rim Association (IORA) and ReCAPP.[23] Last but not least, the EU acts as an observer to the South Asian Association for Regional Cooperation (SAARC).

In addition to these dialogues and training, the EU takes an active part in multilateral military exercises. It participated in the US–China Humanitarian Assistance/Disaster Relief exercise, while EU Member States participated in Thailand's Cobra Gold exercise, India's International Fleet Review, Australia's Pitch Black, and the US RIMPAC. In 2016, the EU was invited for the first time to observe the Indonesian Multilateral Naval Exercise Komodo (MNEK). Along the same lines, Asian countries have already cooperated and are still engaging with the EU in missions such as the EU anti-piracy mission ATALANTA, with e.g., South Korea, Vietnam, and New Zealand having signed participation framework agreements.

Multiple EU Member States have been engaging in training activities on peacekeeping with Asian partners, ranging from the Swedish SWEDINT to the German Armed Forces; complementarily, the European Security and Defense College (ESDC) conducts activities with Asian Strategic Partners including annual courses with the People's Liberation Army (PLA), and seminars alternating between Brussels and Beijing for high- and mid-career–level officials (with the seminars themselves alternating with the EU–China high-level defense and security dialogue). The ESDC regularly organizes orientation seminars with diplomats and militaries from ASEAN countries. Examples of the EU engaging in training and education programs include cooperation with the Indonesian Peace and Security Centre (Sentul) through lectures, and exchange of curricula and sub-contracting courses on Hostile Environment Awareness Trainings (HEAT) for personnel assigned to the region. Particularly the new round of PI projects will actively support capacity-building and cooperation in the region in the key areas of CT, cyber, conflict prevention, and maritime security, in close cooperation with EU Member States.

Caution and criticisms

Skepticism remains, however. With the EU's internal challenges, illustrated by countries being haunted by right-wing populism and the lack of solidarity – let alone a unified voice – between EU Member States, the new "geopolitical" Commission, the still very new service EEAS, and the EU Member States face multiple challenges in order to put words into deeds. The Multiannual Financial Framework had not been agreed upon at the time the new Commission was approved in late 2019. The ongoing refugee crisis in the Mediterranean still puts European naval ambitions under strain. Moreover, Brexit not only binds up multiple human and financial resources, but the EU will also lose one of its most active and potent actors in the Asia-Pacific region. The German Defense Minister Kramp-Karrenbauer announced in November 2019 that he was stepping up the game in Asia and would join France there with a frigate, but given the small number of actually deployable frigates that the German navy has at its disposition, implementation remains in question.

Additionally, concurrent with the transatlantic disenchantment under a Trump administration, the Europeans have also become more alert toward their Asian partners, first and foremost China. The 2019 Joint Communication on China emphasizes the need for China, as "a key global actor and leading technology power with an ever greater presence in the world, including Europe," to take on "greater responsibilities for upholding the rules-based international order, as well as greater reciprocity, non-discrimination, and openness of its system" and the necessity for EU policy to "shift towards a more realistic, assertive, and multi-faceted approach."[24] For the very first time for an official EU document on China, the Joint Communication points out that "China has also increasingly become a strategic competitor for the EU."[25] The paper puts forward ten concrete actions and ends with a clear warning not to compromise 5G networks and the digital infrastructure in the bidding still ongoing in 2019 – a hint toward the demand to ban Huawei from bidding for 5G networks in Europe. But also clashes with China over its handling of the protests in Hong Kong, its Xinjiang detention camps for Uighurs, and increasing uneasiness about Chinese foreign influence and interference in all areas ranging from academia to culture, media, think tanks, and targeting companies – China's sharp power – have soured relations. The outrageous Chinese threats against Sweden upon awarding the free-speech Tucholsky Prize to Gui Minhai, a Swedish publisher currently detained in China, are a point in case to illustrate the difficult relationship.

Difficulties in the EU's and other Asian countries' relationship with the United States as well as with China, however, fuel in return the EU's and these other countries' ambitions for closer cooperation and coordination and have provided more momentum than had been imaginable before, as illustrated by the signing of EU–JPN agreements, that had been negotiated for years without any progress.

Conclusion

In an ever more Asia-centric time, facing a Trump Administration and amidst a US–China rivalry – two of the prime strategic partners for the European Union – the European Union strives to shape its role and pursue its interests of keeping and promoting a rules-based order and avoiding bipolar confrontations. It pursues a strategy of following its interests by aiming for cooperation on security challenges identified as common with its Asian partners in bilateral and multilateral fora, through capacity-building and cooperation on the ground. The EUGS' five key priorities – such as coping with mass migration of disaster- and conflict-induced displacement of people, maritime security, cybersecurity, and counterterrorism – resonate with the challenges of Asian partners, including the EU's Strategic Partners Korea, Japan, India, and China. The concerns about a US policy, seen as unpredictable, volatile, and unreliable spurs, further the interests of cooperation on security challenges. Based on the 2009 Lisbon Treaty, the 2016 EU Global Strategy and subsequent thematic and country strategies, the EU possesses increasingly comprehensive frameworks for interaction and cooperation frameworks signed with Japan, South Korea, Vietnam, and others – with more in the making. The EU can now also draw on more tools provided by the Commission's "Partnership Instrument" to support the European External Action Service with flexible and timely resources. The 2018 Council Conclusions further underline the EU's ambition of enhancing its security presence and role in the Asian region.

However, the EU still ails from a lack of solidarity between EU Member States themselves and vis-à-vis the EU institutions; on how to deal with Asia; on a multitude of significant internal problems from raging populism – now presented in several EU Member States' governments – to Brexit and – last but not least – of a lack of military capabilities, particularly in the naval realm that is so important in Asian military affairs. Also, externally, the EU is still perceived primarily as a potential, not yet as a de facto, security actor in the Asia-Pacific region as a partner in this policy field. Core challenges to the EU's credibility and relevance as a security actor in Asia and with Asian countries are the still-underfunded military capabilities the EU Member States can deploy to the area, the still-maturing processes of coordination between EU Member States, EEAS, and EC Services, underdeveloped, existing security partnerships, and the EU's perceived absence from crucial hot spots in the region, with North Korea being the most striking example, but also the South China Sea as a case in point. To what extent the EU will be able to respond to the new interest coming from its Asian partners and to put the ambitious priorities of the EUGS into practice will impact its credibility and capability; Europe's role in an Asia-centric world and amidst the US–China rivalry will therefore strongly depend on the success of the European Union to reform itself, in a sense, to deliver upon promises – at home as well as in Asia.

Notes

1 This article builds upon a previous article, May-Britt U. Stumbaum, "Eurasian Security Cooperation: Issue Areas and Outcomes," in Christian Echle et al., eds., *Security Architectures Under Threat: The Status of Multilateral Fora, Panorama Insights into Asian and European Affairs, 02/2017* (Singapore: Konrad-Adenauer-Foundation, 2017). 147–157.
2 European Commission, *The von der Leyen Commission: For a Union that Strives for More* (Brussels, 2019), https://ec.europa.eu/commission/presscorner/detail/en/ip_19_5542
3 European Union, *Shared Vision, Common Action: A Stronger Europe. A Global Strategy for the European Union's Foreign and Security Policy* (Brussels: European Union, 2016).
4 European Commission, *The Partnership on Sustainable Connectivity and Quality Infrastructure Between the European Union and Japan* (Brussels, 2019); European Commission; HRVP, *Joint Communication: Elements for an EU Strategy on India* (Brussels: European Commission; HRVP, 2018); European Commission; HRVP,

EU-China – A Strategic Outlook (Brussels, 2019); COUNCIL, G. S. O. T, *Council Conclusions on Implementing the EU Global Strategy in the Area of Security and Defense: Council Conclusions* (November 14, 2016) (Brussels: Council of the European Union, 2016); Council of the European Union, *Council Conclusions on the Global Strategy on the European Union's Foreign and Security Policy* (Brussels, 2016); Council of the European Union, *EU Strategy on China: Council Conclusions* (July 18, 2016) (Brussels: COUNCIL, G. S. O. T, 2016); Council of the European Union, *EU Strategy on India: Council Conclusions* (10 December 2018) (Brussels, 2018); European Union, *Shared Vision, Common Action: A Stronger Europe.*

5 European Union, *EU-China 2020 Strategic Agenda for Cooperation* (Brussels, 2013).

6 European Union, *Shared Vision, Common Action: A Stronger Europe*, 16.

7 Ibid., 37.

8 Council of the European Union, *Enhanced EU Security Cooperation in and with Asia: Council Conclusions* (28 May 2018) (Brussels, 2018).

9 Council of the European Union, *Enhanced EU Security Cooperation in and with Asia*, (28 May, 2018), https://www.consilium.europa.eu/media/35456/st09265-re01-en1 8.pdf

10 Ibid.

11 Council of the European Union, *Enhanced EU Security Cooperation in and with Asia: Council Conclusions* (28 May 2018), 2–3.

12 European Commission, *Elements for an EU Strategy on China* (Brussels, 2016); Council of the European Union, *EU Strategy on China: Council Conclusions* (18 July 2016) (Brussels: COUNCIL, G. S. O. T, 2016).

13 F. Mogherini, *Elements for an EU Strategy vis-à-vis Myanmar/Burma: A Special Partnership for Democracy, Peace and Prosperity* (Brussels: E. E. A. SERVICE, 2016); Council of the European Union, *Myanmar/Burma - Council Conclusions on EU Strategy with Myanmar/Burma* (20 June 2016) (Brussels: COUNCIL, G. S. O. T, 2016).

14 Council of the European Union, *EU Strategy on India: Council Conclusions* (December 10, 2018) (Brussels, 2018b).

15 EU Strategy on Connecting EU and Asia, 2018.

16 European Union and Republic of Korea, "Agreement Between the European Union and the Republic of Korea Establishing a Framework for the Participation of the Republic of Korea in European Union Crisis Management Pperations," *Brussels: Official Journal of the European Union*, L 166, 5 June 2014.

17 European Commission, *DG Trade Statistical Guide 2019* (Luxembourg, 2019).

18 EUROSTAT, *Asylum Statistics*. 2019.

19 IDMC, *Global Report on Internal Displacements 2019.* Internal Displacement Monitoring Centre, 2019.

20 Ibid.

21 A. Chew, "Indonesia on Alert as Isis Fighters Escape Syria to Awaken Sleeper Terror Cells Back Home," *South China Morning Post*, 16 October 2019, 2019, https://ww w.scmp.com/week-asia/politics/article/3033099/indonesia–alert-isis-fighters-escape -syria-awaken-sleeper-terror; Soufan Group, *Foreign Fighters: An Updated Assessment of the Flow of Foreign Fighters into Syria and Iraq.* 2015.

22 Since 2005, the East Asia Summit (EAS) has been held annually at the level of Heads of Government of 18 countries (ASEAN member states, China, Japan, Korea, Russia, Australia, New Zealand, United States, and India) and is seen as the current central forum for discussion of security issues in the Asia-Pacific region on a governmental level. EAS meetings are scheduled back-to-back to annual ASEAN leaders' meetings.

23 ReCAPP – the Regional Cooperation Agreement on Combating Piracy and Armed Robbery against Ships in Asia – represents Asia's first regional government-to-government agreement to promote and enhance cooperation against piracy and armed robbery against ships. The Agreement entered into force on September 4,

2006 and featured, in 2017, 20 States – 14 Asian countries, 4 European countries (UK, Netherlands, Denmark, and the non-EU member state Norway), Australia, and the USA – as Contracting Parties to ReCAAP.

24 European Commission; HRVP, *EU-China – A Strategic Outlook*, 1.

25 Ibid., 5.

12

SINO-RUSSIAN RELATIONS IN AN ERA OF SINO-US RIVALRY

From partnership to alliance?

Jo Inge Bekkevold

Three countries have the potential to impact on the emerging China–US rivalry in significant ways: Japan, as the most important ally of the United States and enabler of its forward posture in the Asia-Pacific; India, with an increasingly prominent strategic position as the Sino-US rivalry is expanding from the Asia-Pacific to the larger Indo-Pacific theater – in a long-term perspective, India is probably the only country with the potential to become a great power along with China and the United States; and the third country is Russia. While Japan is an alliance partner of the United States, and India gradually is strengthening its ties to the United States under pressure from a rising China, Russia is moving closer to China.

This chapter explores the current state of affairs and development of Sino-Russian ties in a new era of China–US rivalry, and whether the growing Sino-Russian partnership can develop further toward a full-fledged military alliance. The forming of a China–Russia military alliance is a concern for the United States,[1] and it would have implications for European security. China's rise is challenging the hegemonic position of the United States, and causing certain unease in Europe that its main security guarantor may give more priority to its transpacific flank than its flank across the Atlantic. The US preoccupation with China would be a lesser concern for Europe if Russia had a strained relationship with China, forcing Moscow to build a credible deterrence on its Asian flank. However, Sino-Russian ties are now better than ever.[2]

Alliances are a means to aggregate power and increase security against adversaries.[3] With the return of a bipolar world structure, revolving around the Sino-US rivalry,[4] alliances will matter less than if we returned to a multipolar structure, because in a bipolar structure no third state is strong enough to add significantly to the resources the two superpowers already possess.[5] Still, some form of strategic alignment with another second-ranked great power could still be useful in a bipolar system, and the obvious historical precedent is the United States playing the "China card" against the Soviet Union in the 1970s and 1980s. When China tilted closer to the United States, the Soviet Union had to balance two flanks, which proved to be a costly undertaking. Likewise, through disarmament on their shared border, China and Russia can today each concentrate forces on their opposite flank facing the United States, and through this posture force the United States to deploy military resources across both its oceanic flanks simultaneously.

This chapter consists of four parts. It starts by examining the current strength of the Sino-Russian partnership, looking at their security ties, defense policies, and economic cooperation. The next part applies balance-of-power theory and geography explaining why China and Russia are moving closer to each other. In the third part, I explore the costs, benefits, and possible gains for China and Russia further deepening their alignment from the current arrangement into an alliance, and discuss what might drive China and Russia closer together, or drive them apart, including if the United States is able to play the "Russia card" against China. The final part of the chapter outlines a few scenarios for the way ahead.

The Sino-Russian partnership

The partnership between China and Russia is now arguably stronger than it has ever been.[6] Russia has moved closer to China, a turn in Russian policy that China has embraced. This shift in Russian policy became evident in the immediate aftermath of the global financial crisis, and was further consolidated following Moscow's annexation of Crimea and Western sanctions. The cooperation between Beijing and Moscow encompasses expanded economic ties, growing energy partnership, deepened policy coordination with close institutional ties at nearly all levels of government, and renewed military cooperation. In addition, the United States continues to be an important common denominator in the Sino-Russian relationship. US relations with Russia are currently at their lowest point since the end of the Cold War, and the strategic rivalry between China and the United States has now risen to unprecedented levels. According to the latest US National Security Strategy from December 2017, "China and Russia want to shape a world antithetical to US values and interests."[7]

Nonetheless, despite Sino-Russian relations growing stronger than ever before, how close is the relationship really? To identify state behavior and the level of cooperation between countries along the balancing–bandwagoning spectrum, the three most essential indicators are security ties (external balancing), military and defense policies (internal balancing), and economic policies, in that order of importance.[8]

Security ties, or alignment policies, can be divided into three categories: strong, moderate, and weak alignment.[9] Strong alignment corresponds with traditional external balancing, and in our case would include China and Russia entering into a formal military alliance, or opening up military bases in each others' countries on a permanent or semi-permanent basis. Moderate alignments are rotational allied troop deployments or limited access agreements, participation in the international military operations of the alliance partner, or conducting joint training and exercises. Weak alignment signals include arms sales, military aid to each other, and statements of support for each other's security policies. These categories offer an indication of the baseline strength of the alignment signal, but the form and degree of cooperation within each category also matter.[10]

The security ties between China and Russia fall short of strong alignment. The Treaty of Good-Neighborliness and Friendly Cooperation between China and Russian signed in 2001 lacks a mutual defense clause, such as that found in the mutual defense treaty that the PRC and Soviet Union signed in 1950.[11] The treaty stresses mutual non-aggression, non-interference, peaceful coexistence, antiterrorism, international law, and respect for national sovereignty, equal security, and territorial integrity. Moreover, they have no military bases or military deployments in each other's countries. Neither does their cooperation tick off many of the indicators signaling moderate alignment; they do not undertake any rotational allied troop deployments, or participate in any of the international military operations of the other alliance partner.

Their military cooperation has expanded significantly in recent years, but mainly through a growing number of joint military exercises, and by Russia reigniting its arms sales to China. Since 2005, Russia and China have been holding Peace Mission exercises, and in 2012 they added the Joint Sea naval exercise series to their growing defense portfolio, which has been conducted in somewhat provocative locations, such as the Baltics and the South China Sea. Although the operational benefits of these exercises have been limited, Russia is the only country conducting large-scale military exercises with China, and they grow in scale and complexity, and involve a wide array of advanced weapons.[12] Their joint missile defense exercise held in May 2016 was clearly a response to the US decision to deploy THAAD in South Korea, a decision that especially rattled the Chinese.[13] And in 2018, Russia for the first time invited China to take part in the Vostok-2018, the largest exercise held in Russia since 1981.[14]

Moscow is now once again transferring some of its most advanced weapons platforms into Chinese hands, highlighting a major shift in Russian thinking from a decade ago.[15] The 2015 agreements selling the S-400 for a total of USD 3 billion, and another for the sale of the Su-35 Flankers for a total of USD 2 billion were the largest transactions between the two since the early 2000s.[16] In 2017, new contracts were signed for the sale of additional aircraft engines,[17] and in October 2019 Putin announced that Russia is helping China to build an early warning system to counter missile attacks.[18]

China and Russia's defense ties further encompass a reciprocal "no first use" nuclear weapons posture, and cooperation against separatism, terrorism, and religious extremism.[19] In 2015, the two countries also signed a cyberspace pact, mainly addressing mutual assurances on non-aggression and upholding the principle of sovereignty in the cyber domain.[20] In sum, although China and Russia have taken major steps improving their security and defense ties over the last 10 to 15 years, if we follow the three categories presented above, their security alignment as of today is one of moderate alignment, and arguably closer to weak rather than strong alignment. China and Russia have a long distance to cover before their cooperation resembles that of an alliance.

The biggest achievement in their security relationship, though, is how both countries have adjusted their military posture. Following normalization in 1989, Russia and China began to gradually draw down the enormous military face-off at their border. By 2000, Russia's forces had been reduced by as much as 85 percent.[21] Despite the growing military imbalance between Russia and China, the two continue to maintain a relatively demilitarized border, allowing them to concentrate most of their forces elsewhere.[22] By reducing its presence on the Chinese border, Russia has provided China with a safe strategic rear, an important prerequisite enabling Beijing to transfer resources into developing naval capabilities and to take on the United States in the maritime theater.[23] Russia's military footprint in its Far East region (RFE) began to change in 2008, but this had more to do with Russia's military reforms and modernization than being caused by the growth of China.[24] Russia's defense posture is mainly targeted toward its European flank. In other words, the main balancing efforts of China and Russia are not pointed toward each other, but toward the United States.

The economic cooperation between China and Russia has over the last 10 to 15 years developed to unprecedented levels, and in the aftermath of the Ukraine Crisis and Western sanctions toward Russia, their economic ties have expanded further. Still, their economic cooperation resembles more that of a normal relationship between two neighboring countries than a special exclusive relationship. Even if China has emerged as Russia's largest trading partner, by 2017 trade with China still accounted for a modest 15 percent of Russia's total trade in goods, and Russia is hardly a top-ten trading partner for China, accounting for only 1.8 percent of China's export and 2.5 percent of its total import of trade in goods.[25]

In 2016, Russia surpassed Saudi Arabia as the largest exporter of crude oil to China, but Europe is still the main market for Russian crude oil production.[26] It is estimated that Russia through the May 2014 agreement between Gazprom and CNPC soon will provide gas deliveries to China in the amount of 38 billion cubic meters per year. In comparison, Gazprom supplied a total of 200.8 billion cubic meters of gas to European countries in 2018.[27]

In addition to growing ties, another development is changing the nature of the Sino-Russian relationship, and that is the growing power gap in favor of China. After losing the Crimean War in the 1850s, Russia regarded Europe as hostile and unwilling to accept Russian greatness, leading several Russian statesmen to advise their country to "turn to China to realize both its great destiny and its civilizing potential."[28] When Russia rolled out its policies on its eastern frontier in the nineteenth century, it did so from a position of relative strength vis-à-vis a fragile China.[29] In December 1949, after victory in the Civil War with the Nationalists, Mao traveled to Moscow to gain support and security against the United States.

Today, the balance in the relationship has changed completely, and when Russia in the aftermath of the 2014 Ukraine Crisis turned to China, it was from a position of relative weakness vis-à-vis a rejuvenated China. In 2015, China's GDP was ten times larger than that of Russia, and according to IMF estimates, the gap seems likely to widen further over the next few years.[30] Russia now only ranks as the eleventh largest economy, with a GDP the same size as Australia and Canada,[31] and its 2018 military expenditure smaller than Saudi Arabia, India, and France.[32] However, Russia has the largest nuclear force, next to the US, and in later years has modernized its conventional forces. Despite economic challenges, the combined effect of Russia's geography, military power, and natural resources still gives it a strategic position in a new era of China–US rivalry. However, within the Sino-Russian relationship, Russia is the junior partner, and this will ultimately shape how these two countries relate to each other.

Even though Sino-Russian economic ties are closer than ever before, it is above all a sign of a normal relationship between two neighboring countries with complementary economic structures, and Russia is in no way economically dependent on China. Their security ties are also strengthening, but do not resemble those of an alliance. The main achievement in the Sino-Russian alignment is that their respective defense postures are targeted away from each other, showing a relatively high degree of mutual trust. In the following I will explain the main basis for this trust.

Explaining the Sino-Russian alignment

The Sino-Russian alignment, and the fact that Russia is moving closer to China despite a growing power gap in favor of the latter, is mainly explained by classical geopolitics, understood as the interplay of geography and power politics.[33] China–Russia relations have to be seen in relation to the United States, and the strategy and policy of the three countries in the China–Russia–US triangle is informed not only by the balance of power between them, but also by their geography, and their respective power position in various strategic theatres.[34]

It is acknowledged that states balance against power, in their vicinity.[35] Russia borders China, as well as NATO forces in Europe, and it faces a larger power gap vis-à-vis NATO and the United States than vis-à-vis China. The combined GDPs of the European Union and China are approximately the same size, but when we add US economic and military might to this picture, Russia faces a larger power imbalance on its European flank.[36] Even though China is rising, the gap between Russia and NATO today is larger than what was the case for the Soviet Union. In 1980, the combined GDP of the United States and the EU4 – the four large European countries (West) Germany, UK, France, and

Italy – was four times that of the Soviet Union. Today, the gap is almost 20 times in favor of the US and EU4.[37] In 1980, the Soviet Union could add the Warsaw Pact countries to this configuration; Russia of today cannot. The changes in the military expenditures gap are not that dramatic, but follows the same trend.[38]

Furthermore, China is in the midst of a massive geopolitical reconfiguration, transforming itself from a traditional land power into a major land–sea hybrid power.[39] China's growing sea power capabilities now challenge the traditional US naval supremacy in the maritime theaters of Asia.[40] China going to sea adds a very important strategic layer to China's rise as the peer-competitor to the United States, and it contributes to fueling Sino-US rivalry.[41] The main thrust of China's sea power development is so far directed toward the East and South China Seas, but it is gradually making waves also into the Indian Ocean, contributing to expanding the theatre of Sino-US rivalry from the Asia-Pacific to the larger Indo-Pacific.[42]

The Russian leadership understands that Beijing's military buildup is directed away from Russia, toward the Western Pacific engaging in a strategic rivalry with the United States. Moscow's arms sales to the PLA are based on the premise that China is much more likely to engage in a maritime conflict with the United States than it is to embark on a land campaign against Russia.[43] As China is channeling most of its resources into the maritime theater facing the United States, Russia can allow itself to accommodate China and channel most of its resources into taking on the United States and NATO.[44] With the Sino-US rivalry drawing the United States deeper into Asia, Russia has more room for manoeuver on its European flank. In fact, we have recently seen a revival of Russian naval activity, and particularly in North Atlantic waters, posing new challenges for NATO's maritime forces.[45] The main achievement in the current Sino-Russian alignment is that both countries keep their rear safe, enabling them to channel resources toward more pressing challenges, which for China is the US, and for Russia is the US and NATO.

In addition, Moscow's diminished threat perception vis-à-vis China owes much to Beijing's policy of reassurance toward Russia since the 1990s.[46] Although, as China's power gap vis-à-vis Russia widens, there is of course no guarantee that China will continue to adhere to a policy of reassurance, or that Russia will be reassured. Yet, they share the same threat perception, of the United States as the main adversary.

A common thread in Sino-Russian security and defense cooperation is non-aggression, with the 2001 Treaty of Good-Neighborliness and Friendly Cooperation as well as the 2015 Cyber Agreement both emphasizing it. Moreover, they are now sharing technology to build missile defense capabilities, and their respective defense postures are pointed away from each other. Their current security arrangement is underpinned by keeping their strategic rear safe, and channeling resources into more pressing theaters, toward the US presence in Asia for China, and the US/NATO presence in Europe for Russia, and they can do this without any significant commitments to each other.

The costs and benefits of a Sino-Russian alliance

In a bipolar world system, the formations of alliances are largely determined by structure.[47] This means either shifts in the balance of power in the international system, or geopolitical changes in the form of major shifts in the geostrategy and defense posture of one of the two superpowers. In other words, the incentive for China and Russia moving from the current arrangement into a full-fledged military alliance, committing them to protecting each other, will most likely be external in the form of increased tension with the United States. As China is the dominant power in the Sino-Russian alignment, any decision to enter into an alliance ultimately rests with China, but for Russia to join, the benefits of joining have to outweigh the costs. The benefits for China and Russia by entering into an alliance will be increased deterrence and military capability to fight a war.

However, with an alliance also follow certain costs, in the form of a more strained relationship with their adversary the United States and its allies in Europe and Asia, and less freedom for China and Russia in their foreign policies due to their commitment to each other.[48] As formal allies, China and Russia would have to deal with their common adversary the United States, and with each other; Snyder calls these the adversary game and the alliance game respectively.[49] The alliance and adversary games proceed simultaneously, and strategies and tactics in the alliance game will have side-effects in the adversary game – and vice versa.[50]

Toughness toward the adversary will cause the adversary to move closer to their own allies, thus solidifying their alliance. Firmness toward the adversary also increases the risk of entrapment by the ally, as the commitment of the alliance partners to each other increases. A tough stance toward the adversary also tends to close off the option of realignment with them.[51] The alliance game is dominated by the tension between the risk of abandonment and the risk of entrapment, and this risk tends to vary inversely: reducing one tends to increase the other.[52] In the following, I will briefly outline some of the main costs for China and Russia associated with the adversary game and the alliance game. Although these are costs that will occur after an alliance has been formed, the concerns about potential costs will still be part of the calculations made before agreeing to join an alliance in the first place.

Strained relations with the adversary

Even though strained relations with the United States would be the very reason for China and Russia entering into an alliance, there is a cost involved in forming such an alliance in the sense that the lines of division between the United States and its allies versus a Sino-Russian alliance would be further consolidated. One very likely outcome is that China and Russia's trade and economic cooperation with the US, NATO members, and possibly also with US allies in the Asia-Pacific, like Japan, South Korea, and Australia, would deteriorate. As the

TABLE 12.1 Trade Dependency (in Percentage of Total Trade, 2017)

		US	NATO8*	Japan	S-Korea	Australia	Total
China	Export	20.0	16.6	6.5	4.1	1.9	49.1%
	Import	8.7	12.8	8.8	9.7	5.5	45.5%
Russia	Export	4.5	26.2	3.5	3.5	0.1	37.8%
	Import	4.9	27.8	3.2	3.2	0.2	39.3%

Source: OEC (2019), accessed 06.12.2019 at https://atlas.media.mit.edu/en/profile/country/chn

*NATO8 is the eight largest economies in NATO; Germany, UK, France, Italy, Spain, the Netherlands, Poland, and Canada (Turkey is excluded from this list).

figures in Table 12.1 indicate, the collapse of economic relations with the US and allies would potentially have a devastating effect on the Chinese and Russian economies.

Entrapment

Entrapment means being dragged into a conflict over an ally's interests that one does not share, or shares only partially, and occurs when one values the preservation of the alliance more than the cost of fighting for the ally's interests. An important determinant affecting both the risk of abandonment and the risk of entrapment is the degree to which the allies' interests that are in conflict with the adversary are shared. If these interests are similar and valued with about equal intensity, both the risk of entrapment as well as abandonment will be minimized, since both parties in the alliance presumably will be about equally ready to fight over them. On the other hand, if their interests are quite different, each partner will worry about being trapped, but each partner will also fear that the other may stand aside if their own interests are threatened. Although both China and Russia see the United States as the main adversary and view the US and allies as encroaching upon their respective spheres of influence, China and Russia have conflictive interests with the US in different geographic theatres; China faces the United States in the Asian maritime theater, while Russia today faces the US and allies in Eastern Europe and in the Middle East. The Soviet Union was a major military force in Asia during the Cold War, but today's Russia is not. By entering an alliance with mutual defense obligations, China and Russia would henceforth face the risk of being dragged into a conflict where it does not necessarily share the same viewpoint.

In Europe, Russia's relationship with the US/NATO started to deteriorate as a result of the Russian invasion of Georgia in 2008, and the tension increased further following the Ukraine Crisis in 2014. From the start of the Ukraine Crisis, China kept a very low profile and shunned any diplomatic initiatives. Adhering to a foreign policy of non-intervention, and loathe to give credence to anything that could be construed as giving sanction to interference in another state's internal affairs, including its own, China has refrained from recognizing South Ossetia and Abkhazia after the Russian invasion of Georgia in 2008, and thus avoided it for the very same reasons during the Ukraine Crisis.[53] Moreover, China didn't want to jeopardize its own close relationship with Ukraine, nor undermine its relations with other Eastern European countries in its 16+1 Initiative launched in 2012[54] or its economic cooperation with the European Union.

It is argued that China's official stand related to Russia and the Ukraine Crisis later turned more toward signs of anti-Western rhetoric, but that this primarily has to be seen as part of a shared Chinese and Russian desire to put up a united front vis-à-vis the United States and other Western countries than as indicative of China supporting Russian policies in Ukraine.[55] Former US President Obama approached China to seek support for a sovereign Ukraine and put more pressure on Russia, but China declined to do so;[56] instead Beijing embraced Putin when his Russia in the aftermath of Ukraine and Western sanctions shifted toward a more pro-China foreign policy.[57] China avoided direct support of Russia on the Ukraine issue, but willingly increased its cooperation with Russia after Ukraine. It would be quite a policy shift for China, moving from keeping a low profile in Russia's conflicts in Georgia and Ukraine to providing military support to Russia in similar conflicts, and it seems very unlikely that China would want to risk this kind of entrapment.

In East Asia, Taiwan, the South China Sea, and the Diaoyu/Senkaku islands dispute in the East China Sea are three flashpoints that could cause tension and even a shooting war between China and the United States. Moscow has traditionally taken a different view from Beijing concerning the Taiwan issue,[58] but Russia upholds Beijing's "One China" principle and it is expected that Russia finds its strategic partnership with Beijing far too important to risk jeopardizing it over Taiwan.[59] On the Diaoyu/Senkaku dispute, it is observed that the Russian debate on the issue considers China's claims more favorably, while Russia retains a position of formal neutrality, and its position on the conflict is not entrenched.[60] In July 2019, four Chinese and Russian bombers approached the Senkaku Islands flying in a joint formation, which is a very unusual exercise.[61]

After China refused to recognize the Permanent Court of Arbitration's 2016 ruling against Beijing's claims in the South China Sea, Russian President Vladimir Putin said that Russia is solidarizing with and supporting China's stance on the non-recognition of the court ruling, but also stated that Russia is not interfering in island disputes in the South China Sea, and that Russia is staying away because "we believe that interference of any non-regional power in the dispute will be bad for the settlement of this problem."[62] The same year, 2016, Russia took part in a naval drill with China in the South China Sea. Still, Russia also sells weapon platforms to Vietnam,[63] and Russian companies are the only ones extracting oil and gas on Vietnamese licenses within China's nine-dash line in the South China Sea.[64]

Russia seems to walk a fine line between supporting China, and at the same time retaining relations with other countries beyond China, to avoid becoming too reliant on its economic, political, and security relationship with China. In this regard, Russia's ties with Japan and India are particularly valuable.[65] Russia has for decades been the main provider of weapons platforms to India, and neither of these two countries want to lose each other as leverage vis-à-vis China.[66] To what extent Russia is able to pursue an independent policy and keep its relationships with Japan and India within a growing Sino-Russian alignment will be important indicators for how far China and Russia can take their relationship.

Another important determinant for entrapment to occur is the content of the alliance agreement. While an ambiguous agreement tends to maximize fears of abandonment, an explicit one that includes full mutual commitment to defend each other increases the risk of entrapment.[67] There is of course a vast difference between China and Russia signing a mutual non-aggression pact, versus a commitment to collective defense if the other part is under attack. A strategy of strong commitment and support will reduce one's bargaining leverage over the ally, and alliance bargaining considerations thus tend to favor a strategy of weak or ambiguous commitment. However, as Snyder notes, a strong commitment to defending each other tends to strengthen their bargaining power vis-à-vis the opponent. [68]

Abandonment

Under bipolarity, abandonment from an alliance is regarded as less likely than in a multipolar world order.[69] Nevertheless, Russia is no ordinary secondary power, and I would argue that in a Sino-Russian alliance there is a risk of abandonment by Russia along the same lines as China toward the late 1950s no longer being willing to accommodate Soviet priorities, resulting in the Sino-Soviet split in 1960.[70] Abandonment may take a variety of specific forms; the ally may realign with the opponent, merely de-align by abrogating the alliance contract, may fail to make good on explicit commitments, or may fail to provide support in contingencies where support is expected.[71]

What could cause Russia to de-align from an alignment with China? One obvious trigger would of course be that China emerges as a larger threat to Russian interests than the US/NATO, either because China's military and economic capabilities surpass those of the US, or as a result of China shifting toward a more offensive defense posture toward Russia. Furthermore, it could be caused by Russian fear of entrapment and reduced independence pursuing its own foreign policy, or by China abandoning its reassurance policy toward Russia, either as a calculated risk or due to miscalculations in Beijing, ignoring or misunderstanding Russian security concerns. An interesting region in this respect is the Arctic.

Russia is adjusting to China's growing influence in Northeast Asia and Central Asia,[72] but in the Arctic, Russia is the dominant power vis-à-vis China. After initial hesitation, Russia has recently facilitated for a growing Chinese presence in the region,[73] and the development of Sino-Russian cooperation in the Arctic is causing concern in Washington, reflected in a number of Arctic strategy papers issued lately by various US government agencies.[74] China's ability to use the Arctic as strategic space will remain limited, and depends on Russian willingness to facilitate for a Chinese presence. While the US is able to make use of NATO allies in the region as forward intelligence posts, China has no equivalent in the region, unless Russia is willing to serve as China's first line of defense.

In its 2019 report on the Chinese military, the US Department of Defense indicates that China seeks a strengthened military presence in the Arctic Ocean, including the possibility of deploying submarines to the region as a deterrent against nuclear attacks.[75] It would be difficult for China to project naval power into the Arctic Ocean through the relatively narrow and shallow Bering Strait undetected, meaning that Russia as well as the United States would be aware of such an operation. Moreover, a long-term deployment of Chinese SSBNs in the Arctic Ocean necessitates some form of Russian support, and possibly China operating a naval base on Russian soil in the Arctic.

If Russia accommodates for China to operate its SSBNs in the Arctic Ocean as part of a Chinese nuclear second-strike capability, the United States and NATO countries would see this as a huge step toward an alliance from the current Sino-Russian arrangement, and military activity in the Arctic Ocean would increase significantly, including from the US Navy. Would Russia be willing to facilitate for such an arrangement, or would it rather lead Russia to push back against China? In 1958, discussing the nature of their military cooperation, the Soviet Union proposed to China the creation of a joint submarine fleet, and the establishing of Soviet naval installations on the Chinese coast enabling Russia to overcome geographic constraints facing its Pacific Fleet in its rivalry with the United States.[76] China's supreme leader Mao Zedong reportedly reacted very strongly against this proposal, and saw it as a Soviet attempt to control and dominate the relationship.[77] This episode was an important factor leading to the Sino-Soviet split.[78] Today, the tables have turned, with China being the dominant part in the Sino-Russian partnership, and a Chinese request for a strong naval presence in the Arctic Ocean or even a base in Russia could contribute to undermining the Sino-Russian partnership rather than strengthening it, and cause tension in the Sino-Russian partnership to such an extent that Russia de-aligned.

The Arctic is literally Russia's backyard, and it has gradually been rebuilding some of its Cold War military and strategic presence in the region.[79] Part of the buildup is for soft security missions and increased activity along the Northern Sea Route, but Russia's main concern in the region is to ensure perimeter defense of the Kola Peninsula, its Northern Fleet, and the survivability of its second-strike nuclear assets.[80]

Russia could in theory turn and realign with the United States, as China ultimately did a decade after the Sino-Soviet split. However, it would be more difficult for the United States to play the "Russia card" against China than it was to play the "China card" against the Soviet Union, for three main reasons. First of all, and most important, Russia is not a great power in Asia, and would thus not be able to counterbalance China the same way as China could contribute to balance Soviet in the Cold War. Russia's economy is now smaller than that of South Korea, and Russia's military posture is US/NATO dominated. While exercises such as Vostok-2018 demonstrated Russia's ability to rapidly reinforce the Russian Far East during peacetime, it is doubtful whether such moves could be replicated in wartime, with insufficient railway systems and airlift capacity to transport large military units rapidly over long distances.[81] Second, despite improved relations between the US/NATO and Russia, Moscow would very likely still want to keep a solid defense posture facing toward NATO, which leads to the third factor; Russia has not forgotten the history of imperial over-stretch during the Cold War. The fact that the Soviet Union had to defend two flanks, facing NATO and China at the same time, contributed to the fall of the Soviet Union. Russia is of course a different animal altogether than the Soviet Union, and a more coherent state, yet Russia would want to avoid the costs involved preparing for a two flank posture.

The way ahead

The existing "strategic partnership" between China and Russia serves both parties well. It allows them to keep their strategic rear safe, and to channel resources into more pressing theaters, without any significant commitments to each other. This security arrangement is a major achievement for both China and Russia. The costs associated with entering into a formal alliance with mutual defense responsibilities might be larger than the benefits. An alliance could damage both Russia and China's hugely important economic ties with the United States and Europe, cause entrapment, and possibly embroil China in Russia's military adventures in Europe and the Middle East, and Russia in China's more assertive policy in Asia. Moreover, the weakest part in the alliance, Russia, would be concerned about growing dependency on China, reducing its own room for maneuver in its foreign policy.

Nonetheless, even though the current Sino-Russian security arrangement serves their geopolitical interests well, it still has a way to go before it resembles an alliance. Thus, there is room for China and Russia to continue improving their security and defense ties under the threshold of an alliance, and without committing to fight each other's wars. They could for instance increase intelligence-sharing, strengthen ties between their defense industries, and increase R&D cooperation. However, if Sino-Russian military ties continue to strengthen, at some point the United States and NATO might perceive their cooperation as passing the threshold of a "de facto" alliance even without a formal alliance agreement.

A Sino-Russian military alliance would move international politics closer toward two confronting blocs, with the United States and allies forming the other bloc. Likewise, the role of the United States as common denominator could intensify, pushing China and Russia closer together. These two developments could easily reinforce each other as great-power rivalry takes on its own dynamic. In fact, the early signs of a possible division into two blocs are evident already, as the United States is considering its economic relationship with China due to rising concerns over the security–economy nexus, with the 5G debate as the most prominent example. At the same time, the US and Europe have economic sanctions in place toward Russia. Economic interdependence, the very fabric that is supposed to promote stability and increase the cost of power politics and alliance formation, could very soon become fragmented and undermined. As China and Russia are authoritarian states, ideology could soon also contribute to further division, between a maritime-based axis of democracies of the United States and allies on one side, facing the two continental-based, more authoritarian powers, China and Russia, on the other side.

Europe has for obvious geographic reasons had a different threat perception than the United States with regard to China's rise, and when the United States announced its "pivot to Asia" a few years ago, European capitals voiced concerns about Washington neglecting European security, with reference to Russia's military modernization. At the time, it was a possibility that China's rise would cause some degree of friction in transatlantic relations. Developments during 2019 contributed to reverse this trend, with the European Union naming China a systemic rival, and later in the year NATO also took an interest in China, moving Europe's take on China closer to that of the United States. A growing Sino-Russian alignment would contribute to further the European perception of China as a possible security threat. Great power politics and rivalry are definitely back, and the Sino-Russian alignment plays a central role in the new configuration of world politics.

Notes

1 For instance, in March 2019, the US–China Economic and Security Review Commission under the US Congress organized a hearing titled "An Emerging China-Russia Axis? Implications for the United States in an Era of Strategic Competition." See also Newth Gingrich, "China-Russia Military Alliance Would Have Incredible Impact on US," *Fox News*, October 27, 2019, https://www.foxnews.com/opinion/newt-gingrich-china-russia-strategic-alliance; and Stephen Blank, "The Russo-Chinese Alliance Emerges," *The Hill*, 21 October, 2019, https://thehill.com/opinion/international/466681-the-russo-chinese-alliance-emerges.

2 Jo Inge Bekkevold and Bobo Lo, eds., *Sino-Russian Relations in the 21ˢᵗ Century* (London: Palgrave Macmillan, 2019).

3 Glenn H. Snyder, "Alliance Theory: A Neorealist First Cut," *Journal of International Affairs*, vol. 44, no. 1 (1990): 106.

4 Øystein Tunsjø, *The Return of Bipolarity in World Politics: China, the United States, and Geostructural Realism* (New York: Columbia University Press, 2018).

5 Kenneth N. Waltz, *Theory of International Politics* (Long Grove, IL: Waveland Press, Inc., 1979).

6 Angela Stent, *Putin's World: Russia Against the West and with the Rest* (New York: Twelve, 2019); and Bekkevold and Lo (2019).

7 White House, *National Security Strategy of the United States* (Washington, DC, December, 2017), 25, https://www.whitehouse.gov/wp-content/uploads/2017/12/NSS-Final-12-18-2017-0905.pdf

8 For a discussion on how to measure state behavior, see Adam P. Liff, "Whither the Balancers? The Case for a Methodological Reset," *Security Studies*, vol. 25 (2016): 420–459; Darren J. Lim and Zack Cooper, "Reassessing Hedging: The Logic of Alignment in East Asia," *Security Studies*, vol. 24, no. 4 (2015): 696–727; Zachary Selden "Balancing Against or Balancing With? The Spectrum of Alignments and the Endurance of American Hegemony," *Security Studies*, vol. 22 (2013): 330–364.

9 Lim and Cooper (2015); Selden (2013) uses the term soft and hard alignment, with formal alliance agreement as proof of hard alignment, and joint exercises as soft.

10 Lim and Cooper (2015), 705.

11 "Treaty of Good-Neighborliness and Friendly Cooperation Between the People's Republic of China and the Russian Federation," July 24, 2001, Ministry of Foreign Affairs (PRC) website at http://www.fmprc.gov.cn/mfa_eng/wjdt_665385/2649_665393/t15771.shtml.

12 Richard Weitz, *Parsing Chinese-Russian Military Exercises* (Carlisle, PA: U.S. Army War College, Strategic Studies Institute, 2015), 28–32.

13 Paul N. Schwartz, "The Military Dimension in Sino-Russian Relations," in Jo Inge Bekkevold and Bobo Lo, eds., *Sino-Russian Relations in the 21st Century* (London: Palgrave Macmillan, 2019), 87–112.

14 Zi Yang, "Vostok 2018: Russia and China's Diverging Common Interests," *The Diplomat*, September 17, 2018, https://thediplomat.com/2018/09/vostok-2018-russia-and-chinas-diverging-common-interests/

15 Schwartz (2019).

16 Ethan Meick, "China-Russia Military-to-Military Relations: Moving Toward a Higher Level of Cooperation," *Staff Research Report of the U.S.-China Economic and Security Review Commission* (Washington, DC, March 20, 2017), 14–15, https://www.uscc.gov/research/china-russia-military-military-relations-moving-toward-higher-level-cooperation

17 Schwartz (2019).

18 Minnie Chan, "Vladimir Putin Says Russia Is Helping China Build a Missile Early Warning System," *South China Morning Post*, October 4, 2019, https://www.scmp.com/news/china/military/article/3031639/vladimir-putin-says-russia-helping-china-build-missile-early.

19 Richard Weitz, "Sino-Russian Security Ties," in Michael S. Chase, et.al., eds., *Russia-China Relations: Assessing Common Ground and Strategic Fault Lines*, The National Bureau of Asian Research Special Report No. 66, July, 2017: 27–36, https://www.nbr.org/publication/russia-china-relations-assessing-common-ground-and-strategic-fault-lines/

20 Government of Russian Federation, "On Signing the Agreement Between the Government of the Russian Federation and the Government of the People's Republic of China on Cooperation in Ensuring International Information Security," April 30, 2015, https://cyber-peace.org/wp-content/uploads/2013/05/RUS-CHN_CyberSecurityAgreement201504_InofficialTranslation.pdf.

21 Jeanne L. Wilson, *Strategic Partners: Russian-Chinese Relations in the Post-Soviet Era* (Armonk, NY and London, England: M. E. Sharpe, 2004), 50.

22 Schwartz (2019).

23 Bernard D. Cole, *The Great Wall at Sea: China's Navy in the Twenty-First Century* (Annapolis, MD: Naval Institute Press, 2010), 16.

24 Schwartz (2019).

25 The Observatory of Economic Complexity (OEC), *China*, accessed 22.06.2019 at https://atlas.media.mit.edu/en/profile/country/chn.

26 US Energy Information Administration, "Russia Exports Most of Its Crude Oil Production, Mainly to Europe," *Today in Energy*, November 14, 2017, accessed 22.06.2019 at https://www.eia.gov/todayinenergy/detail.php?id=33732

27 Gazprom, *Gazprom Export website*, 2019, accessed 22.06.2019 at http://www.gazp romexport.ru/en/statistics/

28 Alexander Lukin, *The Bear Watches the Dragon: Russia's Perceptions of China and the Evolution of Russian-Chinese Relations Since the Eighteenth Century* (New York/London: M. E. Sharpe, 2003), 44–45.

29 John P. LeDonne, *The Russian Empire and the World 1700-1917: The Geopolitics of Expansion and Containment* (New York: Oxford University Press, 1997), 178–199.

30 IMF, *World Economic Outlook*, Database, April, 2019.

31 Ibid.

32 SIPRI, *Military Expenditure Database* (Stockholm: Stockholm International Peace Research Institute, 2018).

33 Nicholas John Spykman, *America's Strategy in World Politics: The United States and the Balance of Power* (New York: Harcourt, Brace and Company, 1942), 8.

34 For an introduction to the importance of geography in power politics, see for instance Stephen M. Walt, *The Origins of Alliance* (Ithaca and London: Cornell University Press, 1978); Jakub J. Grygiel, *Great Powers and Geopolitical Change* (Baltimore, MD: The Johns Hopkins University Press, 2006); and Spykman (1942).

35 See Robert L. Rothstein, *Alliances and Small Powers* (New York: Columbia University Press, 1968), 29; Hans J. Morgenthau, *Politics Among Nations: The Struggle for Power and Peace* (New York: Alfred A. Knopf, 1954), 181–4; Waltz 1979.

36 IMF (2019), SIPRI (2018).

37 IMF (2019).

38 SIPRI (2018).

39 Andrew S. Erickson, Lyle J. Goldstein, and Carnes Lord, eds. *China Goes to Sea: Maritime Transformation in Comparative Historical Perspective* (Annapolis, MD: Naval Institute Press, 2009).

40 Robert S. Ross, "Keeping Up with China's PLAN," *The National Interest*, May/June, 2018, Number 155, 53–61.

41 Øystein Tunsjø, "Global Power Shift, Geography, and Maritime East Asia," in Jo Inge Bekkevold and Geoffrey Till, eds., *International Order at Sea: How It Is Challenged. How It Is Maintained* (London: Palgrave MacMillan, 2016), 41–62.

42 You Ji, "China's Emerging Indo-Pacific Naval Strategy," *Asia Policy*, no. 22, July (2016): 11–19.

43 Alexander Gabuev, "Unwanted but Inevitable: Russia's Deepening Partnership with China Post-Ukraine," in Jo Inge Bekkevold and Bobo Lo, eds., *Sino-Russian Relations in the 21st Century* (London: Palgrave Macmillan, 2019); Schwartz (2019).

44 Gabuev (2019).

45 John Andreas Olsen, ed., "NATO and the North Atlantic: Revitalising Collective Defence," *Whitehall Papers*, March 6, 2017, RUSI.

46 For an in-depth study of Chinese reassurance policies toward Russia, see Christopher Weidacher Hsiung, *Too Big to Fail: China's Russia Policy in the Post-Cold War Period* (PhD dissertation), University of Oslo, 2019.

47 Snyder (1990), 120.

48 See Snyder (1990) for a discussion on benefits and costs in an alliance.

49 Snyder (1984), 468.

50 Ibid.

51 Ibid., 470.

52 Ibid., 467.

53 Niklas Swanström, "China's Stakes in the Ukraine Crisis," *Policy Brief*, Institute for Security and Development Policy, No. 147, March 12, 2014, http://isdp.eu/content/ uploads/publications/2014-swanstrom-chinas-stakes-in-the-ukraine-crisis.pdf.

54 The 16+1 format, also called the China–CEEC (Central and Eastern European Countries) summit, is a Chinese-initiated platform launched in 2012 to expand cooperation between Beijing and a group of 11 EU member states and 5 Balkan countries.

55 D. V. Kuznetsov, "China and the Ukrainian Crisis: From 'Neutrality' to 'Support' for Russia," *China Report*, vol. 52, no. 2 (2016): 92–111.

56 Swanström (2014).

57 Bekkevold and Lo (2019).

58 Jeanne L. Wilson, "China, Russia, and the Taiwan Issue: The View from Moscow," in James Bellacqua, ed., *The Future of China-Russia Relations* (Lexington, KY: The University Press of Kentucky, 2010), 293–311.

59 I-wei Jennifer Chang, "Taiwan and Russia Ties and the China Factor," *The Global Taiwan Brief*, vol. 4, no. 21 (2019): 4–6.

60 James D. J. Brown, "Towards an Anti-Japanese Territorial Front? Russia and the Senkaku/Diaoyu Dispute," *Europe-Asia Studies*, vol. 67, no. 6 (2015): 893–915.

61 The Japan Times, "Chinese and Russian Bombers Flew Near Senkakus in July, Japan Defense Ministry Says," *The Japan Times*, September 28, 2019, https://www.japantim es.co.jp/news/2019/09/28/national/chinese-russian-bombers-flew-near-senkakus -july-japan-defense-ministry-says/#.XefFkUxFwic.

62 TASS, "Putin: Russia Is Staying Out of South China Sea Dispute," Russian News Agency, September 5, 2016, https://tass.com/politics/898040.

63 Reuters, "Vietnam Places Orders for Russian Weapons Worth Over $1 Billion: TASS," *Reuters*, September 8, 2018, https://www.reuters.com/article/us-vietnam -russia-arms/vietnam-places-orders-for-russian-weapons-worth-over-1-billion-tass -idUSKCN1LO08K.

64 Bennett Murray, "Vietnam's Strange Ally in Its Fight with China," *Foreign Policy*, August 1, 2019, https://foreignpolicy.com/2019/08/01/vietnams-strange-ally-in-its -fight-with-china/.

65 Grønning (2019), in Bekkevold and Lo; and Bekkevold (2019).

66 Bekkevold (2019).

67 Snyder (1984), 473.

68 Ibid., 467.

69 Ibid., 485.

70 Andrew J. Nathan and Robert S. Ross, *The Great Wall and the Empty Fortress: China's Search for Security* (New York and London: W.W. & Norton, 1997), 36–46.

71 Snyder (1984), 466.

72 Bekkevold and Lo (2019).

73 Christopher Weidacher Hsiung and Tom Røseth, "The Arctic Dimension in Sino-Russian Relations," in Jo Inge Bekkevold and Bobo Lo, eds., *Sino-Russian Relations in the 21st Century* (London: Palgrave Macmillan, 2019), 167–187.

74 See for instance Department of Defense, *Report to Congress: Department of Defense Arctic Strategy*, Office of the Under Secretary of Defense for Policy (Washington, DC, June, 2019); Chief of Naval Operations, *Strategic Outlook for the Arctic* (Washington, DC: The United States Navy, January 2019), available at https://www.navy.mil/ strategic/Navy_Strategic_Outlook_Arctic_Jan2019.pdf; United States Coast Guard, *Arctic Strategic Outlook* (Washington, DC, April 2019), available at https://www.uscg .mil/Portals/0/Images/arctic/Arctic_Strategy_Book_APR_2019.pdf.

75 Department of Defense, *Annual Report to Congress: Military and Security Developments Involving the People's Republic of China 2019* (Washington D.C.: Office of the Secretary of Defense, 2019b), 114, retrieved 08.10.2019 from https://media.defens e.gov/2019/May/02/2002127082/-1/-1/1/2019_CHINA_MILITARY_POWER _REPORT.pdf.

76 Constantine Pleshakov, "Nikita Krushchev and Sino-Soviet Relations," in Odd Arne Westad, ed., *Brothers in Arms: The Rise and Fall of the Sino-Soviet Alliance 1945–1963*

(Washington D.C.: Woodrow Wilson Center Press with Stanford University Press, 1998), 226–245; Nathan and Ross (1997) 41; John W. Garver, "Review: Mao's Soviet Policies Reviewed Work," [Shi nian lunzhan, 1956–1966, Zhong Su guanxi huiyilu (Ten-Year War of Words, 1956–1966, a Memoir of Sino-Soviet Relations) by Wu Lengxi], *The China Quarterly*, No. 173 (March, 2003): 197–213.

77 Garver (2003), 205.
78 Nathan and Ross (1997).
79 Katarzyna Zysk, "Maritime Security and International Order at Sea in the Arctic Ocean," in Jo Inge Bekkevold and Geoffrey Till, eds., *International Order at Sea. How It Is Challenged. How It Is Maintained* (London: Palgrave MacMillan, 2016), 141–174.
80 Mathieu Boulègue, "Russia's Military Posture in the Arctic: Managing Hard Power in a 'Low Tension' Environment," *Research Paper* (London: Chatham House, June 28, 2019).
81 Schwartz (2019).

PART IV

Crisis management and mitigating conflict

13

REGIONAL SECURITY FLASHPOINTS

New developments in China's crisis management

Zhang Tuosheng

Since the end of the Cold War, the international situation has changed significantly, with peace and development becoming a major trend. But there are still many security hotspots, military conflicts, and local wars. The Korean Peninsula, Taiwan Strait, East China Sea, South China Sea, and the China–India border area emerge as security flashpoints from time to time and they all have a direct bearing on China's security interests. So far, none has erupted into a military conflict or war, for many reasons, a most important one of which is the peaceful foreign policy and increased crisis management on the part of China. This chapter analyzes and summarizes the development and changes of China's crisis management based on five major hot spots around China since 2010.

The Korean Peninsula

Hostility between the North and the South of the Korean Peninsula and between the US and DPRK did not disappear upon the end of the Cold War, which has actually never left the peninsula. This is the origin of the DPRK nuclear program and the nuclear crisis.

In 2009, the DPRK conducted a new "satellite" launch and the second nuclear test, leading to the third nuclear crisis. Despite strong international opposition, the country continued its nuclear and missile tests (including testing of hydrogen bomb and intercontinental ballistic missiles tests) and then crossed the nuclear threshold in 2017.

The third nuclear crisis led to complete suspension of the US–DPRK dialogue and the six-party talks. In 2010, the sinking of the navy frigate *Cheonan* and the shelling of Yeonpyeong[1] further intensified the peninsular situation.

The US and its allies then became increasingly tough toward the DPRK by renewing joint combat plans, frequently conducting large-scale joint military exercises, deploying missile defense systems in ROK, and threatening to attack the DPRK militarily. The peninsula stood at the brink of a military conflict or war.

In the face of escalating tension, China has been insisting on denuclearization, peace, and stability, and peaceful resolution through dialogue and stretched itself to manage crises.

With regard to the *Cheonan* incident, China actively promoted peace and talks, refused to directly condemn DPRK without sufficient evidence, and called on all parties to keep calm, exercise restraint, and refrain from escalating the situation. In the end, the President of the Security Council issued a statement to condemn the attackers and encourage the two sides to resume direct dialogue and consultation.

With regard to the Yeonpyeong Island incident, in addition to immediately sending special envoys to the ROK and the DPRK to push for restraint, the Chinese State Councilor Dai Bingguo also talked with the US Secretary of State Hilary Clinton over the phone, expressing a desire to work with the US to calm the situation down as quickly as possible. The Chinese effort was instrumental to relaxation of the Yeonpyeong Island crisis.

As the DPRK sprinted toward the nuclear threshold and the risk of a military conflict rose drastically, China on the one hand intensified sanctions mandated in UN Security Council resolutions and on the other hand explicitly rejected war and chaos on the Korean Peninsula or any attempt to resolve the Korean nuclear issue by force. In 2017, in order to restart the nuclear talks, China formally put forward the "dual-track" approach (to promote denuclearization in parallel with transforming the armistice to a peace mechanism) and the "suspension for suspension" proposal (with DPRK suspending its nuclear and missile tests and US–ROK suspending large-scale joint military exercises). It supported all parties concerned to seize the opportunities of the Pyeongchang Winter Olympics to improve relations and resume dialogue.

In early 2018, the DPRK initiated a new strategic line and expressed willingness to denuclearize through dialogue so as to focus on economic development. Then talks with countries concerned were resumed and the nuclear crisis markedly eased. A rare historical opportunity to denuclearize the Korean Peninsula has thus emerged.

In the new circumstances, China firmly supports the DPRK's new strategy and has quickly resumed its friendly cooperation with the DPRK. It supports the DPRK and ROK to improve and develop their relations through dialogue and to play a bigger role in the peninsular peace process. China also supports US–DPRK dialogue to overcome obstacles and make gradual, substantive progress with the dual-track approach. It is determined to assume more international obligations so as to advance the denuclearization of the peninsula.[2]

In July 2016, a serious crisis broke out between China and ROK against the backdrop of an intensified DPRK nuclear crisis. It was triggered by the US and ROK's official announcement to deploy THAAD in the ROK despite strong Chinese opposition. Believing that the move seriously undermined its security interests and China–US strategic stability, the Chinese government immediately expressed firm opposition and demanded that the THAAD deployment be stopped and the equipment be withdrawn. With the US and ROK insisting on the deployment, China began to prepare some military countermeasures and decided to suspend all official talks and exchanges with the ROK. Chinese ordinary people started to boycott Korean goods, companies, the "Korean Wave" and travel to ROK, with support even from some state media. The THAAD crisis drove China–ROK relations to their lowest point since establishment of diplomatic ties.

After taking office in the spring of 2017, the new Korean administration under President Moon Jae-in decided to delay the THAAD deployment, then allowed "temporary" deployment, and finally stated three Nos (no to considering additional THAAD deployment, no to joining the American missile defense system, no to developing a military alliance between the ROK, the US, and Japan). China quickly responded positively and agreed to work with the ROK to restore exchanges and cooperation in various fields at an early date. Since then, although the THAAD issue remains unresolved, China has begun to improve and resume relations with the ROK in the overall interest of denuclearization and strategic cooperative partnership.

In December of the same year, President Moon visited China. Bilateral relations were brought back onto the track of normal development. Since early 2018, the two sides have significantly strengthened cooperation in economic, trade, people-to-people exchanges, and denuclearization.

The East China Sea

China and Japan have a long-standing maritime dispute in the East China Sea. When their relations were normalized in 1972, a tacit agreement was reached to shelve the Diaoyu Islands dispute. For quite a long time, the sovereignty dispute had been in a relatively calm state.

After entering the new century, frictions gradually increased. China and Japan held over a dozen consultations and in 2008 reached a principled agreement on cooperation and joint development so as to turn the East China Sea into a "sea of peace, friendship and cooperation" as envisaged by the leaders of the two countries.

However, in 2010 and 2012, two crises happened due to the "ship collision incident"[3] and the "purchase of islands incident,"[4] pushing China–Japan relations to the lowest point since the normalization of relations. The second incident in particular aroused a strong nationalist sentiment in China, with large-scale anti-Japanese demonstrations in many Chinese cities, and even some violent acts against Japanese companies and goods.

The Chinese government reacted strongly to both incidents, lodging serious protests with the Japanese government, demanding immediate rectification, and suspending talks and exchanges. In the second crisis, it adopted a series of countermeasures, including announcing base points and baselines of the territorial sea of Diaoyu Dao and its affiliated islands, conducting normalized cruises in waters off the Diaoyu Dao by law-enforcement agencies, publishing a white paper entitled *Diaoyu Dao, an Inherent Territory of China,* and setting up an East China Sea Joint Operations Command Center to strengthen preparations for a military struggle.

The crisis in 2010 came to an end after the Japanese government released the detained Chinese captain. But the crisis in 2012 lasted several years and even at one point came to the brink of a military conflict. For more than three years, law-enforcement vessels from the two countries faced off inwaters off the Diaoyu Dao. Military aircrafts and warships repeatedly encountered each other in dangerous situations in the East China Sea. Both countries enhanced military preparations and the Japan–US alliance continued to strengthen. China–Japan relations were close to complete breakdown after China's announcement of its ADIZ in the East China Sea in October 2013 and Japanese Prime Minister Abe Shinzo's visit to the Yasukuni Shrine in December 2013.

In these serious circumstances, the Chinese government gradually took a series of crisis-management measures by enhancing persuasion and guidance of Chinese fishing boats in disputed waters, maintaining necessary communication with Japan, trying to guide domestic public opinion (for example by pointing out that "China and Japan will surely have a war" was wrong), regulating maritime law enforcement, making representations with Japan on the dangerous situation at sea and in the air, and investigating cases of dangerous encounters with a view to strengthening crisis prevention.

At the end of 2014, China and Japan reached a four-point principled agreement[5] on handling and improving China–Japan relations and top leaders had a meeting on the sideline of the APEC Summit. It became the turning point after the second crisis. Since then, dialogue and exchanges have gradually resumed and crisis management in the East China Sea has been further strengthened.

In May 2018, Premier Li Keqiang paid an official visit to Japan after attending a trilateral summit in Tokyo. One month later the China–Japan maritime and air liaison mechanism was formally launched. In December that year, Prime Minister Abe came to China for an official visit. It took the two countries six years to steer their relations back onto a normal track. At present, China and Japan are preparing for a possible state visit to Japan by President Xi Jinping next spring.

With the question of history and with structural contradictions, a crisis between China and Japan is much harder to manage than any other crisis. The lessons are worth summing up.

The South China Sea

China has long had disputes with some neighbors over sovereignty and maritime rights and interests in the South China Sea. But for a fairly long time after the end of the Cold War, the situation remained basically stable thanks to the efforts of relevant countries, especially China.[6]

However, in the wake of the global financial crisis in 2018, Vietnam, the Philippines, and other countries stepped up efforts to develop oil, gas and other resources in the disputed waters. More and more Chinese fishing boats got illegally detained in the disputed waters. Against this backdrop, the Chinese government intensified efforts to safeguard its sovereignty. Since 2010, tensions have risen sharply as the US got openly involved in regional sovereign disputes, thus turning the South China Sea into a major security hotspot in East Asia.

In April 2012, a standoff between Chinese and Philippine vessels occurred on Huangyan Island/Scarborough Shoal, triggered by an attempt by a Philippine warship to seize Chinese fishing boats. In December 2013, with the support of the US and Japan, the Philippines unilaterally requested arbitration at the UN International Tribunal for the Law of the Sea, further aggravating China–Philippines relations and the situation in the South China Sea. Between May and July 2014, the worst crisis since their 1988 maritime conflict erupted between China and Vietnam: Vietnam tried to stop China's HYSY-981 oil rig from exploring in waters of Zhongjian Dao, Xisha Islands/Paracel Islands.[7] A military conflict was imminent. From 2013 to 2015, China carried out land reclamation on some of its islands and reefs. The US described the move as "militarization of the South China Sea" and expressed its opposition. But on the other hand, it increased its military presence there, including expanding off-shore military reconnaissance on China, intensifying "freedom of navigation" operations in waters near China's islands and reefs, and conducting more frequent joint military exercises.

In the face of this serious deterioration, the Chinese government made great efforts to stabilize the situation by strengthening crisis management while safeguarding its sovereignty.

In the confrontation over Huangyan Island in 2012, China only sent law-enforcement vessels to rescue fishing boats threatened by the Philippine warship and maintained diplomatic communications all through with the Philippines. After its fishing boats had been rescued and effective control over the Huangyan Island had been restored, China did not take further action against other islands or reefs illegally occupied by the Philippines. In the arbitration case, China expressed firm opposition while insisting that the Philippines should return to the path of resolving the dispute through bilateral talks.

In June 2016, the Duterte Administration came to power and decided to shelve the South China Sea arbitration case and avoid confrontation with China. Seizing the opportunity, China immediately resumed dialogue with the Philippines and their relations quickly returned onto the track of friendly cooperation. Since then, China has quickly become the Philippines' largest trading partner. Bilateral cooperation in other areas has grown rapidly. In 2018, the two sides decided to establish a comprehensive strategic cooperative relationship and signed two memoranda of understanding on jointly promoting the construction of the Belt and Road Initiative and cooperation in oil and gas development. In 2019, the two set up an intergovernmental joint steering committee and an enterprise working group on oil and gas development cooperation. China–Philippines relations have continued moving forward.

In the Sino-Vietnamese "South of Zhongjian Dao incident" in 2014, China sent law enforcement ships to protect its exploration platform against serious threats and to expel the interfering Vietnamese ships, insisted that the exploration must continue, made solemn representations against Vietnam's illegal maritime interference and anti-China violence at home, and demanded that the Vietnamese government rectify its mistakes as soon as possible. At the height of the tension, China sent senior officials to Vietnam for dialogue upon invitation. Despite its military superiority, China exercised a high degree of restraint. In mid-July, after completing its mission, and before an imminent typhoon, the oil rig was withdrawn from the site.

At the end of 2014, China and Vietnam agreed to follow the existing common understanding between their leaders, manage differences on the sea, and maintain the overall interests of their relations and peace and stability in the South China Sea. In 2015, with successful exchanges of visits by top leaders, bilateral relations basically returned to normal.[8]

Vietnam and the Philippines had the most serious maritime frictions with China in the South China Sea. As China has improved its overall relations with them and disputes have been calmed down, the situation in the South China Sea has been significantly eased since the second half of 2016. In addition, important progress has been made in consultation between China and ASEAN to reach an agreement on a code of conduct (COC) in the South China Sea. In August 2019, the China–ASEAN foreign ministers' meeting generated a single-draft COC text for negotiation. The two sides are expected to reach a formal agreement within three years.

Compared with the sovereignty disputes with neighbors, China–US disputes in the South China Sea are more complex and acute, involving deeper issues such as regional power structure and maritime order. They are the focus of China's crisis management.

In recent years, the PLA has strengthened its surveillance and law-enforcement operations with regard to American military vessels and aircrafts illegally entering waters under Chinese jurisdiction. It has earnestly implemented the relevant rules in the two CBM memoranda[9] between China and the US to guard against emergencies. The maritime military security consultation mechanism also continues functioning.

Since 2013, China's construction work on its own islands and reefs has significantly changed its long-standing disadvantaged position, increased its presence and ability to defend, project, and provide public security products there, and enabled a strong counterbalance to the strengthened US military presence in the South China Sea. In addition, in response to the American accusation that China is "threatening freedom of navigation" and "militarizing the South China Sea," China argues that the SLOCs in the South China Sea are always free and unimpeded, that the increased US military presence and activities have driven the militarization of the South China Sea, and that to ease the serious disputes between the two sides, China and the US must have serious and deep strategic dialogue.

In recent years, although military frictions between China and the US in the South China Sea have been on the rise and there have been some dangerous cases, as both sides attach great importance to crisis prevention, serious military crisis has so far been avoided.

China–India border area

China and India have long had territorial disputes and even had a border military conflict in 1962. After the end of the Cold War, the two sides maintained peace and stability on the whole through CBMs and border negotiations. However, from June to August 2017, Indian troops crossed the border to block China's building of a road in the Doklam area, leading to the longest military standoff since 1962.

For more than two months, hundreds of Indian border troops, with weapons, tents, and bulldozers, crossed the Sikkim sector of the border into Chinese territory to obstruct China's road construction activities, thus going into tense confrontation with Chinese border troops.

After the Indian invasion, the Chinese government urgently lodged solemn representations with India through diplomatic channels, demanding that it immediately withdraw its troops. A number of Chinese government departments and state media also voiced their strong protest and condemnation against the illegal transgression. But for some time, instead of withdrawing its troops, India continued to increase its forces. The illegal behavior aroused strong indignation among the Chinese public and many on Chinese social media called for military operations against India.

In these circumstances, while further strengthening military deployment to create a strong deterrence against India, China also continued with great restraint to engage with India and strive for a negotiated solution. In addition, China also issued a government document to fully explain the truth and demonstrate China's solemn position to win understanding and support from the international and domestic public for China's efforts to safeguard sovereignty and seek peaceful settlement of disputes.

On August 28, 2017, India withdrew all its personnel and equipment to its side of the border. The 71-day standoff came to an end. Chinese border troops continue to patrol and garrison the Doklam area. In September, Indian Prime Minister Modi attended the BRICS summit in Xiamen, China and held talks with President Xi. In 2018, the Indian leader paid two more visits to China. Leaders of the two countries agree that a sound China–India relationship will be an important positive factor for world stability. China–India relations, which were severely damaged by the Doklam incident, have been quickly restored and improved.

The peaceful resolution of the Doklam crisis is an ideal outcome for both countries. In terms of power, if they go to war, China will win in the battlefield, but a battlefield victory will not necessarily be a true victory for China. A Sino-Indian military conflict will likely drive India into a formal alliance with the US, Japan, and Australia, which will completely alter the geopolitical landscape.[10]

The Taiwan Strait

After the end of the Cold War, the situation across the Taiwan Strait was strained due to the development of pro-independence forces in Taiwan and the promotion of relations with Taiwan by the US. The third military crisis between China and the US broke out in the Taiwan Strait in 1995–1996. After Ma Ying-jeou of the Kuomintang came to power in 2008, the two sides of the Taiwan Strait agreed to uphold the 1992 Consensus and oppose Taiwan's independence, resulting in a trend of peaceful development.

However, since the regime change in Taiwan in the spring of 2016, the newly elected DPP Tsai Ing-wen's administration has refused to accept the 1992 Consensus and promoted gradual and cultural independence, poisoning cross-strait relations again. More seriously, in the three years since 2017, the US congress has passed a number of Taiwan-related bills that seriously undermine the "one China principle" and elevate relations with Taiwan. In addition, since the summer of 2018, US warships crossing the Taiwan Strait have become a regular sight. In this situation, the possibility of another crisis is increasing.

In the face of this serious situation, the Chinese mainland has comprehensively intensified the struggle against Taiwan independence. Since 2017, PLA military planes and warships have flown and sailed around the island and begun to fly across the central line in the Taiwan Strait to deter the pro-independence forces. The Chinese mainland has also increased its constraints on Taiwan's "international space."

The Chinese government still adheres to the policy of peaceful reunification and keeps three direct cross-strait links and non-governmental economic cooperation. In January 2019, in his five-point proposal for peaceful reunification, President Xi proposed that the two sides should work together to promote national rejuvenation, jointly explore a plan of "two systems" adapted to Taiwan, and deepen integrated development of the two sides.

Between China and the US, the first round of the Sino-American struggle after President Trump took office was the Taiwan issue.[11] After repeated solemn representations from China, President Trump reiterated that the US would stick to the "one China policy" in the first phone conversation with his Chinese counterpart. Since then, while continuously making solemn representations and expressing firm opposition to the various Taiwan-related acts passed by the US congress and the increased American military activities in the Taiwan strait, the Chinese government has started to comprehensively strengthen military preparations with a view to preventing foreign military interventions in Taiwan.

At present, on the Taiwan question, China and the US and their militaries are still engaging with each other, and crisis management is still an important topic in their communications. In May 2019, during the 3rd Asia-Pacific security consultation, the two militaries stressed the need to maintain open and clear communication, especially in times of crisis. The Chinese and American defense ministers have agreed in several meetings to deepen communication, strengthen risk and crisis management, and make the Mil-to-Mil Relationship a stabilizer of bilateral relations. There is no doubt that the Taiwan Strait is the top priority for crisis management between China and the US.

However, it must be pointed out that the Chinese government always considers the Taiwan question an internal rather than an international affair. China will strive, to the best of its ability, for peaceful reunification with the utmost sincerity, but will not undertake to renounce the use of force. China will be forced to use force if Taiwanese independence forces or external interfering forces want to separate Taiwan from China.

New developments in China's crisis management: Evaluation and summary

The overview given in the previous sections clearly indicates many new developments in China's crisis management under the guidance of an independent foreign policy of peace. These practices have played an important role in China safeguarding national security, preventing conflict or war, and maintaining regional peace and stability.

These new developments are mainly manifested in four aspects.

The first is a significantly higher crisis-management awareness.

Historically, although the older generations of Chinese leaders also experienced a lot of international crises and had rich practice in dealing with them, crisis management was, for a long time, not an important part of Chinese diplomatic and military strategy.

In the new international situation after the end of the Cold War and through a series of security crises with the US, the Chinese strategic research circle started to study crisis management seriously and the Chinese government also began to attach more importance to it. At the turn of the century, China set up top-leader hotlines with the US and Japan and agreed to carry out military maritime security consultation with the US. The momentum was kept up in the first decade of the new century.

However, for China, a significant increase in crisis-management awareness came after 2010. A number of hotspots in the surrounding area, emerging almost at the same time – in particular, the two successive crises with Japan – played a catalytic role in Chinese leaders and government departments becoming more crisis-aware.

In 2014, China and Japan reached a four-point principled agreement, one of which points was to establish a bilateral crisis management mechanism and to avoid unforeseen events. This was a major step forward. In 2015, China published a white paper on China's military strategy, and for the first time strengthening crisis management became a part of its military strategy. In the same year, the new National Security Law was promulgated, with a clear statement that "the state shall establish a national security crisis management system featuring unified leadership, coordination, order and efficiency." Since then, the diplomatic and defense services have increasingly called for the strengthening of crisis management. Crisis management has become part of the curriculum in many colleges and universities, especially military colleges.

Second, the principles of crisis management have been enriched and developed. Historically, the old generation of Chinese leaders developed some basic crisis-management principles in dealing with lots of military crises, such as, "despise the enemy strategically and attach importance to the enemy tactically," "on just grounds, to our advantage and with restraint," "two hands to two hands" and so on.

In the several crises with the US in the early years after the end of the Cold War, Chinese leaders at that time put forward some new principles, such as "give top priority to conduct dialogue, increase trust and avoid confrontation," "always bear in mind the overall situation of bilateral relations even during the struggles," "fight without breaking up," and strictly observe and make full use of the norms of international law.

In the past ten years, under the new security situation, while generally adhering to the above principles, the new generation of Chinese leaders has also put forward some new propositions, such as "no conflict, no confrontation," to "strengthen the management of differences," "adhere to the bottom-line thinking, focus on preventing and resolving major risks," and "military preparation" is "an important guarantee to contain crisis."

Third, the construction of crisis management mechanisms has been further strengthened. Improved crisis management mechanisms will be the fundamental guarantee for effective crisis management. In the past decade, China has made great progress in this regard:

1) By strengthening the core role of the top party and state leader, establishing the Central Leading Group on Maritime Rights and Interests (2012) and the Central National Security Commission (2013), and strengthening the role of the Central Foreign Affairs Commission (2018),[12] the security decision-making and crisis management capacity of the top level of the CPC and the national government has been further strengthened.

2) External communication mechanisms have been widely established. In addition to hotlines and security talks with Russia, US, France, and Japan, China has also set up various hotlines and security talks and dispute-consultation mechanisms with India, ROK and ASEAN countries. Sending special envoys has become an important means of communication in emergencies.

3) Great progress has been made in establishing bilateral and multilateral military and security CBMs with relevant countries. For example, China signed two CBM MOUs and the relevant annexes with the US in 2014 and 2015, adopted the Code for Unplanned Encounters at Sea (CUES) at the

Western Pacific Naval Symposium in 2014, reached an agreement with ASEAN countries on the application of CUES in the South China Sea in 2016, and signed the MOU on maritime and air liaison mechanism with Japan in 2018.

4) China has become increasingly active in participating in and hosting regional multilateral security dialogues, such as ARF, ADMM plus, Shangri-La Dialogue, SCO summits, Beijing Xiangshan Forum, CICA, and WPNS.

Fourth, crisis-management capability has been strengthened. Successful crisis management requires not only soft capabilities such as awareness, principles, and mechanisms but also hard power in terms of the economy, the military, science and technology, intelligence, and law enforcement.

Over the past decade, China's economy has continued to grow. In the crisis response, it has employed the roles of both hard power and soft power.

Ongoing national defense and military reform drives the growth of China's military power, giving the country a more credible military deterrence in crises, which is essential to contain crises and avoid military conflict.

With technological development and the restructuring of intelligence institutions, China's ability to collect information and intelligence and conduct comprehensive research and analysis has been strengthened, providing a stronger guarantee for improved crisis management.

The establishment of the China Coast Guard in 2013 and the integration of maritime law enforcement capabilities have completely changed the past situation in which maritime law enforcement forces were dispersed and weak. This restructuring has played an important role for China to strengthen maritime rights protection and conduct relevant diplomacy and crisis management.

In addition, in recent years, the Chinese government's ability to guide domestic public opinion has also gradually strengthened.

While fully recognizing the positive progress China has made in crisis management in the past decade, to be frank there are still some shortcomings and room for improvement in China's crisis management as follows:

1. Hotlines became unavailable prior to or during some crises when they were needed most.
2. In certain crises, due to domestic public opinion not being guided in a timely manner, under the influence of strong nationalist sentiment some violent and unlawful acts occurred during domestic demonstrations and protests, resulting in negative international influence.
3. In some crises, countermeasures were upgraded drastically within a short period of time and even all dialogue and exchange with the other side were suspended, which intensified the crisis situation instead of resolving the disputes.
4. Some decisions to maintain sovereignty and rights and interests were made without thorough consideration, coordination or a contingency plan, leading to unexpected emergencies and danger.

5. Insufficient attention was paid to the interconnections between various security flashpoints and crisis events in the surrounding areas. As a result, at one point, China had to face multiple crises at the same time, which obviously made it more difficult to manage these crises.

Compared with the positive progress, these shortcomings are obviously secondary and arguably an inevitable price to be paid in achieving progress. But it is very important to recognize these shortcomings, be courageous enough to sum up the lessons and find practical improvement measures. Only by so doing will China do a better job in future crisis management.

In *Chinese International Military Security Crisis Behavior Analysis* published in 2010, I wrote, "In more than 60 years, with evolving international situation and domestic and foreign policies, China's international military security crisis behavior has changed dramatically, drawing a trajectory from military confrontation to crisis management and from conflict avoidance to win–win." It was a summary of the fact that China was involved in many conflicts and wars in the early stages of the Cold War, had basically avoided military conflicts since the start of reform and opening up (except for one on the border with Vietnam) and had not had any military conflict after the end of the Cold War.

Yet it was from that year that China began to face increasing security challenges in its neighboring area. In 2014, the year of the one-hundredth anniversary of the outbreak of World War I, some international analysts even compared the situation in East Asia to that on the eve of World War I and believed that a military conflict between China and Japan was inevitable. Almost five years have passed, and, although interest differences and disputes still exist, there has been no military conflict in East Asia and the situations in the East China Sea and the South China Sea and on the Korean Peninsula have apparently eased. China's foreign policy of peace and its crisis-management ability have stood the test.

In the future, to achieve a peaceful rise, China has to properly resolve its disputes with many countries, especially with its neighboring countries and the USA. China's long-term goal is to develop a new type of international relations featuring mutual respect, mutual benefit and win–win, and finally build a community of a shared future for humanity. There is a long way to go. In this long journey, strengthening crisis management remains an important task for China. But it will not stop there. To better integrate crisis management with dispute resolution and seek common development will be the unswerving direction of China's foreign policy.

Notes

1 On March 26, 2010, the South Korean navy frigate *Cheonan* exploded and sank while patrolling in the Yellow Sea. Later South Korea and the United States suspected the ship had suffered military attack by North Korea. On November 23, 2010, North and South Korea exchanged artillery fire when South Korean artillery performed a drill near Yeonpyeong Island.

2 Following the repeated deadlock of the US–DPRK nuclear talks, China put forward the draft UN Security Council resolution with Russia in December 2019. The main content of the draft included: reaffirming the commitment of all parties to the denuclearization of the Korean peninsula; urging the US and the DPRK to continue dialogue, and calling for the resumption of the six-party talks; and deciding to lift some sanctions against the DPRK based on its compliance with the resolution.

3 On September 7, 2010, a Chinese fishing boat collided with two Japanese coast guard patrol boats in waters off the Diaoyu Dao. Japan arrested the captain of the Chinese fishing boat on suspicion of "obstructing official duties" and later decided to file a lawsuit against him.

4 In early 2012, the governor of Tokyo Shintaro Ishihara, a major representative of Japan's right-wing forces, launched a campaign to "raise money to buy the island." On September 11, 2012, the Noda administration of the Democratic Party of Japan "purchased" part of the Diaoyu Islands and nationalized them in the name of "maintaining administration of the islands in a stable manner" despite the repeated solemn representations and objections of the Chinese government.

5 The four-point principled agreement includes adhering to the spirit of the four political documents between China and Japan, overcoming historical obstacles, establishing a crisis management mechanism, and resuming dialogue. See "China, Japan Reach Four-Point Principled Agreement," Xinhua News Agency, November 7, 2014.

6 In the early 1990s, China's proposition of "shelving disputes and engaging joint development" and its position of peacefully resolving disputes in accordance with international law and the principles of the UNCLOS were welcomed by ASEAN countries. In 2002, China and ASEAN signed the Declaration on the Conduct of Parties in the South China Sea.

7 At the time, hundreds of Chinese and Vietnamese ships were locked in a fierce maritime confrontation. There have also been violent attacks on Chinese companies in several provinces and cities, leading to the evacuation of large numbers of Chinese nationals from Vietnam.

8 In 2017 and 2019, China and Vietnam faced off again over Vietnam's attempt to develop oil and gas in cooperation with other countries in waters of Vanguard Bank of the Nansha/Spratly Islands. The two standoffs were less tense than the one in 2014 and both ended with Vietnam stopping unilateral drilling.

9 The two CBM memoranda were signed in 2014. One is about the mechanism for notification of major military activities and the other is about the rules of behavior for safety of air and maritime encounters. In 2015, China and the US expanded the memoranda through adopting the air encounter annex and the crisis communication annex.

10 Zheng Yongnian, "Did China Lose in the Doklam Crisis?," *Phoenix International Think Tank*, August 30, 2017.

11 On December 2, 2016, President-elect Donald Trump broke with usual practice since the establishment of diplomatic relations between China and the US to have a phone call with the Taiwanese leader Tsai Ing-wen. Soon afterwards, he also publicly questioned the "one China policy" on Twitter.

12 In 2018, the CLGMRI was incorporated into the CFAC.

14

US–CHINA MARITIME SECURITY FLASHPOINTS IN THE NEW ERA

Isaac Kardon

Introduction

The commercial interests that long served as ballast on the ship of US–China relations have been heaved overboard in this uncertain "new era" of great-power competition. Chinese and American economic officials and corporate executives have lately come to share in the suspicion, hostility, and appetite for confrontation long harbored by the military and defense communities.[1] Once-cheerful advocates of globalization now contemplate "decoupling" of key industries and the advent of an "economic iron curtain" separating the two superpowers.[2] Multinational supply chains that systematically linked China's labor and land to American capital and consumption are unraveling.[3] The entity once called "Chimerica" now seems to be a historical artifact;[4] instead, major Chinese and American firms are being blacklisted on dueling "entities" lists[5] that would have been unthinkable in the "old era" of wary but willing pursuit of a symbiotic bilateral relationship.

Competition, not cooperation, is the watchword of the "new era" in US–China relations.[6] Does this newly adversarial high-level direction in bilateral foreign policy entail increased risk of militarized conflict? Are the security flashpoints in East Asia more volatile or more numerous now that Washington and Beijing are engaged in a trade war? Does the absence of the typical diplomatic gestures toward harmony and cooperation portend deteriorating security dynamics?

This chapter addresses those questions by (i) canvassing some major flashpoints in maritime East Asia – namely, the perennial risk of conflict over Taiwan's sovereign status, and the disputes in the South and East China Seas,[7] and then (ii) focusing on the potential for unintended conflict arising from maritime or air encounters between American and Chinese vessels and aircraft. It concludes by

(iii) assessing the prospects for conflict mitigation and sustained peace in East Asia in light of these security dynamics, new and old. Overall, the several long-standing flashpoints of potential US–China crisis and conflict in the maritime domain are now more risky because of increasing capabilities, higher stakes, and growing geopolitical competition.

Sino-US maritime flashpoints in East Asia: More capability, more stability?

The major security flashpoints of East Asia are those specific issues with the lowest thresholds for producing militarized interstate conflict involving the US and China.[8] These acute areas of dispute are distinct from the broad structural issues addressed elsewhere in this volume, which contemplate tectonic changes to the balance of power that might lead one or both nations to opt strategically for confrontation. Flashpoints, by contrast, refer to the most likely sources of accidental, inadvertent, or at least not entirely intentional escalation to violence involving ships and aircraft operating in close proximity.[9] To place this terminology in the context of other commonly used terms, flashpoints are those areas that are prone to crisis; such crises, in turn, are the crucibles for the use of force and escalatory dynamics that may lead to war. This chapter focuses on specifically maritime flashpoints.

As Thomas Christensen argued nearly 20 years ago, and Avery Goldstein elaborated more recently,[10] the relative capabilities either side can bring to bear is not determinative of the decision to use limited force to achieve a political objective.[11] Indeed, quite independent of the epochal conflict predicted by some "power transition" theorists,[12] there are conditions under which China or the United States might elect to use force against the other without intending escalation to a general war that would decisively test their relative power. Contingencies involving Taiwan, the South China Sea, the East China Sea, and American Freedom of Navigation Operations (FONOPs) are such flashpoints, listed in descending order of the potential severity of the crises that these flashpoints could spark. This section considers the new dynamics evident in each case, focusing especially on how deteriorating Sino-US relations affect the likelihood of unintended conflict.

Taiwan

Topping the list is the "original sin" in US–China relations: the wicked problem of Taiwan. The basic contradiction in 2019 is the same as it has been since late June 1950, when the US elected to deploy the Seventh Fleet to defend Taiwan from mainland invasion at the outset of the Korean War.[13] The US–China bilateral relationship's lowest points are punctuated by the series of crises attending real or perceived changes in Taiwan's sovereign status.

Yet, since the early 2000s, if not earlier, the balance of power across the Taiwan Strait has so favored Beijing over Taipei that it is primarily the "strategic ambiguity" of possible US intervention that deters a PRC attack. The first responders would inevitably be that same Seventh Fleet. Because of the preponderance of mainland capability, Taiwan gets a vote only in some variants of this contingency.[14]

Are US commitment and capability still sufficient to deter that conflict? Would the election of another pro-independence Democratic Progressive Party (DPP) administration in 2020 convince Beijing that the window of opportunity is closing for it to bring about "unification" by force? Does the internal stability of Xi Jinping's regime depend on some kind of timetable for unification? Some rough assessment of these questions can be undertaken by considering the interaction of three factors: the military balance, the degree of cross-strait integration, and intra-elite calculations in Beijing.

The first of these factors is almost certainly a bad one, raising the probability of an inauspicious *fourth* Taiwan Strait Crisis. Under virtually any set of assumptions, the mainland's military capability relative to Taiwan will continue to increase and, *ceteris paribus*, incentivize Beijing to compel unification.[15] Such mounting incentives do not necessarily mean Chinese civilian leaders will opt for military force, but they do increase the likelihood of more severe political coercion that might ultimately provoke a militarized crisis. A mitigating factor is the specificity of the campaign that would be required to subdue the island by force: an opposed amphibious invasion is an exceedingly high-risk operation, and one for which the People's Liberation Army (PLA) force structure and doctrine are not optimized.[16] That said, there are a range of military operations short of a beach landing that could incite spiraling conflict involving the US and China in and around Taiwan.

The second factor is a more hopeful indicator that blunts the effects of the military asymmetry, that perennial liberal workhorse of economic integration. Deeper economic ties raise the costs of engaging in political coercion or military force. PLA leaders are fond of reminding Pollyannish observers who believe the costs are too high that China would "fight at all costs – all costs – for national unity,"[17] as Minister of Defense, Wei Fenghe, told a large international audience at the Shangri-la Dialogue in June 2019. This resolve may well hold true if military force has already been used, but prior to the initiation of hostilities, the opportunity costs of choosing war will loom large. PRC civilian leadership will need to consider whether to forego not just the economic benefits of stable trade and investment with Taiwan, but the possibility of major international economic disruption, potential blockade, and extraordinary sanctions as likely consequences for use of force against Taiwan. Thus, while the relative military balance may breed growing confidence in the capability of the PLA to deliver victory before American intervention, the opportunity cost of using force mitigates that risk. Despite Beijing's episodic restrictions on mainland tourism to Taiwan, DPP initiatives to "Look South" and diversify their economic partners, and a general diminution of Taiwanese officials' enthusiasm for new initiatives in cross-strait economic integration, there is no evidence of a meaningful downturn in economic relations.[18] As Beijing meets further obstacles to its access to American semiconductors and other high tech products, Taiwan's relatively advanced tech sector and its massive investment in and trade with the mainland will further mute tendencies to disrupt cross-strait economic ties.

The decisive third factor is the type and degree of political urgency felt in Beijing. Xi Jinping's strength as the "core" of the fifth generation of CCP leadership is also the party's weakness. Xi's consolidation of power (marked, though hardly defined by elimination of term limits on the PRC presidency) has hollowed out the sixth generation of leadership. There are no obvious candidates to lead after Xi Jinping. There is now no easy way to kick the Taiwan can down the road, as has been the practice for all previous generations of leadership who handled this intractable problem.

Especially as the 20th Party Congress approaches in 2022, it is inconceivable that there will not be mainland elite demands for changes in cross-strait policy; these will be heightened if the economic tensions with the US persist and China's economy slows – both likely circumstances. If the Taiwan issue has not been decisively resolved by then (also a high probability circumstance) the question of why Xi has not brought that about will be one of only a few avenues open for criticizing his leadership. There are bound to be elite CCP circles who prefer Xi's power circumscribed, and the Taiwan issue is perhaps the only remaining political leverage they can deploy against an increasingly powerful and consolidated Xi-dominated regime. Decisive action on Taiwan may prove irresistible, a worrisome dynamic for the "new era" of cross-strait relations.

South China Sea

The sovereignty disputes over the Spratly and Paracel islands, as well as the maritime jurisdictional disputes connected to them, are among the premier flashpoints in maritime East Asia. Over the last decade, they have become a perennial irritant in US–China relations. In the midst of the trade tensions, SCS issues have been sidelined to a degree, but some of their "new era" dynamics are worrisome and trending towards an ever-lower threshold for flaring up into open conflict. There are two principle arenas where these disputes are prone to conflict, one involving Vietnam and the other involving the Philippines.

On the western side of the SCS, the "new era" is marked by growing hostility between China and Vietnam, and increasing warmth between Vietnam and the US. Vietnam remains the most likely participant in unintended escalation in maritime East Asia—and this time the US may be compelled to enter the fray. The China–Vietnam dyad is the one most prone to militarized conflict in recent history (recall Sino-Vietnamese bloodshed at the 1974 Battle of the Paracels, the 1979 PRC invasion, and the 1988 armed clash at Johnson Reef in the Spratlys). It is also the locus of more disputes than any other claimants: Vietnam claims *all* of the features in the SCS, and occupies some 29 of them; it has active programs to exploit oil and gas within range of China's ambiguous "nine-dash line" claim; and Vietnamese maritime militia forces, coast guard, and a handful of potent naval assets (including Kilo-class submarines) are, like their opposite Chinese numbers, incentivized by a strong central party-state to take risks in defending national sovereignty. The testy situation during the summer of 2019 involving Vietnamese law enforcement vessels in close quarters with Chinese survey and coast guard vessels is only the latest in a long series of close encounters between Chinese and Vietnamese vessels in the western (and southern) SCS.[19]

The fact that Vietnam is not a treaty ally of the US makes Sino-Vietnamese escalation somewhat more likely, but does not rule out the possibility that the US would be drawn into the conflict. Exxon, a US-based firm, has leases on oil and gas fields that border on Chinese claimed waters, and is one of several vectors by which American decision-makers may be confronted with difficult choices about the degree to which US naval forces or diplomats should go to bat for Vietnam. American defense leaders are increasingly keen on cultivating defense ties with Vietnam, and these feelings are largely mutual. China plainly resents this development and may opt for coercion of Vietnam to sever these ties, with unpredictable results in Washington as it considers its appetite for risk against China.

On the eastern side of the SCS, the dynamics are likewise not trending toward increased stability. The comity between the Duterte administration of the Philippines and the PRC is one worrisome trend, because it introduces uncertainty into Beijing's calculus of how hard it can push in sovereignty and jurisdictional disputes with the Philippines. That it will almost certainly give way to a period of anti-China politics in the Philippines, by now a familiar cycle, augments this uncertainty and creates incentives for Beijing to seek more gains now before a less accommodating Philippines leadership.

There was visible discomfort on the face of Zhang Gaoli as the recently elected Rodrigo Duterte stood in the Great Hall of the People and pronounced his nation's "separation" from the US and declared that the Philippines would be going with China's (and Russia's) "ideological flow."[20] Capitalizing on this over-eager Philippines courtship, Chinese leadership is energetically attempting to make a bilateral arrangement for oil and gas development and perhaps fisheries before the end of the Duterte regime,[21] but will encounter challenges once the staunchly pro-alliance defense and foreign policy establishment of the Philippines regains influence over policy. Although Duterte was content to largely ignore the arbitral award handed down in July 2016, his successors are likely to use it as leverage in future negotiations with China, potentially inflaming Beijing and triggering disproportionate responses from the increasingly capable China Coast Guard, and maritime militia forces under the direction of the PLA.

The attempted resupply of the marine platoon on the rusting hulk of the Sierra Madre on Second Thomas Shoal,[22] or a renewed PRC attempt to build upon Scarborough Shoal are two conceivable flashpoints as the Philippines regresses to the mean in its relations with the US and the PRC. The US treaty alliance with the Philippines is explicitly inferior to that with Japan,[23] affording somewhat more flexibility for American decision-makers in the event of a flare-up. Is the Sierra Madre a "government vessel" or a disputed maritime feature? Would a "militarization" of the Scarborough Shoal be met with a forceful US counter? Diplomacy has failed in both instances, but China's actions have remained below the flashpoint threshold. Unfortunately, that threshold is a moving target and may become more rather than less easy to cross. The likely US response to more aggressive PRC actions against its erstwhile ally cannot be easily predicted as attitudes toward the PRC harden in Washington.

The East China Sea

Among China's many maritime disputes, the dispute with Japan over the sovereignty of the Senkaku/Diaoyu Islands and delimitation of the exclusive economic zone (EEZ) and continental shelf (CS) between the two East Asian rivals is comparatively stable. Among the characteristics of the "new era" in PRC foreign policy is renewed effort beginning in 2014 to establish stable, if not especially warm, diplomatic ties and a bilateral maritime dialogue to manage potential crises between Beijing and Tokyo.[24] The US–Japan treaty alliance is another stabilizing factor in this theater, introducing a credible risk of major escalation in the event of a militarized exchange that diminishes incentives for either side to shoot first.

A less promising recent development, however, is the persistent operation of China Coast Guard (CCG) vessels and aircraft,[25] as well as maritime militia and other "motivated" PRC fishing vessels in and around the territorial seas and contiguous zone surrounding the Senkaku/Diaoyu islands. The Japanese Coast Guard (JCG) lacks the capacity to monitor all of China's regularized (定期) sea and aerial patrols, and periodic massed intrusions of Chinese fishing vessels.[26] These activities take place in an area "administered" by Japan – and are therefore explicitly covered under the US–Japan Mutual Defense Treaty, Article 5. Similarly, the Japanese Air Defense Force cannot sortie enough aircraft to monitor all of the overflights into Japan's air defense identification zone (ADIZ), which now has significant areas of overlap with China's own ADIZ, declared in 2013. While American presidents have vocally endorsed that the disputed islands are within the scope of US security commitments under the treaty in recent years,[27] China appears to calculate that its actions are unlikely to trigger armed response by Japan or the American treaty obligation.

The fine calibration of PRC incursions into Japan's claimed waters, however, is more art than science. The limitations of Japan's capacity[28] to intercept or monitor these incursions raises the possibility of, inter alia, a landing on one or more of the Senkaku/Diaoyu islands by Chinese forces. Such an operation would likely not be conducted by PLA, but rather maritime militia or other civilians with semi-plausible deniability about acting under direct orders from Beijing.

Other more likely scenarios involve attempted JCG law enforcement against Chinese fishing vessels that could trigger escalatory responses from proximate CCG or PLAN. Notably, in 2010 the PRC opted to restrict rare earth exports in response to an incident between a Chinese fisherman and Japanese coast guard vessels.[29] That choice to escalate horizontally in an unrelated economic domain, rather than bringing vessels in close proximity, may be less attractive now that CCG and other capable PRC forces could potentially join the fray on short notice. The instruments available to Beijing to coerce Tokyo are now more numerous, and only prudence keeps the situation from producing another crisis.

Indeed, growing Chinese capacity to deploy "white hulls" (maritime law enforcement vessels) as well as naval vessels and maritime militia vessels is a feature of the "new era" that introduces new risk. Since the tense weeks in late 2012, when Japan's government "nationalized" (国有化) several of the Senkaku/Diaoyu Islands to head off their acquisition by right-wing nationalists, there has been a contradiction in this theater. It becomes more problematic as time goes on because of the strain on Japan's capacity to monitor and intercept the huge volume of Chinese vessels and aircraft operating in and around the Senkakus. Nonetheless, the US–Japan treaty alliance and steady Sino-Japanese efforts to develop maritime protocols make this a lesser flashpoint, at least relative to the South China Sea disputes.

FONOPs and other close Sino-American air and maritime encounters

The risk of unintended escalation due to the close proximity of US and Chinese aircraft and vessels in maritime East Asia is growing in the "new era," if only because of the greater scope for miscalculation. While US naval and air assets have long operated in the region, Chinese forces are now capable of monitoring, intercepting, and interfering with their activities – and have done so in unsafe fashion on numerous occasions. PLA Navy (PLAN) vessels now regularly shadow the USN vessels on maneuver, and PRC spokespeople now publicly denounce the USN operations. These encounters are further pressurized by the high degree of media attention now accorded to once-banal US Navy (USN) Freedom of Navigation operations (FONOPs), one of several modalities of US military presence in the region. Audiences in both countries, and around the globe, fixate on these relatively low-key operations as a window into the intensifying US–China rivalry in the maritime domain. It is this attention – far out of proportion to the operational importance of FONOPs – that creates troubling dynamics in this new era of Sino-US maritime interactions.

FONOPs are hardly the only potential flashpoint interactions between US and Chinese aircraft and vessels. The USN has operated between 700 to 900 ship-days per year in the SCS in recent years.[30] In the course of these regular deployments of task forces and strike groups operating and exercising throughout the exclusive economic zones (EEZs) and high seas of the SCS, the Navy's Pacific

Fleet infrequently tasks a vessel or two to conduct a FONOP within 12 nautical miles of a disputed feature or within claimed territorial sea straight baselines (there have been 21 such operations since 2015 – see Table 14.1). Typically, these operations consist of a single Arleigh Burke–class destroyer conducting an "innocent passage" through territorial seas, though some involve minor operations such as launch of a helicopter or a man overboard exercise, intended to assert that the waters in question are not lawfully territorial seas. Though the number and type of vessels have begun to vary in recent years, these are not operations designed to put targets in the Chinese mainland at risk, but rather, to assert defined navigational rights and freedoms under the UN Convention on the Law of the Sea (UNCLOS).[31]

This flashpoint does not typically involve third parties who also "get a vote" in whether incidents arise and escalate. It may therefore be evaluated as a direct function of the worsening state of bilateral US–China relations. This bilateral dynamic is on balance a mitigating factor: American and Chinese officers are in command of the vessels and aircraft involved, and both chains of command would be reticent to initiate hostilities in the course of such routine and non-threatening engagements.

Yet, despite long-standing efforts to deconflict these operations, both parties' willingness to introduce friction and accept risk is now fully evident. When the USN began conducting these operations to contest excessive Chinese claims (the Pentagon's open source reports catalog operations beginning in 1991),[32] the PLA lacked adequate intelligence, surveillance, and reconnaissance capability to anticipate and monitor the operations. A much more modest Chinese fleet with no surface vessels or aircraft based out of the Paracel and Spratly Islands targeted by USN assertions also lacked the capacity to intercept. Unplanned encounters were unlikely to occur because there was virtually no PLAN in play. Now, with four large bases in the South China Sea (one at Woody Island in the Paracels, one each at Mischief Reef, Fiery Cross Reef, and Subi Reef in the Spratlys) and capable long-range vessels based out of Hainan and Zhanjiang, it is routine for PLAN to shadow USN vessels at visible range throughout their operations in the SCS.

Compounding this augmented Chinese presence and domain awareness is a wide variety and large number of Chinese vessels operating in the area. The vast expansion of the CCG and its aggressive posture in facing off against rival claimants is the most salient change;[33] Chinese fishing vessels operating as maritime militia forces are also tasked with a range of duties, including interfering with USN operations.[34] Now that the USN is explicitly designating CCG and maritime militia forces as possible combatant forces,[35] commanders simply abiding by standard rules of engagement may provide sufficient basis for an armed exchange. A number of close calls, notably the near-collision of the USS *Decatur* when a PLA frigate intercepted it at 45 yards and forced an emergency stop,[36] reinforce the judgment that very little stands in the way of unplanned escalation.

There are, however, good reasons to think that as the Sino-US dance surrounding FONOPs becomes routinized, both parties may find it easier to anticipate and manage potential clashes. Even as the frequency and intensity of FONOPs have increased (after a hiatus of perhaps three years during the prior administration), there has been only one reported recent close encounter (September 2018, involving the USS *Decatur*). While it is impossible to observe "dogs that didn't bark" – i.e., close encounters that went unreported – in open sources, it is likely that near-misses like the *Decatur* would not escape publicity from one or both sides, now eager to show their assertiveness to an attentive international audience.

Table 14.1 lists the operations since the FONOP program resumed in the SCS in late October 2015, noting the dates, vessels, which country first reported the operation, and which spokesperson delivered the message to public media.

Of the 21 FONOPs since 2015, PRC spokespeople have been the first to publicly comment on 9 of them (red shading). These messages were first broadcast by the civilian MFA, then by the non-operational MND, and finally by the operational command for the SCS. All such Chinese statements denounce the actions as "illegal" and refer to the "expulsion" of the offending vessels, though there is no evidence that FONOPs have been interrupted or curtailed by PLA interception. A new mode of transmitting these messages was adopted in November 2018, with the PLA's Southern Theater Command (itself established in February 2016) publishing its remarks to the popular online platform "WeChat."[37] The eagerness of the PLA to publicize FONOPs is a notable development.

Equally notable, in each of the record-high 8 FONOPs in 2019, the US Pacific Fleet or its component numbered fleet, the Seventh Fleet, have been the first to announce the FONOP to the press. This dynamic in publicity for the operations reflects the symbolic value both sides and interested observers now evidently attach to these operations.

Why might the PRC want to call public attention to such a large proportion of operations that, by virtue of being conducted well offshore, are unlikely to be witnessed by anyone other than naval personnel?[38] One obvious conclusion is that PRC leaders view the FONOPs as a diplomatic opportunity. That is, they offer a chance for Beijing to promote a narrative that it is the United States, not China, that is responsible for "militarizing" the SCS. It follows from this narrative that China's artificial island bases are "defensive" responses to US encroachment.

Meanwhile, the US is also changing its approach to these operations with the much-increased tempo of FONOPs, employment of multiple vessels instead of the single destroyer, and quick publicity offered by the ships' operational commands. These efforts indicate the US desire to seize the narrative. In the eyes of many observers, these operations are a proxy for the US resolve to counter Chinese assertiveness in the region, so proactive messaging is designed to signal this and reassure allies and partners (whether or not the operations themselves deter any Chinese activities).

TABLE 14.1 US Navy Freedom of Navigation Operations (October 2015–May 2019)

Date of FONOP	USN vessels	Location of FONOP	First report
26 Oct 2015	USS *Lassen* (DDG-82)	Subi Reef, Spratlys	PRC Foreign Minister, Wang Yi, on CCTV
30 Jan 2016	USS *Curtis Wilbur* (DDG-54)	Triton Island, Paracels	US DOD
10 May 2016	USS *William P. Lawrence* (DDG-110)	Fiery Cross Reef, Spratlys	US DOD
21 Oct 2016	USS *Decatur* (DDG-73)	Triton and Woody Islands, Paracels	PRC Ministry of Foreign Affairs
24 May 2017	USS *Dewey* (DDG-105)	Mischief Reef, Spratlys	US DOD
2 Jul 2017	USS *Stethem* (DDG-63)	Triton Island, Paracels	US PACFLEET
10 Aug 2017	USS *John S. McCain* (DDG-56)	Mischief Reef, Spratlys	US DOD
10 Oct 2017	USS *Chafee* (DDG-90)	Paracels	PRC MFA
17 Jan 2018	USS *Hopper* (DDG-70)	Scarborough Shoal	PRC MND and MFA
22 Mar 2018	USS *Mustin* (DDG-89)	Mischief Reef, Spratlys	PRC MND
27 May 2018	USS *Higgins* (DDG-76) and USS *Antietem* (CG-54)	Paracel Islands	PRC MND
30 Sep 2018	USS *Decatur* (DDG-73)	Gaven and Johnson Reefs, Spratlys	PRC MND
26 Nov 2018	USS *Chancellorsville* (CG-62)	Paracels	PRC Southern Theater Command
7 Jan 2019	USS *McCampbell* (DDG-85)	Paracels	US Pacific Fleet
10 Feb 2019	USS *Spruance* (DDG-111), USS *Preble* (DDG-88)	Mischief Reef	US Seventh Fleet
7 May 2019	USS *Preble* (DDG-88), USS *Chung Hoon* (DDG-93)	Gaven and Johnson Reefs, Spratlys	US Seventh Fleet
20 May 2019	USS *Preble* (DDG-88)	Scarborough Shoal	US Seventh Fleet
28 Aug 2019	USS *Wayne E. Meyer* (DDG-108)	Fiery Cross & Mischief Reefs	US Seventh Fleet
13 Sep 2019	USS *Wayne E. Meyer* (DDG-108)	Paracel Islands	US Seventh Fleet
20 Nov 2019	USS *Gabrielle Giffords* (LCS-10)	Mischief Reef	US Seventh Fleet
21 Nov 2019	USS *Wayne E. Meyer* (DDG-108)	Paracel Islands	US Seventh Fleet

China's fighter- and bomber-capable airfields, hardened hangars, anti-ship and surface-to-air missile batteries, and extensive electromagnetic and radar facilities now emplaced across the SCS islands provide capability superior to that of the small number of USN vessels conducting FONOPs. This mismatch is not lost on the US operators, who recognize the risks to their survivability operating in a theater where PLA capability to deny them is plain and growing. The USN, then, with near certainty would not elect to escalate through the instrumentality of a FONOP. Similarly, China is highly unlikely to misinterpret a FONOP anywhere within the first island chain as a prelude to an offensive operation. Therefore, questions of whether there are dangerous incentives for a first strike should be withheld for more volatile circumstances.[39] FONOPs themselves are not flashpoints likely to generate wider US–China conflict.

Nonetheless, FONOPs are a proxy for a structural, balance-of-power rivalry that is addressed elsewhere in this volume: namely, the question of whether China intends to evict US forward-deployed forces from maritime East Asia. At a minimum, it seems clear that Beijing intends to raise the costs to USN vessels operating in proximity of its large coast guard and vast maritime militia forces, with which a collision or other incident could conceivably generate a militarized crisis. In the "new era," FONOPs are probably not the vector for uncontrolled escalation, but they do reflect a wider bilateral circumstance that has removed some of the brakes on military conflict.

A final consideration regarding FONOPs is the increasing cooperation and presence of American allies in the SCS, some potentially mounting FONOP-like challenges alone or in tandem with the USN. France, the United Kingdom, and Australia have all committed to join the USN in this venture to some degree. In the SCS alone this year, the British frigate HMS *Argyll* (F-231) operated alongside the USS *McCampbell* (DDG-85) in mid-January 2019; another British frigate HMS *Montrose* (F-236) joined USS *Guadalupe* (T-AO-200) in mid-February 2019, and even more recently, an Australian navy frigate HMAS *Melbourne* may have joined USS Preble in a full-fledged FONOP. The French defense minister committed to sail French navy vessels through the SCS "more than twice a year."[40] The Taiwan Strait transit of a French frigate *Vendémiaire* earned it a disinvitation from the PLAN 70th anniversary fleet review,[41] reflecting China's sensitivity to foreign military operations judged to be supporting America's persistent presence. These modest allied contributions are likely to irritate Beijing, but are unlikely to generate escalatory dynamics.

The perception in Beijing of a balancing coalition willing to take on risk to operate in the SCS, however, will further increase the strategic tensions in the region. Beijing is unlikely to step back from its claims or curtail the operations of its CCG or PLAN forces in the region, so the net effect of these additional foreign navies operating in the region is to expand the scope for miscalculation and conflict. The relative professionalism of navies compared to non-naval vessels, however, means this flashpoint is not one prone to flaring up independently.

Conclusions: A new era of mutual denial?

The preceding analysis of four potential maritime security flashpoints in East Asia identifies some of the new dynamics that might precipitate a militarized exchange between the US and China. On balance, despite some newly worrisome factors, there appears to be stable deterrence. This is largely the result of the extraordinary capability both sides bring to bear in each of these maritime arenas, and the corresponding unacceptability of the anticipated costs of conflict. However, the flashpoint concept is intended to highlight the possibility for mistaken, inadvertent, or otherwise unintended escalations. What specific bilateral mechanisms exist to head off such potential crises?

In 2014 and 2015, the United States and China concluded a series of bilateral military "memorandums of understanding" (MOUs) on air[42] and maritime[43] encounters and on prior notification of military activities.[44] As a complement to the 1998 Military Maritime Consultative Agreement and a host of other fixed bilateral civilian and military arrangements (e.g. the Defense Policy Coordination Talks and Joint Staff Dialogue Mechanism), these non-binding, basically duplicative agreements are welcome but not particularly meaningful. The hotlines and institutionalized dialogues are not especially helpful in crisis if the PLA is unwilling to use the mechanism, as was the case in the 2001 EP-3 crisis.[45] Likewise, the PLA's 2014 agreement to abide by the multilateral Code for Unalerted Encounters at Sea (CUES)[46] provides yet another set of norms and standards that, if followed by all vessels and aircraft, will diminish the risk of unintended conflicts.

The more pertinent question is whether or not the policy and operational patterns adopted by American and Chinese civilian and military leaders introduce greater scope for miscalculation due to the frequency and intensity of at-sea interactions. If so, then even the best crafted mechanisms and codes are mitigating an increased risk of conflict. Even as China's military professionalism and sophistication about crisis-management[47] approach the US standard, the absolute number of potential crises has increased. Some of these involve what Chinese leaders refer to as "core interests" – most notably Taiwan – for which risk-acceptant behavior might prevail despite other mitigating factors noted earlier.

The new era does not bode particularly well for US–China maritime flashpoints, even as the costs of such an event mount. Given the growing capability fielded in the region and its increasing points of contact on the water, in the air, and in the public arena, the perceived stakes are larger. While mechanisms for communication exist and in some cases have been improved, the scope for cooperation appears to be narrowing as both sides adopt more adversarial postures. China's insecurity along its maritime frontier and US persistence in seeking access to those vulnerable points breed a spiraling dynamic. In this new era of great power competition, some of the brakes on conflict are being tested. The maritime flashpoints of East Asia are increasingly important sites to watch and manage some acute risks of Sino-US miscalculation and potential conflict.

Notes

1 It bears noting that neither the Xi nor the Trump administration marks the beginning of this shift. In some industries, "decoupling" long predates the current tensions: Google concluded as early as 2005 that it could not do business in China. By 2010, American corporate leaders like GE's CEO Jeff Immelt had concluded that China was not the place for the world's biggest manufacturer to conduct commercial operations, telling Italian business leaders that "I am not sure that in the end [China] wants any of us to win, or any of us to be successful." ("Immelt Blasts China," *The Economist*, July 2, 2010, https://www.economist.com/schumpeter/2010/07/02/immelt-blasts-china In China, meanwhile, the resistance to close economic integration with the United States has always been right at the surface of public discourse. For example, even at the high tide of financial globalization in 2006, conservative voices in China were arguing against openness to foreign capital. Yang Bin, a prominent "New Left" economist, argued that "as we implement bank and stock market reforms, we must never believe in the financial liberalization promoted by the Americans, and we certainly should believe in the necessity of 'linking up with international practice' and blindly open to markets" (李瑞英 [Li Ruiying], "警惕新自由主义思潮 [Be alert to the "Neoliberal" thought trend,"光明日报, November 9, 2004, http://m.aisixiang.com/data/12651-2.html The Global Financial Crisis of 2008-2009 marked the ascendance of these "New Left" voices in rejecting the neoliberal capitalist model and pursuing a distinctive path that kept US firms at arms length. See, for example, 魏源 [Wei Yuan], "金融危机后美国与中国经济政策及其效果研究 [Research on Chinese and American Economic Policy After the Global Financial Crisis], "当代经济, May 20, 2017.

2 Enda Curran, "Paulson Warns of 'Economic Iron Curtain' Between US, China," *Bloomberg*, November 6, 2018, https://www.bloomberg.com/news/articles/2018-11-07/paulson-warns-of-economic-iron-curtain-between-u-s-china

3 Chad Bray, "US-China Trade War Pushes Firms to Accelerate Supply Chain Shift to Asean, Citigroup Says," *South China Morning Post*, November 5, 2018, https://www.scmp.com/business/banking-finance/article/2171598/us-china-trade-war-pushes-firms-accelerate-supply-chain

4 E.g., Zachary Karabell, *Superfusion: How China and America Became One Economy and Why the World's Prosperity Depends On It* (New York: Simon & Schuster, 2009).

5 In May 2019, the US Department of Commerce listed Huawei Technologies, Inc. on a list of "entities" involved in "activities contrary to the national security or foreign policy interests of the United States," see "Addition of Entities to the Entities List," *Federal Register*, May 21, 2019, https://www.federalregister.gov/documents/2019/05/21/2019-10616/addition-of-entities-to-the-entity-list China responded by establishing a list of "unreliable entities" – that is "foreign enterprises, organizations and individuals that do not comply with market rules, violate contracts, block or cut supplies to Chinese firms with non-commercial purposes, and seriously damage the legitimate rights and interests of Chinese enterprises," see "China to Establish a List of Unreliable Entities: MOC," *Xinhua*, May 31, 2019, http://www.xinhuanet.com/english/2019-05/31/c_138106866.htm

6 National Security Council, "National Security Strategy of the United States of America," December 2017, https://www.whitehouse.gov/wp-content/uploads/2017/12/NSS-Final-12-18-2017-0905.pdf

7 Other possible flashpoints on China's immediate periphery include a range of contingencies involving North Korea, a renewed Sino-Indian standoff at Doklam, or deployment of PLA to central Asian states for counterterrorism missions. These are left for fuller treatment elsewhere, as the focus of this chapter remains on the maritime security dynamics of the new era in US–China relations.

8 The focus on thresholds is essential to the "flashpoint" concept, which points to the lowest level of political strife that could give rise to use of force. Avery Goldstein,

"First Things First: The Pressing Danger of Crisis Instability in US-China Relations," *International Security*, vol. 91, no. 6 (2013): 49–89, focuses on intra-crisis bargaining – that is, the incentives faced by both sides to use military force *once a crisis is already underway*. This analysis focuses on a still earlier stage, namely the conditions that produce onset of the crisis itself. We should thus be attuned to the political or operational factors in each issue area that could unexpectedly produce a crisis in which the use of military force becomes a viable option.

9 The prospects for de-escalation or crisis management are also a different subject, though inevitably they bleed into one another in the operationally oriented analysis that follows. For a very thorough analysis of this distinction between initiation of a crisis and escalation during a crisis, see Goldstein (2013). Goldstein convincingly calls attention to the prior question of each side's calculation of the efficacy of using force rather than continuing to bargain "non-kinetically" under conditions of intense time pressure and thus limited information.

10 Goldstein (2013).

11 Thomas Christensen, "Posing Problems Without Catching Up: China's Rise and Challenges for US Security Policy," *International Security*, vol. 5, no. 2 (Spring, 2001): 10–17. Christensen is referring to the relative weakness of China, quite pronounced in 2001, but this logic ought to apply equally in those contingencies in which it is the United States that brings relatively less firepower to bear, as in conceivable scenarios within range of Chinese coastal missile batteries.

12 E.g., Graham Allison, *Destined for War: Can America and China Escape Thucydides's Trap?* (New York: Houghton Mifflin Harcourt, 2017).

13 For the strategic factors attending this decision, see Thomas J. Christensen, *Useful Adversaries: Grand Strategy, Domestic Mobilization, and Sino-American Conflict, 1947-1958* (Princeton, NJ: Princeton University Press, 1996): 138–193.

14 See Michael Chase, "Averting a Cross-Strait Crisis," *Council on Foreign Relations*, Contingency Planning Memorandum No. 34, February 26, 2019, https://www.cfr.org/report/averting-cross-strait-crisis

15 This logic is elegantly laid out in Scott L. Kastner, "Is the Taiwan Strait Still a Flash Point?: Rethinking the Prospects for Armed Conflict Between China and Taiwan," *International Security*, vol. 40, no. 3 (2014/15): 54–92.

16 "There is also no indication China is significantly expanding its landing ship force at this time – suggesting a direct beach-assault operation requiring extensive lift is less likely in planning," Office of the Secretary of Defense, "Military and Security Developments Involving the PRC," 2019, 88–89.

17 Wei Fenghe, Speech at Shangri-La Dialogue, Fourth Plenary Session, "China and International Security Cooperation," Singapore, June 2, 2019, https://www.youtube.com/watch?v=OSoQ0_Grauk

18 According to Taiwanese data, trade has grown year on year since 2016; the mainland remains the largest target for Taiwan's direct foreign investment. See Republic of China Bureau of Trade and Statistics, https://cus93.trade.gov.tw/FSCE050F/FSCE050F

19 James Pearson, and Khanh Vu, "Vietnam, China Embroiled in South China Sea Standoff," *Reuters*, July 17, 2019, https://www.reuters.com/article/us-vietnam-china-southchinasea/vietnam-china-embroiled-in-south-china-sea-standoff-idUSKCN1UC0MX

20 Elena Holodny, "Philippine President Rodrigo Duterte Announced His 'Separation' from the US – Here is What it Means", *CtPost*, October, 21, 2016, https://www.ctpost.com/technology/businessinsider/article/Philippine-President-Rodrigo-Duterte-announced-10046627.php

21 Jay Batongbacal, "The Philippines-China MOU on Cooperation on Oil and Gas Development," *AMTI*, December 5, 2018, https://amti.csis.org/philippines-china-mou-cooperation-oil-gas-development/

22 Jeff Himmelman, "A Game of Shark and Minnow," *NYT Magazine*, October 27, 2013, http://www.nytimes.com/newsgraphics/2013/10/27/south-china-sea/index.html

23 Jim Gomez, "Philippines Worried It May Get Involved in a War at Sea for US," *Associated Press*, March 5, 2019, https://www.apnews.com/c8d36e22d5af478b9fe4bb 9b8dd3743b

24 Leika Kihara and Sui-Lee Wee, "China's Xi, Japan's Abe Hold Landmark Meeting," *Reuters*, November 9, 2014, https://www.reuters.com/article/us-china-japan/chinas -xi-japans-abe-hold-landmark-meeting-idUSKCN0IU08420141110
"Japan, China Launch Maritime-Aerial Communication Mechanism," *The Mainichi*, June 8, 2018, https://mainichi.jp/english/articles/20180608/p2a/00m/0na/002000c

25 CCG vessels operate regularly in the contiguous zone and have periodically entered the territorial seas, where their operations are potentially illegal (only innocent passage is permitted in a foreign territorial sea under international law and Japanese domestic law); a variety of PRC aircraft operate nearby Japan's territorial airspace; aircraft operated by the civilian State Oceanic Administration (former parent ministry to the CCG) periodically enter Japan's territorial airspace and generate demand for Japanese Air Self-Defense Force scrambles: "Trends in Chinese Government and Other Vessels in the Waters Surrounding the Senkaku Islands, and Japan's Response: Records of Intrusions of Chinese Government and Other Vessels into Japan's Territorial Sea," *Japan Ministry of Foreign Affairs*, May 16, 2019, https://www.mofa.go. jp/region/page23e_000021.html;
"Chinese Activities Surrounding Japan's Airspace," *Japan Ministry of Defense*, https:// www.mod.go.jp/e/d_act/ryouku/

26 A large deployment in 2016 of maritime militia vessels to the contiguous zone surrounding the Senkaku/Diaoyu has been confirmed by DOD. See Office of the Secretary of Defense 2019, 54.

27 Obama was the highest-level official to affirm that the treaty indeed covers this dispute: "And let me reiterate that our treaty commitment to Japan's security is absolute, and Article 5 covers all territories under Japan's administration, including the Senkaku Islands", see The White House, "Joint Press Conference with President Obama and Prime Minister Abe of Japan," *Office of the Press Secretary*, April 24, 2014, https://obamawhitehouse.archives.gov/the-press-office/2014/04/24/joint-press -conference-president-obama-and-prime-minister-abe-japan; A joint statement in 2017 reaffirmed that "Article V of the U.S.-Japan Treaty of Mutual Cooperation and Security Covers the Senkaku Islands", see White House, "Joint Statement from President Donald J. Trump and Prime Minister Shinzo Abe," *Statements and Releases*, February 10, 2017, https://www.whitehouse.gov/briefings-statements/joint-statem ent-president-donald-j-trump-prime-minister-shinzo-abe/

28 For a detailed assessment of Japan's capability and capacity in this domain, see Desmond Ball and Richard Tanter, *The Tools of Owatatsumi: Japan's Ocean Surveillance and Coastal Defence Capabilities* (Sydney: Australian National University Press, 2015): 99–104.

29 The September 2010 incident in which a Chinese fishing boat captain rammed two Japan Coast Guard Vessels generated a minor diplomatic crisis, establishing that pattern as a potentially escalatory one in the event of future such incidents.

30 Andrew Galbraith, "US Commander Says Ships on Course for More Days in the South China Sea," *Reuters*, June 15, 2017, https://uk.reuters.com/article/uk-china- usa-defense-idUKKBN1961GT

31 See Peter A. Dutton and Isaac B. Kardon, "Forget the FONOPs – Just Fly, Sail, and Operate Wherever International Law Allows," *Lawfare*, June 10, 2017, https://ww w.lawfareblog.com/forget-fonops-%E2%80%94-just-fly-sail-and-operate-wherever -international-law-allows

32 U.S. Department of Defense Oceans Policy Advisor, "DoD Annual Freedom of Navigation (FON) Reports," http://policy.defense.gov/OUSDPOffices/FON.aspx

33 See Ryan Martinson, "Echelon Defense: The Role of Sea Power in Chinese Maritime Dispute Strategy," *CMSI Red Book*, no. 15, 2018, https://digital-commons.usnwc. edu/cmsi-red-books/15

34 See Conor M. Kennedy and Andrew S. Erickson, "China's Third Sea Force: The People's Armed Forces Maritime Militia – Tethered to the PLA," *CMSI China Maritime Report*, no. 1, 2017, https://digital-commons.usnwc.edu/cmsi-maritime-re ports/1/

35 Demetri Sevastopulo and Katherine Hille, "US Warns China on Aggressive Acts by Fishing Boats and Coast Guard," *Financial Times*, April, 28 2019, https://www.ft.com /content/ab4b1602-696a-11e9-80c7-60ee53e6681d

36 Ben Werner, "Destroyer USS Decatur Has Close Encounter with Chinese Warship," *USNI News*, October 1, 2018, https://news.usni.org/2018/10/01/37006

37 The PLA Southern Theater Command's WeChat feed is available at https://xw.qq .com/m/author?id=5116892

38 There is a possibility that Chinese fishing vessels would witness these transits and report them independently, to Beijing's embarrassment, but this is a low probability given the vast spaces in question and the superior radar and ISR platforms employed by USN vessels that keep them well away from civilian vessels.

39 The question of whether the extensive missile forces arrayed throughout coastal China, and their potential targeting by US forces, creates a "use it or lose it" scenario, and thus the potential for first-mover advantages, is worth considering. However, the proverbial "Battle of the First Salvo" is quite unlikely to arise accidentally, and there are many options available to the USN short of launching all out strikes that could control escalation – for example, pulling most of their assets out of the missile envelope of PLA forces rather than going after their missile platforms and triggering general war.

40 French Minister of Defense, Speech, "Discours de Florence Parly, ministre des Armées_Allocution au Shangri-La Dialogue", *Ministry of Defense, France*, June 6, 2019, https://www.defense.gouv.fr/salle-de-presse/discours/discours-de-florence-p arly/discours-de-florence-parly-ministre-des-armees_allocution-au-shangri-la-dia logue

41 Minnie Chan, "China Withdraws PLA Navy Anniversary Invitation to French Warship After Taiwan Strait Trip," *South China Morning Post*, April, 25, 2019, https ://www.scmp.com/news/china/military/article/3007647/china-withdraws-pla-nav y-anniversary-invitation-french-warship; NB - reportedly, an Indian Navy frigate made the same transit en route the fleet review but was not disinvited.

42 US Department of Defence, "US–China Air Encounters Annex," November 9, 2014, https://dod.defense.gov/Portals/1/Documents/pubs/US-CHINA_AIR_ENC OUNTERS_ANNEX_SEP_2015.pdf

43 US Department of Defence, "Memorandum of Understanding Between the Department of Defense of the United States of America and the Ministry of National Defense of the People's Republic of China Regarding the Rules of Behavior for Safety of Air and Maritime Encounters," November 9, 2014, https://digital.library.u nt.edu/ark:/67531/metadc949788/

44 US Department of Defence, "Memorandum on Notification of Major Military Activities," October 31, 2014, https://dod.defense.gov/Portals/1/Documents/pubs /141112_MemorandumOfUnderstandingOnNotification.pdf

45 John Keefe, "Anatomy of the EP-3 Incident, April 2001," *Center for Naval Analyses*, January 2002.

46 Western Pacific Naval Symposium, "Code for Unplanned Encounters at Sea," https ://www.jag.navy.mil/distrib/instructions/CUES_2014.pdf

47 Iain Johnston, "The Evolution of Interstate Security Crisis-Management: Theory and Practice in China," *Naval War College Review*, vol. 69, no. 1 (2016): 29–44.

15

AN UNCERTAIN FUTURE

Conventional arms competitions in Asia and their effect on Europe

Ian Bowers

When US Secretary of Defense Mark Esper visited the Indo-Pacific region in early August 2019, he quickly sought to exploit the US withdrawal from the Intermediate-Range Nuclear Forces (INF) treaty. The Defense Secretary stated that the United States would seek to deploy intermediate range weapons systems in the region as soon as possible.[1] Despite a frosty initial response from some of the US' closest regional allies, the Pentagon continues to push for such a deployment in its bid to meet the challenge posed by an increasingly powerful China.[2]

The decision to develop and in the future deploy such assets, including conventional intermediate range ballistic missiles (IRBM) garnered significant attention with arguments both for and against such a shift in US policy.[3] However, much of the debate has missed the forest for the trees. Future US intermediate range weapons are but one component in what is an increasingly complex and potentially dangerous conventional arms competition in East Asia.

An arms competition is an arms dynamic between two states where "both chip away at the status quo and constantly seek to improve their position."[4] This definition fits the contemporary arms dynamic between Chinese conventional missile doctrine and technology on the one side and the US counter-response of intertwined offensive and defensive measures.[5] This chapter argues that this conventional arms dynamic coupled with potential technological and doctrinal advances are sources of increasing uncertainty and therefore have the potential to undermine strategic stability. Further, these sources of uncertainty, while being developed for the Asian theater of operations have substantial implications for European stability.[6]

Strategic stability is a concept born out of the Cold War. Based on the destructive power of nuclear weapons, it is broadly defined as existing when two or more opponents have sufficient confidence in their ability to inflict devastating damage on their opponent even after sustaining a nuclear strike.[7] Strategic instability arises when either a crisis incentivizes one side to strike first (crisis instability) or when one side fears that the other is developing or has developed weapons that could undermine mutual vulnerability (arms race instability).[8] While never easy to achieve, strategic stability in the contemporary world is even more complex. Technological, doctrinal, and geopolitical developments ensure that nuclear capabilities can no longer solely define strategic stability. Instead, it crosses domains where conventional systems including precision conventional strike capabilities, missile defenses, and cyberweapons can now influence previously bounded strategic dynamics.

The China–US arms competition

In East Asia, the primary source of instability centers on China's and the US' search for conventional arms competition advantage. On one side, China has developed an array of conventional capabilities designed to deny the United States and its allies a secure operating space in East Asia. At the heart of these capabilities is a range of conventional ballistic and cruise missiles that can hold at risk US and allied military assets and bases. As a counter to this capability, the US is developing a new strategy centered on an Integrated Air and Missile Defense (IAMD) doctrine. Publicly articulated in the Trump administration's *2019 Missile Defense Review*, this doctrine is designed to "to prevent an adversary from effectively using its offensive air and missile weapons through the integrated combination of deterrence, active and passive defenses, and attack operations."[9] This combination of capabilities reflects the fallibility of existing missile defense technology and the consequent need to target C4ISR nodes and launch facilities before the opposition fires the majority of their missiles. By raising the possibility of offensive operations, the US is developing an operational doctrine underpinned by advances in arms technology that will target weak points in China's conventional ballistic missile architecture in any conventional scenario such as a crisis in the Taiwan Strait or the South China Sea.

China's conventional missiles systems form a vital part of its military and deterrent strategy. Multiple authors have demonstrated that the People's Liberation Army Rocket Force (PLARF) has grown in importance and is now at the core of PLA operations. Writing in 2012, Chase and Erickson argued that China's missile and rocket forces, then under the auspices of the Second Artillery Force (SAF), was "one of the most important elements of Chinese military modernisation".[10] Seven years later, Gill and Ni wrote that the establishment of the PLARF, the successor to the SAF, and continued investment in its forces "solidified China's missile forces as a critical element of China's evolving strategic deterrent posture".[11] Indeed, according to China's 2019 Defense White Paper, the PLARF "plays a central role in maintaining China's national sovereignty and security".[12]

These conventional systems have two core strategic and operational roles that explain their centrality in PLA defense planning. A large proportion of China's short-range missiles are targeted at Taiwan, holding the small territory in a state of constant hostage. They are one of Beijing's best coercive tools when dealing with Taipei, acting as constant latent threat to deter a declaration of independence or any other political or strategic move that may challenge China. Additionally, in any warfighting scenario they would play a substantial role both in diminishing Taiwanese defensive capabilities and hindering or even deterring US intervention in such a scenario.

Relatedly, these missile capabilities are tasked with securing Chinese advantage in its strategic relationship with the US. China's so-called anti-access/area denial strategy (A2/AD) seeks to deny the US and its allies the secure use of the sea and land in China's near abroad. This would include the East and South China Sea's (the first island chain) and arguably the Western Pacific in the open seas between Japan and Guam. This strikes at the heart of the US' power projection capacity and therefore the basis of their strategic position in East Asia. To enact such a strategy China must have the ability to overwhelm missile defenses and still disrupt significant facilities such as airfields, C4ISR nodes, ports, and ships at sea. The PLARF's conventional missile capabilities therefore provide Beijing with a powerful tool to shape the battlefield should war break out or a potent first-strike capability aimed at degrading the enemy's capabilities before they can respond.

China's current phase of modernization seems to have made substantial inroads into undermining US defense capabilities. In numerical terms, the Chinese missile forces have grown substantially over the last 20 years with estimates on the number of short-, medium-, and intermediate-range ballistic missiles now ranging between 3900 and 7450.[13] Numerical growth is only one element of China's missile modernization. Recently introduced capabilities include multiple and maneuverable, highly accurate terminal stages/warheads designed to evade missile defenses and strike moving targets such as warships. Complementing these missiles systems is a growing array of networked ISR capabilities that allow for more accurate over the horizon detection of moving naval vessels and other targets. These systems include increasing numbers of advanced imaging and maritime surveillance satellites with higher fidelity and the capacity to provide near constant coverage of strategically important areas such as the East and South China Seas and the Western Pacific. Additionally, China is investing in surface and sky wave over the horizon radar.[14] These radars have the potential to detect US vessels and aircraft and missile launches out to range of approximately 3000km.[15]

Of course, the US has not stood still in the face of China's missile development. Washington has, with arguably a quickening pace, sought to build and deploy capabilities that can, if needed, enact its IAMD strategy. By combining offensive and defensive elements into one missile defense doctrine, IAMD fits within the operational-level Joint Concept for Access and Maneuver in the Global Commons (JAM-GC) that is specifically designed to overcome advanced A2/AD environments such as the one that China has operationalized in East Asia.[16]

Recent developments in missile defense technology are now making this once virtually impossible task more viable. Despite setbacks such as the cancellation of a key upgrade to the US-based Ground Midcourse Defense system, the US continues to invest in these systems which are increasingly capable of detecting, targeting, and destroying incoming ballistic missiles.[17] The current arrangement of sensors and missile defense systems combined with ongoing development pathways including artificial intelligence, higher-fidelity sensors, and even lasers that can improve tracking and interception, speak to a future where missile defense will become increasingly effective.[18]

Currently deployed capabilities include the Patriot Missile, which in its PAC-3 and PAC-3 MSE versions includes a new interceptor specifically designed for ballistic missile interception and a series of other upgrades including greater connectivity and better search, detection, tracking, and discrimination abilities.[19] Beyond Patriot, the THAAD missile system with its powerful X-band radar is currently deployed in South Korea and Guam, while X-band radar units are also deployed in Japan providing US forces with coverage of the Korean Peninsula and Eastern China. Further, the US continues to invest in its sea-based AEGIS missile defense system, jointly developing the SM-3 Block IIA interceptor with Japan, which will have greater speed and accuracy than previous missiles in the SM family. In addition, the US Navy is almost ready to deploy the AN/SPY-6(V) radar, which is a substantial upgrade on the AN/SPY-1 used on today's AEGIS ships. The radar will allow vessels to track smaller targets at much greater distances. Indeed, in 2019 the US Navy again deployed a laser aboard one of its vessels. While this technology is still nascent and is currently likely designed to intercept swarms of boats or drones, future and more powerful lasers will render incoming missiles increasingly vulnerable.[20]

Ongoing investments also highlight how the US military is actively augmenting its offensive capabilities for the specific task of countering Chinese conventional intermediate-range systems by developing its own systems linked to advanced ISR capacities.[21] The US already possesses superior targeting and intelligence capabilities which if leveraged will provide US forces with the ability to find and destroy Chinese fixed and mobile capabilities with conventional weapons.[22] Investments in stealth capabilities including the F-35 Joint Strike Fighter, upgrades to the B2 Spirit Bomber, and the future B-21 Raider heavy bomber are intended to ensure that the US can penetrate high-density enemy defenses such as those possessed by China. Additionally, improved and future versions of the Tomahawk cruise missile and AGM-158 JASSM provide the US with increased ability to attack targets from greater distances. Although the US may struggle to deploy IRBM on the shores of its allies, it can deploy them on Guam, adding this capability, when developed, to its now growing arsenal of offensive systems.

Conventional competition and strategic stability

The interaction between Chinese conventional missile capabilities and US responsive strategies is already producing an arms competition. Advances in US counter-systems in part influence China's pursuit of numerical and technological improvements in its conventional missile force. US government reports confirm that China continues to build new capabilities specifically designed to bypass missile defenses.[23] Given the strategic and operational importance of Chinese conventional missile forces and the US' focus on countering them combined with the technological and economic resources of both sides, it is likely that they will continue to design around each other's advances.[24] Such efforts suggest that even in its relatively embryonic stage this form of arms competition may lead to arms race instability.

New technologies across domains will likely accelerate this arms competition and magnify strategic uncertainty, as neither side can be sure of the advances of the other and their own capacity to catch up to such advances.[25] Two examples of this kind of technologically driven uncertainty are hypersonic and cyber-weapons.[26] Hypersonic boost and glide vehicles (HGV) are weapons capable of traveling at over Mach 5 thereby reducing a defender's response and decision-making time and making missile defense an even more difficult exercise.[27] They have raised fears of increasing the risk of miscalculation by increasing strategic ambiguity given their ability to carry both conventional and nuclear warheads at high speeds to destinations that may be difficult to initially determine.[28] HGV systems will form the backbone of the US Prompt Global Strike initiative that aims to provide its military with the ability to conduct a conventional strike anywhere in the world within one hour.[29]

The operational potential of cyberweapons is introducing further uncertainty into the US–China dynamic. Both sides possess offensive cyber capabilities and the US has already revealed the capability to disrupt hardware as shown by the Stuxnet attack on Iranian nuclear facilities and the rumored disruption of North Korea's ballistic missile program.[30] It is likely that both the US and China have the capacity to attack each other's C4ISR capabilities thereby disabling or damaging the sophisticated targeting systems and data networks required for a conventional warfare.[31] However, the secretive nature of such weapons means that neither side can be certain of the true capabilities of their opponent. This fact, combined with the unregulated space that is the cyber domain and the pressure on policy-makers to make strategic decisions with incomplete or ambiguous information, heightens uncertainty and undermines US-China strategic stability.

The operationalization of these technologies has further implications for crisis stability. Vitally, for Beijing, ongoing and future improvements in US missile defense capabilities in Asia have strategic implications beyond conventional capa-bilities. Writing in 2015, two experts in Chinese capabilities, Fiona Cunningham and Taylor Fravel, convincingly argued that the Chinese strategic community fear that US missile defenses could undermine China's nuclear deterrent by "pos-ing a direct threat to its retaliatory capability" and that these systems were part of a US effort to reduce or remove nuclear vulnerability.[32] Beijing's reaction to the deployment of THAAD on South Korean territory in 2016 and more importantly the deal that was struck with South Korea a year later suggests a distinct discom-fort with the growing array of networked sensors that now encircle China.[33]

This chapter has demonstrated that a conventional arms competition is emerging from US efforts to counter China's growing conventional missile capabilities. Future weapons technologies will both intensify this arms competition and reduce strategic stability as advanced missile defence doctrines undermine Chinese conceptions of the surety of mutually assured destruction. Exacerbating this fear is the challenge of new and improved precision strike capabilities. For Beijing these capabilities raise the possibility that the US may have the capacity to either intentionally or unintentionally degrade a substantial part of China's nuclear forces in any conventional scenario.[34] US attacks on Chinese conventional systems including C4ISR nodes, supporting military infrastructure, air and missile bases risks damaging Chinese nuclear systems. This, Caitlin Talmadge argues, means that any degree of nuclear degradation arising from conventional warfare in East Asia may force the Chinese leadership into thinking that nuclear escalation is the only possible option.[35]

Implications for Europe

The conventional arms competition that is now underway in East Asia has implications for European security. Although Russia and the United States have their own strategic dynamic that has multiple unique strategic characteristics, many of the same dynamics that drive uncertainty in Asia are now at play in Europe.

Russia is in the midst of its own buildup of new and potentially highly effective conventional and nuclear missiles that are specifically designed to counter US missile defense capabilities. These include the Iskander-M IRBM – the missile that drove the US to end the INF treaty – and a range of air, ground, and sea-launched hypersonic missiles. Some of these systems are dual-warhead capable and are undergoing testing.[36] Both Russia and the US are also now pursuing a broad modernization of their nuclear arsenals in a bid to remove obsolescent technology and manage modern missile defense threats.[37]

While the extent to which what is happening in Asia is driving this arms dynamic in Europe is open for debate, one key point must be understood. Although the challenge posed by China is likely the primary driving force behind the acceleration of US weapon and doctrinal development, the capabilities that will result from this development will have strategic utility in Europe. Core concepts such as Prompt Global Strike, JAM-GC, and IAMD have global applicability and therefore influence the Russia–NATO dynamic. As the arms competition in Asia continues it will not remain confined to that region. Because the doctrines and weapons being developed have global implications, it is likely that Russia as a third party is now being in forced to respond to ensure its own strategic interests are met.

The Russian strategic community seems to share many of China's concerns about the US approach. Senior Russian leadership figures have articulated their perception of the threat that these US offensive and defensive capabilities pose to Russian strategic capabilities. For example, while Moscow views the current level and capabilities of US and NATO missile defense as unable to affect their nuclear deterrent, it does believe that future capabilities built on the growing global network of sensors will pose a higher threat.[38] Indeed, in a sign of Russia's near paranoia about this topic, some Russian strategists even fear that extant missile defense facilities located in Europe could be repurposed to launch cruise missiles in areas close to Russia territory.[39]

Similarly, Moscow has repeatedly stated that US offensive doctrines, in particular Prompt Global Strike, are a direct threat to strategic stability. Russia believes that a substantial proportion of its nuclear infrastructure would be vulnerable to future US conventional strike operations. Anatoly Andolov, Russia's then Deputy Minister of Defense, argued in 2013 that the US mating of hypersonic weapons within its Prompt Global Strike architecture would mean that conventional weapons "will be capable of performing tasks that today are supposed to be carried out by strategic nuclear arms."[40] Indeed Russia fears that in the future it may be difficult to determine if such missiles are carrying nuclear or conventional warheads, that they would reduce warning and therefore decision-making time and that they may even reduce the threshold for politicians to consider attempting a strategic strike against a nuclear power such as Russia.[41] The rapid development of Russian hypersonic capabilities can be considered a direct response to US developments in this area.

Importantly the China–US arms competition introduces further uncertainty into the US–Russia dynamic and vice versa. In the words of one analyst, "a three way-relationship can be deeply confusing."[42] As an example, the potential ambiguity of new weapons including hypersonics and cyber capabilities raises the risk of inadvertent escalation due to difficulties of attack attribution.[43] Moreover, arms control treaties between Russia and the US will inevitably be impacted by China's capabilities. For example, including China with its smaller nuclear arsenal in something such as New START would require substantial and difficult concessions.

An uncertain future?

The long-term consequences of the China–US arms competition cannot yet be fully understood. The technologies involved, and the doctrines used to operationalize them, are either too secretive or not mature enough to allow for a complete insight into their effect on strategic stability. This chapter is therefore not arguing that conflict or war is inevitable. Rather it builds upon a growing literature on the future of strategic stability to clearly annunciate concerns regarding contemporary arms competitions and their impact on strategic stability in East Asia. It is evident that both China and the US are engaged in an arms dynamic that may have unforeseen consequences in the conventional and nuclear realms. The level of strategic uncertainty may even increase as technology matures and both sides view the contemporary and future military balance with some trepidation. While there are few clear current off-ramps, arms control may not be impossible but will involve difficult choices for all involved including "non-like-for-like-exchanges" and limiting new technologies such as HGV.[44]

European policymakers should view this conventional arms competition with increasing concern. The consequences will not only be felt in Asia. This chapter has shown that while Chinese capabilities inform new US doctrine and technologies, these operational and strategic approaches will be replicated in Europe and thus Russia is and will continue to respond. Moreover, as NATO builds up its missile defense capabilities in Europe it argues that this does not affect Russian strategic interests. However, advances in these technologies, alongside the introduction of more sophisticated European strike capabilities such as the F-35, may not be seen in such a benign manner in Moscow. As conventional capabilities advance and China and the US continue to push doctrinal boundaries in multiple domains, European strategic elites should be fully aware of the uncertainty that this will introduce to strategic stability in their own backyard.

Notes

1 Lolita C. Baldo, "Esper: US to Soon Put Intermediate Range Missile in Asia," *Military Times*, August 04, 2019, https://www.militarytimes.com/news/pentagon-congress/2019/08/04/esper-us-to-soon-put-intermediate-range-missile-in-asia/

2 Franz-Stefan Gady, "Australia, South Korea Say No to Deployment of US INF-Range Missiles on Their Soil," *The Diplomat*, August 06, 2019, https://thediplomat.com/2019/08/australia-south-korea-say-no-to-deployment-of-us-inf-range-missiles-on-their-soil/; Taketsugu Sato, "New Missile Deployment in Asia Raised at Japan-U.S. Talks," *The Asahi Shimbun*, October 22, 2019, http://www.asahi.com/ajw/articles/AJ201910220029.html

3 Andrew S. Erickson, "Good Riddance to the INF Treaty: Washington Shouldn't Tie Its Own Hands in Asia," *Foreign Affairs* (August 29, 2019), https://www.foreignaffairs.com/articles/china/2019-08-29/good-riddance-inf-treaty; Tom Countryman and Kingston Reif, "Intermediate-Range Missiles Are the Wrong Weapon for Today's Security Challenges," *War on the Rocks*, August 13, 2019, https://warontherocks.com/2019/08/intermediate-range-missiles-are-the-wrong-weapon-for-todays-security-challenges/; Joshua Nezam, "Can New U.S. Missiles in Asia Deter China and Increase Security on the Korean Peninsula?," *War on the Rocks*, October 25, 2019, https://warontherocks.com/2019/10/can-new-u-s-missiles-in-asia-deter-china-and-increase-security-on-the-korean-peninsula/

4 Barry Buzan and Eric Herring, *The Arms Dynamic in World Politics* (Boulder, CO: Lynne Reinner Publishers, 1998), 80.

5 Caitlin Talmadge argues that while concern over new technologies and escalatory pressures is reasonable, it is how they are used within operational strategies and doctrines that is more important in driving conflict escalation. See: Caitlin Talmadge, "Emerging Technology and Intra-War Escalation Risks: Evidence from the Cold War, Implications for Today," *Journal of Strategic Studies*, vol. 42, no. 6 (2019): 864–887.

6 Zenel Garcia, "Strategic Stability in the Twenty-First Century: The Challenge of the Second Nuclear Age and the Logic of Stability Interdependence," *Comparative Strategy*, vol. 36, no. 4 (2017): 355.

7 Robert Axelrod, "The Concept of Stability in the Context of Conventional War in Europe," *Journal of Peace Research*, vol. 27, no. 3 (August 1990): 249.

8 Heather Williams, "Asymmetric Arms Control and Strategic Stability: Scenarios for Limiting Hypersonic Glide Vehicles," *The Journal of Strategic Studies*, vol. 42, no. 6

(2019): 792; Aaron R. Miles, "The Dynamics of Strategic Stability and Instability," *Comparative Strategy*, vol. 35, no. 5 (2016): 425.

9 US Department of Defense, *2019 Missile Defense Review* (Washington, DC: US Department of Defense, 2019), 33.

10 Michael S. Chase and Andrew S. Erickson, "The Conventional Missile Capabilities of China's Second Artillery Force: Cornerstone of Deterrence and Warfighting," *Asian Security*, vol. 8, no 2 (2012): 115.

11 Bates Gill and Adam Ni, "The People's Liberation Army Rocket Force: Reshaping China's Approach to Strategic Deterrence," *Australian Journal of International Affairs*, vol. 73, no 2 (2019): 161.

12 The State Council Information Office of the People's Republic of China, *China's National Defense in the New Era* (Beijing: Foreign Language Press, 2019).

13 Ashely Townshend, Brendan Thomas-Noone, and Matilda Steward, *Averting Crisis: American Strategy, Military Spending and Collective Defence in the Indo-Pacific* (Sydney: The United States Studies Centre, 2019), 17; US Department of Defense, *Annual Report to Congress: Military and Security Developments Involving the People's Republic of China 2019* (Washington, DC: US Department of Defense, 2019), 47.

14 US Department of Defense, *Annual Report to Congress: Military and Security Developments Involving the People's Republic of China 2019*, 47.

15 Lee Kil-Seong, "China Sets Up More Long-Range Radars," *The Chosun Ilbo*, March 14, 2017, http://english.chosun.com/site/data/html_dir/2017/03/14/201703140 1319.html

16 See: Michael E. Hutchens, William D. Dries, Jason C. Perdew, Vincent D. Bryant, and Kerry E. Moores, "Joint Concept for Access and Maneuver in the Global Commons A New Joint Operational Concept," *Joint Forces Quarterly*, vol. 84, no. 1 (2017): 134–139.

17 Jen Judson, "Pentagon Terminates Program for Redesigned Kill Vehicle, Preps for New Competition," *Defense News*, August 21, 2019, https://www.defensenews.com /pentagon/2019/08/21/dod-tanks-redesigned-kill-vehicle-program-for-homeland -defense-interceptor/

18 Michael O'Hanlon, *Forecasting Change in Military Technology, 2020-2040* (Washington, DC: Brookings Institute, 2019), 20.

19 The first US PAC-3 system was deployed in Okinawa in 2006 but current numbers and location positions in Japan are classified.

20 Joseph Threvitick, "Navy Amphibious Warfare Ship USS Portland Spotted Heading to Sea with New Laser Turret," *The Warzone*, December 03, 2019, https://www.the drive.com/the-war-zone/31309/navy-amphibious-warfare-ship-uss-portland-spot ted-heading-to-sea-with-new-laser-turret

21 John A. Tirpak and Gen. Charles Q. Brown, "Questions and Answers: Towards a Seamless Pacific," *Air Force Magazine*, October 2019, 8–9.

22 Austin Long and Brendan Rittenhouse Green, "Stalking the Secure Second Strike: Intelligence, Counterforce, and Nuclear Strategy," *The Journal of Strategic Studies*, vol. 38, no. 1 (2015): 60–64.

23 US Department of Defense, *2019 Missile Defense Review*, IV; US Department of Defense, *Annual Report to Congress: Military and Security Developments Involving the People's Republic of China 2019*, 44.

24 Edward Rhodes, "Conventional Deterrence," *Comparative Strategy*, vol. 19, no. 3 (2000): 222.

25 Williams, "Asymmetric Arms Control and Strategic Stability" 790.

26 Other future technologies include artificial intelligence and unmanned systems: See: James S. Johnson, "Artificial Intelligence: A Threat to Strategic Stability," *Strategic Studies Quarterly*, vol. 14, no. 1 (2020): 16–39.

27 See: Joshua H. Pollack, "Boost-Glide Weapons and US-China Strategic Stability," *The Nonproliferation Review*, vol. 22, no. 2 (2015): 155–164.

28 Williams, "Asymmetric Arms Control and Strategic Stability," 797.

29 Mark Hilborne, "Conventional Prompt Global Strike: Enhancing Deterrence?," *Air Power Review*, vol. 20, no. 2, 182–190, (2017).

30 David E. Sanger and William J. Broad, "Trump Inherits a Secret Cyberwar Against North Korea Missiles," *The New York Times*, March 04, 2017, https://www.nytimes.com/2017/03/04/world/asia/north-korea-missile-program-sabotage.html

31 Eric Heginbotham, et al., *US-China Military Scorecard: Forces, Geography, and the Evolving Balance of Power 1996-2017* (Santa Monica: Rand Corporation, 2015), 267.

32 Fiona S. Cunningham and M. Taylor Fravel, "Assuring Assured Retaliation: China's Nuclear Posture and U.S.-China Strategic Stability," *International Security*, vol. 40, no. 2 (Fall 2015): 16–20.

33 The Moon administration agreed with Beijing that there would be no additional THAAD deployments, no networking with US missile defense systems, and no trilateral alliance with the US and Japan. See: Byong-su Park, "South Korea's "three no's" Announcement Key to Restoring Relations with China," *Hankyoreh*, November 02, 2017, http://english.hani.co.kr/arti/english_edition/e_international/817213.html

34 See: Caitlin Talmadge, "Would China Go Nuclear? Assessing the Risk of Chinese Nuclear Escalation in a Conventional War with the United States," *International Security*, vol. 41, no. 4 (2017): 50–92.

35 Ibid.

36 Franz-Stefan Gady, "Russia: Avangard Hypersonic Warhead to Enter Service in Coming Weeks," *The Diplomat*, November 14, 2019, https://thediplomat.com/2019/11/russia-avangard-hypersonic-warhead-to-enter-service-in-coming-weeks/; Kyle Mizokami, "Russia's Navy Will Be the First to Use Hypersonic Weapons," *Popular Mechanics*, September 23, 2019, https://www.popularmechanics.com/military/weapons/a29192213/russia-hypersonic-weapon/

37 Jeffrey Lewis, "The Last Nuclear Weapons Treaty Between the US and Russia is About to Fall – and No One Seems to Care," *Prospect Magazine*, December 07, 2019.

38 Charles K. Bartles, "Russian Threat Perception and the Ballistic Missile Defense System," *The Journal of Slavic Military Studies*, vol. 30, no. 2 (2017): 154–155.

39 US defense officials have denied this, saying that unlike its seaborne equivalent the Aegis Ashore system does not have this capability. See: Larry Luxner, "Top Pentagon Official Disputes Russian Claims that Aegis Ashore Violates INF Treaty," *Atlantic Council*, June 26, 2015, https://www.atlanticcouncil.org/blogs/new-atlanticist/top-pentagon-official-disputes-russian-claims-that-aegis-ashore-violates-inf-treaty/

40 Anatoly Antonov, "Russia Forced to Develop Global Prompt Strike Weapons," *Security Index: A Russian Journal on International Security*, vol. 19, no. 3 (2013): 5.

41 James M. Acton, "Russia and Strategic Conventional Weapons," *The Nonproliferation Review*, vol. 22, no. 2 (2015): 145–147.

42 Lewis, "The Last Nuclear Weapons Treaty."

43 James S. Johnson, "Artificial Intelligence: A Threat to Strategic Stability," 26.

44 For a framework of arms control under the conditions described in this chapter, see: Williams, "Asymmetric Arms Control and Strategic Stability," 801–811.

16

CONCLUSION

The United States, China, and
Europe in an age of uncertainty

Robert S. Ross

The chapters in this volume address the impact of the US–China power transition on the international politics of East Asia and Europe. A recurring theme throughout the book is the uncertainty throughout East Asia and Europe over the trends in the power transition has contributed to policy fluidity and instability among key countries in East Asia and Europe. In East Asia, uncertainty over the regional balance of power has contributed to a transition in secondary state alignments. And in reaction to these developments, America's commitment to European security is in doubt, eliciting policy instability among the European powers.

In the aftermath of World War II, there was great stability in international politics. The US–Soviet Cold War competition, despite its high degree of insecurity and frequent crises, created a bipolar system with considerable certainty in great power security commitments and regional alignments. Despite the US defeat in Vietnam and the US–China rapprochement, the US–Soviet competition dominated international politics and it informed the security polices of secondary states not just in East Asia and Europe, but also in the Middle East, South Asia, and Latin America. The European distribution of power did not fundamentally change and the commitment of the Soviet Union and the United States to maintaining the balance of power was unquestioned.

Similarly, in the three decades after the Cold War, despite a brief period of early uncertainty, the international politics of East Asia and Europe was characterized by stable unipolarity. The United States possessed unchallenged preeminence in both Europe and maritime East Asia and it a maintained a consistent commitment to strategic and economic cooperation with its regional allies and it was the foundation of a stable institutional global order.

The chapters in this volume make clear that the period of post–Cold War great-power stability and certainty in international security affairs is over. The world is no longer unipolar and international politics is now characterized by increasing instability. The East Asian and European security and economic orders are in flux, with heightened uncertainty among the regional countries over great power commitments. The source of this instability and uncertainty is the changing US–China balance of power, reinforced by domestic political change and leadership characteristics. Together, these developments contribute to diminished confidence in US security commitments in East Asia. But because since World War II the United States has been a great power in both East Asian and European balance of power politics, developments in East Asia necessarily influence European security. Thus, the changing US–China balance of power has affected the Europe's great power politics and national defense policies.

The US–China balance of power, national leadership, and East Asian security affairs

Power transitions among the great powers are always difficult. Incorporating a new power into the international security order is the most difficult and most destabilizing political process in international politics. The US–China power transition is not an exception to this historical trend. The rise of China, and the corresponding decline of the United States, is transforming contemporary international politics.

The power transition sets the parameters of US and Chinese security policies, but leadership politics exacerbate the challenge of the transition. Contemporary Chinese and American leaders possess activist agendas and they are prepared to use coercive instruments to shape the course and outcome of the power transition to optimize their national security interests.

The new balance of power

In balance-of-power politics, the most important factor is the distribution of military power in war-fighting capabilities. As the gap between the first and second most powerful great powers significantly narrows, a power transition takes place that destabilizes international security affairs. The chapters by Avery Goldstein, Robert Ross, Joshua Shifrinson, and Øystein Tunsjø address these dynamics in in the US–China balance of power.

Whereas in the 30 years following the Cold War the United States was the sole maritime great power in East Asia and exercised maritime hegemony, in less than a decade China has challenged US interests on multiples fronts. Especially since 2012, under President Xi Jinping's leadership, China has pursued a rapid and ambitious development of Chinese national power. In security affairs, Chinese military has acquired multiple modern naval platforms, accurate conventional ballistic missiles targeting Taiwan and US bases and naval facilities in East Asia, and militarily relevant advanced communications and targeting technologies. It employs its new capabilities to establish a significant military presence in the coastal waters of US security partners. The result is that China has significantly narrowed the gap in the US–China balance of power. China's navy and conventional missiles challenge US ability to contend with Chinese forces in East Asian waters, and US missile defense systems remain ineffective against China's regional missile capabilities.

Under Xi Jinping, China has also challenged US global economic presence. Its large and growing domestic market, its Belt and Road Initiative (BRI), its Asian Infrastructure Investment Bank, and its growing foreign aid program attest to China's capability and intent to assume a leadership role in the global economy and in global governance. China's market and investment capital have become significant sources of growth and development for most countries throughout East Asia and for many countries throughout the world.

A decade ago, US concern for China's emergence as a peer competitor was speculative, based on assumptions about China's future capabilities. But the United States no longer dismisses Chinese great-power capabilities and its challenge to the regional and global security and economic orders. The US Navy cannot operate with impunity in East Asian waters and it cannot anticipate merely low-cost hostilities with the Chinese Navy. On the contrary, as the US–China capabilities gap continues to narrow, China confronts the United States with the likelihood of a costly war with an uncertain outcome. As it now stands, the United States does not plan to operate its surface fleet in the South China Sea in wartime and it is developing basing options for its navy and air force in the Indian Ocean and the Western Pacific, far from Chinese territory and East Asia's internal seas.

Moreover, the power transition will continue to develop, because the United States lacks the financial resources to match the pace of China's growing naval fleet and stabilize the maritime balance. In economics, the trade war reflects US impatience with China's reluctance to adopt the trade and investment norms of the advanced industrial economies and the domestic regulatory advantages that China enjoys that have contributed to its rise. Nonetheless, the United States is not confident that the trade war can compel China to submit to US demands or that a protracted trade war will not benefit China's relative economic rise vis-à-vis the United States.

The result of the power transition is the emergence of a bipolar East Asian maritime structure. Whereas US maritime hegemony once dampened the incentives for conflict and competition, military bipolarity now accentuates mutual great-power suspicions and competition. Moreover, the growing parity in US and Chinese GDP establishes the underlying basis for bipolarity and suggests consolidated bipolarity in the coming decades. Acutely concerned that China's growing military and economic capabilities and its strategic objectives directly challenge US strategic presence in East Asia, rather than target another great power in a multipolar system, the United States perceives heightened threat perception and develops single-minded resistance to China's rise.

This trend in the balance of power has necessarily transformed all elements of US policy toward China. Leaders matter, but the power transition to a bipolar structure establishes the parameters of US policymaking, limiting the range of choice. No longer confident that it can maintain the strategic status quo and its alliance system in East Asia, during the past decade Washington's China policy has done an about-face. The United States is no longer interested in maximizing US–China cooperation, much less pursuing engagement. Rather, in the face of rising China, since the Obama administration's rebalance to Asia the United States has developed policies that increasingly aim either to contain China's rise or to reverse its rising power trajectory.

US effort to contend with rising China is reflected in Washington's reduced concern for Chinese interests, including regarding Taiwan. This evolution in US policy is analyzed in the chapters by Isaac Kardon, Zhang Tuosheng, and Ian Bowers. Whereas in the past the United States had encouraged Taiwan to expand cooperation with the mainland, it now encourages Taiwan to resist Chinese "bullying" and to maximize its distance from the mainland economy. US naval transits through the Taiwan Strait and sales of high-technology weaponry to Taiwan signal US resolve to balance the rise of China, rather than deterrence of Chinese use of force. Similarly, frequent and high-profile US freedom-of-navigation operations in close proximity to Chinese-claimed features in the South China Sea reflect US competition with China over the regional balance of power more than they reflect Chinese challenges to freedom of navigation. Overall, US high-profile naval activities in East Asia, its interest in a larger navy, its deployment of missile defense systems in South Korea, its earlier leadership of the Trans-Pacific Partnership, a regional trade agreement that excluded China, and then its initiation of the US–China trade war, including a quest for "decoupling" in manufacturing and advanced technologies, and its anti-communist diplomatic polemics all reflect a response to rising China and US resistance to a change in the strategic status quo.

But the rise of China has also transformed Chinese policy. No longer constrained by US maritime hegemony, China now seeks greater security by reordering regional security affairs. It seeks, at minimum, military parity with the United States in East Asia and it has been willing to use its improved military and economic capabilities to compel the region's secondary states to accommodate Chinese interests regarding territorial disputes and security cooperation with the United States. Moreover, US responses to China's rise have reinforced China's perception of US effort to contain China and undermine Chinese security, thus eliciting greater hostility. Even as the United States has sought to establish its resolve to its East Asian security partners, heightened Chinese naval and air power presence around Taiwan and periodic Chinese tension and crises with South Korea, the Philippines, and Vietnam reflect Chinese insistence that the region's secondaries restrain their cooperation with US security policy against Chinese interests.

Leadership and power transitions

Regional bipolarity and US–China strategic competition will characterize long-term US–China relations. There not be a return to the past levels of cooperation between the US and China; the potential for reduced competition and greater cooperation will be constrained by the bipolar balance of power and mutual suspicion based on the distribution of capabilities. Nonetheless, leaders matter in policymaking, so that there continues to exist potential for reduced US–China trade conflict and restored cooperation on such issues as climate change, narcotics trafficking, human trafficking, the World Trade Organization, and nuclear non-proliferation.

Donald Trump and "America First"

President Donald Trump is a revisionist leader who seeks both to turn back the course of the power transition and to overturn the post–World War II international economic order. Rosemary Foot's chapter underscores how these policy preferences necessarily contribute to heightened US–China competition and tension.

The Trump administration's imposition on China of coercive tariffs seeks more than advancing US leverage to compel China to adopt economic reforms. China's domestic trade, finance, and investment regulations challenge the norms of the economic order among the advanced industrial countries. But the Trump administration is content with the long-term consolidation of mutual high tariffs. Its promotion of "decoupling" of manufacturing and high-technology supply chains, its "all-of-government" approach to contending with China's rise, and its ideologically tinged rhetoric that seeks to marshal US domestic and international resistance to China's rise all seek to establish US resolve to engage in competition reminiscent of the early Cold War. The Trump administration has minimal interest in cooperation with China on any bilateral or global issue and it seeks to impose such long-term high costs on China that its domestic political and economic systems cannot sustain resistance to US pressure.

The Trump administration's approach to global institutions is revisionist and disruptive. It has a unilateralist "America first" and zero-sum approach to realizing US interests. It has undermined the World Trade Organization and it opposes multilateral cooperation on trade, nuclear proliferation, and climate change.

Leaders matter in policymaking and contemporary US–China policy is policy with "Trump characteristics." Whereas the administration resists cooperation with China and the American public sees China as a competitor, 60 percent of the American people support cooperation with China. The trade war is highly controversial in the United States, with opposition from domestic groups in the high-tech, agricultural, and manufacturing sectors. Democratic Party candidates in the United States oppose China's economic policies, but they also oppose the trade war. They also have strong commitment to cooperation on climate change and they resist greater defense spending to contend with the rise of the Chinese navy, preferring to increase funding for social welfare programs. And they support US membership in international organizations.

Thus, just as there is fluidity in the course of the power transition, US leadership politics is uncertain, with implications for US policy and for trends in US–China economic and strategic competition and bilateral cooperation. Under different leadership, the United States could both compete and cooperate with China, rather than pursue a "whole-of-government" approach to competition with China.

Xi Jinping and Chinese great-power activism

Chinese foreign policymaking is as idiosyncratic as US policymaking and it is equally susceptible to leader characteristics. Thus, the transition from Hu Jintao to Xi Jinping was transformational. Recent China foreign policy reflects Xi's personal imprint of Chinese policymaking. Xi Jinping's predecessors had pursued peaceful rise and maintained a "low profile" in international affairs. But under Xi, the era of peaceful rise ended and China is no longer concerned with attracting international attention and controversy. Xi proudly proclaims that China is now a great power and that it seeks regional and global great power status, on par with the United States, and he is not reluctant to push back against US resistance and endure heightened US–China competition. And under Xi, China is prepared to wage a protracted trade war, despite the implications for slower Chinese economic growth. Xi's China has also consistently challenged East Asian countries that challenge Chinese security.

Xi Jinping has adopted a similarly activist agenda for the global order. After World War II, China was excluded from the global order. But despite the recent rise of China, Beijing has been denied a leadership role in the US-led institutional order. Under Xi Jinping, China's BRI, its development of the Asian Infrastructure Investment Bank, its large bilateral foreign aid budget, and its active diplomacy for multiple multilateral regional trade agreements attests to its effort to become a leader in the global economic and development orders, challenging US hegemonic leadership. But, as with the strategic order, China's emerging leadership of the global and regional economic orders is in flux. Despite China's rhetorical support for the WTO and multilateral cooperation on climate change, its vision for the global order remains fluid and in development. And, as Wang Dong's chapter explains, it has long resisted claims that the "liberal" international order has represented a global consensus.

Chinese leaders have amended the state constitution to allow unlimited five-year terms for the Chinese president. Nonetheless, Shi Yinhong's chapter stresses that because China's recent foreign policy agenda reflects Xi's personal dynamism, it remains unclear whether China's could become even more assertive under Xi's leadership, or perhaps less assertive with a new, more risk-adverse leadership. Whatever the course of Chinese leadership politics, there will be implications for China's contribution to international security affairs and global cooperation.

International uncertainty: East Asia and Europe

The East Asian balance of power is developing into a US–China bipolar maritime structure. But whereas by 1947–1948 the European Cold War bipolar balance was stable, characterized by entrenched armies along the border between Eastern and Western Europe and entrenched US and Soviet spheres of influence in Europe, the East Asian balance of power continues to evolve. There remains considerable fluidity in the US–China maritime balance of power; the distribution of power has yet to consolidate into a long-term stable structure. There is also considerable international attention to national leaderships and leadership preferences and to succession politics in both China and the United States. This evolving situation has created uncertainty in East Asia and in Europe over regional and global issues.

The power transition and uncertainty in East Asia

In bipolar East Asia, the trend from US hegemony to bipolarity has required adjustment from every East Asian country. But strategic adjustment is not easy, as leaders have struggled to maintain defense cooperation with the United States while minimizing Chinese opposition to their cooperation with US security policy and, thus, its containment of China. The result is region-wide uncertainty in the secondary countries over maintaining their security amid the changing great-power balance of power.

Since the early 2000s, South Korean presidents have struggled to develop a consistent security policy that can maintain traditional South Korean security ties with the United States while accommodating rising China's security interests. Presidents Kim Dae-jung and Roh Moo-hyun initiated South Korea's effort to improve relations with China, but President Lee Myung-bak moved policy back toward a more pro-US position. Park Geun-hye then tried to develop a balanced policy toward the United States and China, but finished her presidency with a decidedly pro-US tilt, ignoring Chinese warnings and agreeing to US deployment of the terminal high-altitude area defense (THAAD) missile defense system in South Korea. Her successor, Moon Jae-in, has made improved relations with China and North Korea a South Korean priority, agreeing to oppose additional THAAD deployments and cooperation with the US–Japan alliance, despite the Trump administration's increasing US resistance to the rise of China and its ongoing sanctions against North Korea.

On Taiwan, similar policy instability has followed presidential successions. In the late 1990s and 2000s, Lee Teng-hui and then Chen Shui-bian developed active policies of promoting Taiwan independence. But Chen's successor, Ma Ying-jeou, opposed independence and he developed closer economic cooperation and political relations with the mainland. Following Ma's presidency, Taiwan's current president, Tsai-Yong-wen, has resisted cooperation with the mainland while promoting greater security cooperation with the United States.

In the Philippines, in the early 2010s, following heightened China–Philippine tension over fishing in the disputed Scarborough Shoal in the South China Sea, President Benigno Aquino III cooperated with the United States to challenge the legality of Chinese claims before the international Permanent Court of Arbitration at The Hague. Although the court ruled in favor of the Philippines, Aquino's successor, Rodrigo Duterte, publicly dismissed the policy importance of the court's ruling and of the importance of the United States to Philippine security; he quickly moved to improve relations with China. In Malaysia, Prime Minister Najib Razak developed close political and economic ties with China. In the 2018 presidential election campaign, Mahathir Mohamad criticized Najib's China's policy as excessively accommodating to Chinese demands and he criticized China's "totalitarian" government and its colonial practices. But after he became president, Mahathir improved Malaysia's political and economic relations with China.

Vietnam, despite its stable leadership, has, since 2011, repeatedly tried to use improved military cooperation with the United States to challenge Chinese claims in disputed waters in the South China Sea. But in 2014 and 2019, following episodes of Sino-Vietnamese heightened military tension in the South China Sea, Vietnam ended its overt challenge to Chinese claims and improved relations with China.

But the power transition is simply one element contributing to policy uncertainty in East Asian countries. Donald Trump's unilateralism and "America first" policies have exacerbated regional uncertainty over US commitment to East Asian security and have accelerated the region's accommodation of rising China. Compared to past administrations, the Trump administration has sent relatively junior officials to attend annual regional leadership meetings, signaling that it does not prioritize US diplomacy with East Asian countries. The administration has threatened trade sanctions against Japan and South Korea and asserted that the stability of the US alliances with Japan and South Korea requires them to increase significantly their monetary contributions to US defense presence in their countries. The United States has thus signaled Tokyo and Seoul that the alliances are not vital to US security and that they cannot depend on the US defense commitments to contend with rising China, contributing to their interest in improving relations with Beijing.

The impact of US politics on regional diplomacy is especially clear in Japanese policymaking. As the largest and most advanced country in maritime East Asia, Japan is the most important US ally in the world. Japan should thus be confident in the stability of the US–Japan alliance and in its contribution to US and Japanese security. Moreover, the Sino-Japanese sovereignty dispute over the Diaoyu/ Senkaku islands in the East China Sea is a growing concern for Japanese security. Nonetheless, Japanese uncertainty over US–Japan security ties has encouraged Tokyo to improve relations with China. Sino-Japanese relations had been frozen since 2011. In 2012, the Japanese Government purchased a disputed island in the East China Sea, incurring Chinese retaliation. But in 2019 Prime Minister

Shinzo Abe visited Beijing and Xi Jinping agreed to visit Tokyo in 2020. China and Japan have also made significant progress toward a trade agreement.

The power transition and European uncertainty

The US–China power transition in East Asia has had a profound effect on European policymaking. Gerlinde Groitl's contribution examines how US relative decline and its preoccupation with the rise of China in East Asia has created doubt among European leaders over America's ability to sustain its post–World War II defense posture in Europe and thus its commitment to NATO and its credibility to provide for the defense of Europe. Moreover, these doubts over American resolve are developing just as Russia is developing a more assertive defense policy in the Caucuses and in European waters and as instability in the Middle East continues to challenge European security and its reliable access to Middle East energy resources. And, as is the case among the East Asian countries, the Trump administration's economic and security unilateralism and its "America first" approach to its security partners and the international order have exacerbated uncertainty among America's traditional European allies, contributing to policy adjustment.

Since 2010, the priority for US security policy has been responding to the rise of China in East Asia. There is a robust debate in the United States over American grand strategy in the context of the rise of China. But the only economically viable options call for prioritizing US interests in East Asia over its interests in Europe and in contending Russian power. Thus, the Obama administration's "rebalance to Asia" called for a greater concentration of US naval ships in East Asia, at the expense of US naval presence in other regions, including in European waters. Trump administration officials have similarly declared that to contend with China's growing naval capabilities, the US Navy must concentrate a greater share of ships in East Asia. Concern for the rise of China has also contributed to US interest in winding down its military presence in Afghanistan and Syria and reducing the burden on its navy in defending sea lanes for energy shipments through the Persian Gulf.

US domestic politics have exacerbated European uncertainty over the trends in great-power relations. As in his approach to US alliances in East Asia, President Trump has questioned the value of NATO to US security and his demands for increased European annual contributions to NATO operations signal US policy that the alliance is expendable. Moreover, Trump's apparent ambivalence toward Russian advances in the Ukraine and Syria and its growing Russian naval activism suggests appeasement of Russian demands and that European security concerns are of no concern to the United States.

The Trump administration's economic policies exacerbate European concerns. The administration's unilateral imposition of adversarial tariffs on French and German products and its attacks on the WTO amount to attacks on political cooperation with long-standing US allies, placing US economic interests over its security interests. Moreover, Washington's disinterest in stable US–Europe economic cooperation occurs just as China's BRI is expanding Chinese penetration of European economies, particularly in the Southern, Central, and Eastern European countries. Philippe Le Corre's chapter observes that whereas US economic presence in Europe is declining, many European countries increasingly rely on Chinese infrastructure investment and their industries' investments in China to promote economic growth.

European countries share with United States a concern for China's state-led economic policies, growing trade imbalances with China, and the vulnerability of their technologies sectors to Chinese espionage. May-Britt Stumbaum's chapter examines the European Union's response to China's growing economic influence in Europe. In 2019 the European Union labeled China a "strategic competitor" and stressed the importance of developing a "more realistic" and "assertive" approach to China. The EU has also moved to diversify its trade partnerships. Since 2016 it has concluded trade agreements with Canada, Japan, Singapore, and Vietnam.

Nonetheless, European uncertainty over the direction of US and Russian security policies and China's growing importance for the prosperity of the European economies have also led European countries to restrain cooperation with US trade policies toward China, while they compete with each other for preferential access to Chinese capital and the Chinese market. Whereas the United States has demanded that other countries follow the US lead and ban China's Huawei technology company from investing in its national cell-phone architecture, many European countries, including France and Germany and Great Britain, have opted for more discriminant polices, banning Huawei from their governments' communication infrastructure, while allowing it to compete with other providers in the civilian sector.

More generally, the United States has sought to deny Chinese technology firms access to US markets, for fear that China's technology capabilities will advance faster than US capabilities. European countries have been reluctant to adopt policies as restrictive as US policies. Moreover, since 2017, involved in their own trade war with the United States, the European countries have increased their exports from China, undermining the Trump administration's effort to use sanctions on Chinese exports to compel China to negotiate changes in its economic system. The EU plans to expand infrastructure links with Asia, which will contribute to greater trade with China.

Jo Inge Bekkevold's chapter examines the impact of the US–China power transition on Europe's response to Russia's growing role in European security. Uncertainty over the US security commitment to European security occurs just as Sino-Russian cooperation has increased against the United States and Russia has challenged European stability. And instability in the Middle East has grown as US retrenchment from the region and growing Chinese cooperation with Middle East oil-producing countries challenges European access to energy resources. China has expanded its presence in the North African countries.

There is thus growing concern over rising China's capabilities and intentions throughout the Mediterranean and the Middle East, Europe's "backyard." As the US retreats from Europe and its periphery, Russia and China are on the march.

These trends have encouraged European countries to reconsider their defense postures and the share of their national budgets they allocate for defense to contend with Russian activism. In contrast to the widespread stagnation in European defense spending since the end of the Cold War, in 2018 and 2019 the defense budgets of Norway, England, France, and Germany, for example, increased more than the US defense budget.

Multiple European countries are developing enhanced defense capabilities that, over the long term, will contend with Russian power and shape the European balance of power. The Cold War in Europe was a bipolar system characterized by the US–Soviet competition. In the twenty-first century, the diminution of Russian power and US preoccupation with the rise of China in East Asia combine to increase the relative regional power of Europe's larger countries, contributing to an emerging multipolar European order in which no one or two European states can dominate security affairs.

Conclusion

Strategic and economic uncertainly will persist in East Asia and Europe for the coming decades. The stable Cold War European balance of power reflected the enduring stalemate along the ground border between Eastern and Western Europe and the US and Soviet substantial ground-force presence in their respective spheres of influence, which consolidated alignments and served as trip wires to deter use of force. In contrast, the maritime balance in East Asia is fluid. Naval deployments are spread out over vast oceans and seas and changes in the balance of naval forces can create insecurity among the secondary states over the commitment of the great powers to their defense. Moreover, although the pace of China's rise will slow, its great-power capabilities in East Asia will endure.

Persistent US–China bipolar competition and uncertainty in East Asia will shape European security affairs. America's concern for the changing US–China balance of power will constrain long-term US involvement in European security affairs and American ability to contend with Russian assertiveness in Europe. There will thus be growing uncertainty in Europe regarding regional security and ongoing policy instability.

But the fluidity and uncertainty of East Asian security affairs will diminish the pressures toward a polarized regional order. The United States and China will not experience Cold War competition characterized by economic, social, and cultural warfare. And the island states of East Asia will experience moderate to minimum fear of an amphibious invasion and occupation by a great power, in contrast to the intense concern in NATO and the Warsaw Pact over a decisive surprise ground-force attack. Thus, polarized secondary states' alignment in East Asia is not necessary for secondary states' security. Regardless of the trends in the maritime balance of power, both the United States and China will enjoy security and economic cooperation with states throughout East Asia and the secondary states will benefit from foreign policy flexibility and security and economic cooperation with the United States and China.

In Europe, Russia is not the dominant imperial power that was the Soviet Union. Its population, economy, and military capabilities are similar to other European countries. Going forward, it will simply be one power among many in a fluid security order. And, as in East Asia, a fluid European regional order will enable the United States to cooperate with all countries in Europe, despite contending security alignments.

Policymaking is easier in regional orders characterized by strategic certainty. Spheres of influence are clearly demarcated and states know which states are their allies and which states are their adversaries. Nonetheless, strategic uncertainty has the benefit of fluid regional orders, in which all states experience less fear of a devastating war and they all enjoy the benefits of multifaceted cooperation with all countries, big and small. Uncertainty will persist in East Asia and Europe, but the benefits of uncertainty will outweigh the costs.

INDEX